Risk-Based Internal Auditing for Depository Institutions

Principles and Standards

William T. Thornhill, President
Thornhill Consulting Services
Barrington, Illinois

Bankers Publishing Company
Rolling Meadows, Illinois

Library of Congress Catalog Card Number: 89-82207

Printed in the United States of America.

No. 225   ISBN: 01-55520-172-5

In dedication to my daughter Karen, my son Thomas, and my stepson Mark for their continuing support.

"What we see depends mainly on what we look for."
John Lubbock

Contents

List of Figures

Preface

This book was written to inform senior and intermediate management, including those in internal auditing, of a new dimension in internal auditing, namely, the concept of "risk-based" internal auditing. This concept adds a new dimension to the principle of internal auditing being "constructive." It truly results in internal auditing being "a management tool" and "of service to all levels of management," as stated in the "creed" of The Institute of Internal Auditors, Inc. It concentrates on *(a)* determining the "risks," relative to any activity, function, product, service, entity, facility, work-task, or duty, *(b)* having management identify what are "acceptable levels," for each "risk" under *(a)*, and *(c)* developing policies, procedures, practices, and standards to bring the "risks," as identified under *(a)* to the levels that are "acceptable" to management, as under *(b)*.

While traditional audit reviews continue to be performed, the interim between such reviews is extended, so that more frequent reviews can be performed in the areas of "above average risks" to "very high risks" to assure that they are being controlled by levels considered acceptable by management.

This combination audit approach, by adding "risk-based" to "traditional" internal auditing, will result in the function being recognized as a "management tool." It is the first internal audit concept which, in both theory and practice, can result in identified benefits, to the institutions, exceeding the total, direct and indirect costs, of the function. It is structured to accomplish the following:

(a) Improved efficiency, effectiveness, and economy.

(b) Changes in organizational structure so as to accomplish the objectives, as under *(a)*, as well as assuring proper assignment of authority and responsibilities, while establishing clear-cut accountabilities, and, finally, assuring that management and staff are competent to perform their duties, properly utilize their authority, and fulfill their responsibilities.

(c) Identification of "risks," in all aspects of accounting, administration, finance, operations, planning, security, and systems (i.e., manual and automated/computerized).

(d) Require management to establish acceptable levels, relative to all identified "risks," as under *(c)*, and make decisions relative to each as to (1) self-insurance, (2) co-insurance, and deductible acceptable to institution, and (3) total insurance, with no liability retained.

(e) Initiate actions necessary to bring the identified "risks," as under (c), to the levels established by management as acceptable, as under (d).

These benefits are in addition to those normally expected to result from traditional auditing. They make "risk-based" internal auditing, which is both proactive and reactive, the most effective use of audit dollars by any institution!

Part I
Overview of Standard
Internal Audit Methodologies

1

Historical Summary

"Historians believe that recordkeeping originated about 4000 B.C., when ancient civilizations in the Near East began establishing organized governments and businesses.[1] They began with an accounting system to record receipts, taxes due, and disbursements. They recognized the need for establishing controls, including audits, "to reduce errors and fraud on the part of the incompetent or dishonest officials."[2] The Bible describes "several modern forms of internal control," which is generally viewed as the logic behind instituting controls, in the period 1800 B.C. through A.D. 95. It indicates the same degree of professional audit skepticism expected of auditors today. "Specifically, the Bible discusses dual custody of assets, the need for honest employees, restricted access, and segregation of duties." Some other stages of audit evolution are:

1. The Zhao dynasty (1111-256 B.C.) in China had an elaborate budgetary process and audits of all governmental departments.

2. In the 5th Century B.C. in Athens, the popular Assembly (comparable to our U.S. House of Representatives) controlled the receipt and disbursement of public funds. The system included government auditors who examined the records of all officeholders at the expiration of their terms.

3. Managers of estates, private and public, conducted audits of the accounts.

4. Public finances in the Roman Republic, which were under the control of the Senate, were examined by a staff of auditors supervised by the treasurer. The Romans maintained segregation of duties between the officials who authorized taxes and expenditures and those who handled receipts and payment.

"The oldest surviving accounting records and references to audits, in the modern sense of the word, of English-speaking countries are those of the Exchequers of England and Scotland, which date from 1130 A.D."[3]

---

[1] Jerry D. Sullivan, Richard A. Gnospelios, Philip Defliese, and Henry R. Jaenicke. *Montgomery's Auditing*, 10th ed. (New York: Ronald, 1985), pp. 9-11.
[2] *Ibid.*, pp. 9-11.
[3] *Ibid.*, pp. 9-11.

The city of London was found to have been audited in the 13th Century. By the 14th Century, auditors were among the elected officials. From that time on, there is extensive evidence that the value of audits was widely recognized and that the accounts of municipalities, private landholds, and craft guilds were audited regularly."[4] The 13th and 14th Century audits were primarily of two types:

1. "Audits of cities and towns were held publicly before the governing officials and citizens and consisted of the auditors' hearing the accounts"[5] read by the treasurer; similarly, audits of guilds were heard before the membership. Over time the auditors would use a quasicertification concept by annotating the accounts with phrases such as "heard by the auditors undersigned," a preliminary form of "audit certificate."

2. These audits involved a review of the "charge and discharge" accounts as maintained by the officers of large manors. Upon completion, their audit efforts were "followed by a 'declaration of audit,' that is, an oral report before the lord of the manor and the council. Typically, the auditor was a member of the manorial council, and thus was the precursor of the modern internal auditor."[6]

During the next 200 years, with growth of towns, manors, factories, new guilds, and widespread commerce, a number of new accounting concerns were identified. "[They] focused on the ownership of property and the calculation of profits and losses in a business sense. Auditing also began to evolve from an auditory process to a close examination of written records and the testing of supporting evidence." In the 17th Century, "the first law was enacted (in Scotland) prohibiting certain officials from serving as auditors of a town, thus introducing the modern notice of auditor independence . . . "[7] It was not until the 19th Century [that] the professional auditor became an important part of the business scene.

In point of fact, "There is evidence that auditing of a sort was done in ancient times. The fact that early rulers required that their household accounts be kept by two scribes independently is evidence that some measures were taken to prevent defalcations in these accounts. As commerce developed, so did the need for independent reviews to ascertain the accuracy and reliability of the records kept of the various commercial ventures."[8]

---

[4]*Ibid.*, pp. 9-11.
[5]*Ibid.*, pp. 9-11.
[6]*Ibid.*, pp. 9-11.
[7]*Ibid.*, pp. 9-11.
[8]James A. Cashin, ed. *Handbook for Auditors.* (New York: McGraw-Hill, 1971), pp. 1-9.

"Professional auditing was enhanced through the British Companies Act of 1862 and the general recognition, during the period leading up to the act, that an orderly and standardized system of accounting was desirable for both accurate reporting and fraud prevention."[9] Also, there was "a general acceptance of the need for an independent review of the accounts for both large and small enterprises."[10] "From 1862 to 1905, professional auditing grew and flourished in England, and it was introduced in the United States around 1900. In England considerable emphasis was placed on the detection of fraud, but auditing in the United States took an independent turn away from fraud detection as a primary objective of auditing."[11]

In the early part of the 20th Century, during a period that "might be called the formulative days of auditing, students were taught that the chief objectives of an audit were:

1. Detection and prevention of fraud.

2. Detection and prevention of errors.

However, in recent years there has been a decided change in demand and service. Present-day purposes are:

1. To ascertain actual financial condition and earnings of an enterprise.

2. Detection of fraud and errors, but this is a minor objective."[12]

From the beginning of the century through about 1940, disagreement arose as to whether the British or U.S. approach to audit, as described, was the proper direction for auditing. By 1940, most U.S. auditors had accepted "that the auditor could not and should not be primarily concerned with the detection of fraud."[13] Also, there was general agreement that the "primary objective of an independent audit should be to review the financial position and results of operations as indicated by the financial statements of the client so that an opinion on the fairness of such presentation can be rendered to the many publics of the client."[14]

"In most professions it is rather difficult to predict the future, but there are some significant trends revealed by the history of auditing

---

[9]Robert H. Montgomery. *Auditing Theory and Practice,* 8th ed. (New York: Roland Press, 1912), p. 13.
[10]R. Gene Brown. "Changing Audit Objectives and Techniques." *The Accounting Review,* October, 1962, pp. 697, 700, 708.
[11]Cashin, *op. cit.,* pp. 1-9.
[12]Brown, *op. cit.,* pp. 697, 700, 708.
[13]*Ibid.,* pp. 697, 700, 708.
[14]Cashin, *op. cit.,* pp. 1-9.

which should carry forward into succeeding years. Interpreted to be in line with changing audit objectives and techniques, these trends seem to indicate:

1. The first and foremost audit objective will remain the determination of the fairness of financial statement assertions.

2. Reliance on the system of internal controls will increase. The audit will be primarily a system of audit procedures. Detailed testing will take place only insofar as it is required to detect irregularities and errors, or to evaluate the effectiveness of the internal controls.

3. Since the fairness of the financial statement assertions is affected by all material misstatements, there will be acceptance of the general responsibility of the auditor to perform tests to detect material defalcations and errors if they exist. This will be incorporated as a supplementary audit objective."[15]

"Parallel to the growth of independent auditing in the United States, internal and governmental auditing developed and became part of the field of auditing. As independent auditors recognized the importance of good internal control and its bearing on the extent of testing necessary in the independent audit, they supported the growth of auditing departments within client organizations [that] would be charged with the development and maintenance of good internal control procedures apart from the general accounting department. Progressive companies fostered the expansion of the activities of internal audit departments into areas which are beyond the scope of the accounting system. Today, many internal audit departments are reviewers of all phases of a corporation's operations, of which financial operations are a part."[16]

In 1921, the Congress of the United States established the General Accounting Office (GAO) formally recognizing governmental auditing. "This law . . . directed the Comptroller General, among other things, to investigate all matters relating to the receipt, disbursement, and application of public funds."[17] Later legislation extended and clarified the Comptroller General's audit authority, particularly with respect to government corporations. However, it was the 1921 law which laid the primary foundation for a broad scope of auditing that went beyond accounting, financial matters, and legal compliance. The scope of the audit mandate given by Congress to

---

[15] Brown, *op. cit.,* pp. 697, 700, 708.
[16] Cashin, *op. cit.,* pp. 1-9.
[17] *Ibid.,* pp. 1-9.

the Comptroller General continues to grow, sometimes on a "reactive" basis (e.g., overbillings, based on estimated percent of completion on a project; duplicate payments, accidently and, possibly, on purpose; improper accounting, such as billing a "cost plus" contract with expenses that properly belong to a "fixed cost" contract). On other occasions, the Comptroller General acts on a "proactive" basis striving to get improved systems and controls in place relative to (a) internal administration and operational practices of governmental entities; and (b) the administrative and operational practices of contractors who have signed contracts to provide work and/or services, meeting stipulated quality control standards and specifications. By the early 1970s, a survey showed there were more than 75 separate audit organizations in the federal government. By now the number is probably a 100 or so. The Department of Defense itself has nearly 4,000 auditors. Some of their recent publicized events have included (a) Rockwell International booking "fixed cost" contract amounts to "cost plus" contracts; (b) Sunstrand Corp. paying penalties in the nine figures; and (c) heavy penalties against other defense contractors that had to pay assessed penalties or be barred from bidding on government contracts.

The American Institute of Accountants (AIA), now the American Institute of Certified Public Accountants (AICPA), (a) published in 1917 a pronouncement that referred to "balance sheet" audits; (b) they revised it in 1929 with a pamphlet entitled "Verification of Financial Statements," which still emphasized the balance sheet audit but also discussed income statement accounts indicating an increasing interest in results of operations and, finally, the pronouncement also covered reporting practices and stressed reliance on internal controls; and (c) a 1936 revision that was entitled "Examination of Financial Statements by Independent Public Accountants." The change to the word "examination" rather than "verification" indicates the fundamental changes in auditing theory and practices that had occurred. It indicated the "testing of selected items," rather than implying a detailed audit of all data. The era of audit-standard setting began in earnest in 1939, when the AICPA created the Committee on Auditing Procedure. They issued the first Statement on Auditing Procedures (SAP) shortly thereafter and had issued 54 SAPs before its name was changed to the Auditing Standards Executive Committee, later renamed the Auditing Standards Board, which codified all the SAPs in its Statement on Auditing Standards (SAS) No. 1. The SAS pronouncements continue to the present, in many instances.

The AICPA properly has concluded, through its Commission on Auditors' Responsibilities, that:

"Audited financial statements cannot be perfectly accurate, in part be-cause of the ambiguity of the accounting concepts they reflect . . . [Also,] accounting results—the financial statements—cannot be more accurate and reliable than the underlying accounting measurement methods per-mit. For example, no one, including accountants, can foresee the results of many uncertain future events. To the extent that the accuracy of an accounting presentation is dependent on an unpredictable future event, the accounting presentation can be no more accurate, for the auditor cannot add certainty where it does not exist."[18]

In the late 19th Century and early 20th Century a new concept called "operational auditing" came into being. Its intent was to fill a need for a management tool that could be involved with day to day administrative and operational matters, not just financial matters, to help management keep informed on all areas of its respon-sibilities.

My favorite definition of "operational auditing," which is pre-ferred over that of the one used by The Institute of Internal Audi-tors, is:

"Operational auditing is using common sense, or logical audit tech-niques, with management perspective, and applying them to company objectives, operations, controls, communications, and information sys-tems. The auditor is more concerned with the who, what, when, where, why, and how of running an efficient and profitable business than just the accounting and financial aspects of the business functions."[19]

Another related definition is:

"Central to the whole concept of operations auditing is the idea that, if they are to operate incisively and creatively, managers need some kind of early warning system for the detection of potentially destructive prob-lems and opportunities for improvement. That is, modern business has had to develop ways to anticipate and cope with the heightened risks and more sophisticated resources involved in reaching its objectives."[20]

While most think of operational auditing as new, one speaker summarized its history as:

"It seems likely that the operational audit is even older than double-entry bookkeeping, inasmuch as it is purely the product of applied common sense."[21]

---

[18] "Reports, Conclusions, and Recommendations." Statement of AICPA Commission on Audi-tors Responsibilities, 1978, p. 7.

[19] Anton Steven, "Operational Audits of Construction Contracts." *The Internal Audit*, v. 30, May-June, 1973, p. 10.

[20] Flesher and Siewert. *Independent Auditor's Guide to Operational Auditing*, (New York; Ronald Press, 1982), pp. 5, 6, 8.

[21] Reginald H. Jones. *"Audit of the Future."* Unpublished speech before New York Chapter of the Institute of Internal Auditors, February, 1969.

Evidence has been found that The Krupp Company in Germany was using some form of operational auditing as far back as 1875. Its company audit manual then stated:

"The auditors are to determine whether laws, contracts, policies and procedures have been properly observed and whether all business transactions were conducted in accordance with established policies and with success. In this connection, the auditors are to make suggestions for the improvement of existing facilities and procedures, criticisms of contracts with suggestions for improvement, etc."[22]

In the United States about 1919, a leading railroad used its internal auditors to perform operational audits of dining-car service.[23] The audit report on such efforts outlined a wide range of inefficiencies, extravagance, and incidents of dishonesty.

In 1941, Brad Cadmus and some associates formed The Institute of Internal Auditing (IIA), with the objective of establishing internal auditing as a recognized profession. In 1959, the organization adopted "operational auditing" as the basic internal auditing approach they would promote. The basic objective of all internal auditing, not just those using "operational auditing," was and is the desire to provide management with an expanded control over all activities of the organization, on a reasonable basis.

In 1957, the IIA established the following Statement of Responsibilities:

"NATURE OF INTERNAL AUDITING. Internal auditing is an independent appraisal activity within an organization for the review of accounting, financial, and other operations as a basis for service to management. It is a managerial control which functions by measuring and evaluating the effectiveness of other controls."[24]

"OBJECTIVE AND SCOPE OF INTERNAL AUDITING. The overall objective of internal auditing is to assist all members of management in the effective discharge of their responsibilities by furnishing them with objective analyses, appraisals, recommendations, and pertinent comments concerning the activities reviewed. The internal auditor therefore should be concerned with any phase of business activity wherein he can be of service to management."[25]

To achieve the quoted objectives, the internal auditor must:

1. Review and appraise soundness and adequacy of accounting, financial, administrative, and operating controls.

---

[22] Flesher and Siewert, *op. cit.*, pp. 5, 6, 8.
[23] *Ibid.*, pp. 5, 6, 8.
[24] *Ibid.*, pp. 5, 6, 8.
[25] *Ibid.*, pp. 5, 6, 8.

2. Affirm compliance with policies, plans, procedures, and regulatory requirements, as applicable to the business.

3. Assure adequate controls are in place to affirm reasonably that company assets are accounted for and adequately safeguarded.

4. Ascertain reliability of accounting and other company data.

5. Appraise performance, at all levels, in fulfilling assigned responsibilities.

In summary, the internal auditor is charged with evaluation, compliance, and verification of accounting, financial, administrative, and operational activities, procedures, and practices of the business.

As "operational auditing" became increasingly accepted, internal auditors striving to broaden ways they could assist senior management began to see how they could accomplish that worthwhile objective. As a result, "operational auditing" expanded increasingly into assisting directly with management activities (e.g., strategic planning, budgeting, new product or service introduction). This progressed so far that a second higher tier of "operational auditing" came into being. It has been called "management auditing" or "management-oriented auditing." The American Institute of Management (AIM), now defunct, came up with the term "management auditing" in the 1950s, and it was commonly used until near the end of the 1960s when AIM folded. Actually, it was more a form of "management analysis" than true auditing. In 1983, IIA published a booklet entitled *Elements of Management-Oriented Auditing*, written by Lawrence B. Sawyer. The terms "management auditing" or "management-oriented auditing" in this text will be synonymous. However, because of AIM, the latter term is preferred to describe the second higher tier of "operational auditing."

With the broadened perspective of auditing, and the formulation of standards for internal auditing by IIA, the American Accounting Association (AAA) Committee on Basic Auditing Concepts in 1973 came up with the following to describe both the process and purposes of auditing:

> "Auditing is a systematic process of objectively obtaining and evaluating evidence regarding assertions about economic actions and events to ascertain the degree of correspondence between those assertions and established criteria and communicating the results to interested users."

AAA wanted a definition that was intentionally broad as it encompassed "the many different purposes for which an audit might be conducted and the variety of subject matter which might be focused on in a specific audit engagement."

Auditing has evolved to where creativity is encouraged. This has resulted in new approaches and techniques, for both external and internal auditors. Some examples:

1. External Auditors

   (a) Development and implementation, by many, of the "cycle" concept, which will be described in some detail throughout this book.

   (b) Movement of "internal controls" up from *a necessary evil*, of minimum audit value, as I viewed it when in public accounting in the 1950s, to the point where its rightful importance is recognized and duly emphasized starting in the 1970s, and it continues to grow in importance when evaluating accounting, finance, administration, and operations.

   (c) Development of far better perspective and understanding of any activity, function, product, service, facility as well as accounting, finance, administration, and operations relative to any upcoming audit during the familiarization phase, the first phase of an audit examination.

   (d) Betterment of training, at all levels, relative to the criteria under points *(a)* through *(c)*.

2. Internal Auditors

   (a) Improvement of staffing standards.

   (b) Greater discipline in environment on programs, checklists, flow charts, audit techniques, and approaches, to be as nearly comparable in this regard to external auditors.

   (c) Greater focus on efficiency, effectiveness, and economy.

   (d) Assurance of sound internal controls and checks existing, relative to all phases of the involved business, while validating that such controls and checks are cost/risk or value/risk effective, unless reasons are valid for bypassing such standards.

   (e) Development and implementation of "early warning" standards and criteria (e.g., "anticipatory auditing"; use of broader exception reports through automated systems when unusual or irregular conditions are identified, either in nature of transaction or amount; and adding dimensions of psychological control—polygraph, when appropriate and where allowed; psychological testing; improved interviewing; and, where appropriate, interrogation, and more "hands-on" auditing by physically observing what is going on in the environment under audit).

(f) Adoption of "cycle" auditing concepts developed and used by the external auditors, on an increasing basis.

(g) Use of computer software to make inquiries into and extract data from computers. Audit through and not around the computers (e.g., input, processing and storage, and output).

(h) Utilization of tools such as message recording, cameras, etc., to provide both evidence of events or to focus on areas of concern.

(i) Use of the risk management concept of auditing to focus on human resources to hold *risks* at levels acceptable to management. This is relative to *any* aspect of the business.

Figure 1
Historical Perspective of Auditing

Date	Event
4000 B.C.	First audits involving scribes and tax collections in areas of Middle East.
1900 B.C. - 95 A.D.	Biblical references to internal controls and surprise audits.
1130 A.D.	Audits of revenue and expenditures by Exchequers of England and Scotland
1500s	Manorial accounts audited by member(s) of council (really precursor of internal auditor).
17th Century	Law prohibiting town officials in England from serving as auditors (first indication of auditor independence).
1854	Creation of the "chartered accountant" (CA) designation in Scotland.
1887	Establishment of American Institute of Accountants (AIA) now the American Institute of Certified Public Accountants (AICPA) in United States.
1896	New York State passed first CPA law; creation of the CPA designation.
1900	Annual audits made compulsory for limited companies in Britain.
Early 1900s	Evolution of U.S. audits from "detailed" audits to "test" audits—in effect a change from examination to verification.
1921	General Accounting Office (GAO) created by the Budget and Accounting Act.
1936	Revised auditing pronouncement entitled "Examination of Financial Statements" by independent public accountants.
1939	First Statement on Auditing Procedures issued.
1941	Institute of Internal Auditors (IIA) founded.
1959	IIA adopts "operational auditing" as the internal audit standard.
1978	Foreign Corrupt Practices Act (FCPA) places increased responsibility on auditors, external and internal, as to ethics in the conduct of business.
1980s	The Treadway Commission again increased the responsibilities of both external and internal auditors to be more diligent relative to the reality of fraudulent activities in any company.

2

Traditional (Vertical) Internal Audit Methodology

Definitions

VERTICAL. "... Pointing straight down...; lying in the direction of an axis: Lengthwise (up - down)... Plumb stresses an exact verticality determined (as with a plumb line)..."[26]

For audit purposes, a vertical review of any activity, function, product, service, facility, or organizational unit, relating to any or all of the following (1) accounting, (2) finance, (3) administration, (4) operations, (5) security, and (6) controls, is normally self-contained and involves comparing one thing (e.g., general ledger, trial balance) with another (e.g., subsidiary records supporting a trial balance or general ledger figure; or confirming by count cash and/or securities to a control figure in related records).

ATTEST. "To affirm to be true or genuine...; to authenticate officially..."[27] "To authenticate formally, as in a report; to express, after careful investigation, an opinion of correctness."[28]

ATTEST FUNCTION. "Refers to the extention of the" auditor's role "to any situation where he may be called upon for an objective statement of fact or opinion that may assist in the making of judgments by others."[29]

CERTIFY. "Attest applied to oral or written testimony usually from experts or witnesses. ... To attest authoritatively. ... To attest as being true or as represented or as meeting a standard."[30]

Attest Reviews and Controls

The concept of attest review represented the first known form of auditing. In some instances, where only one scribe (bookkeeper) was used, some other person would be designated to take a physical inventory (e.g., Armory: swords, spears, shields; Warehouses: bags of wheat and other grains, bolts of cloths; Treasury: units of coins,

---

[26]*Webster's Ninth New Collegiate Dictionary.* (Springfield, Mass.: Merriam-Webster, 1986), p. 1311.
[27]*Ibid.*, p. 115.
[28]Eric L. Kohler. *A Dictionary for Accountants*, 4th ed. (Englewood Cliffs, N.J.: Prentice-Hall, 1970), p. 39.
[29]*Ibid.*, p. 39.
[30]Webster's, *op. cit.*, p. 223.

bullion of precious metal, gemstones; Household Items: specific items in particular locations; Fields: numbers of various types of livestock).

The independent count would then be compared with the continuing record as kept by the scribe. Differences, if any, would be followed up to affirm the accuracy of the records or whether thefts of the goods counted had occurred. If the records were found incorrect, and the reason identified, a simple correction would be made to adjust the record. If the difference was material and the reason was unknown, another person would take a second inventory. When that was done, the two inventories would be compared. If they did not agree then the two inventory takers would take a third inventory together. It was normal practice to accept the counts where two or more of the inventories taken were the same, or take the lowest count if all three inventories differed on the same item. The second or third counts may be made only for items where the first counts did not agree with the records. Where one or more of the counts did not agree with the records, a transactions review may have been made to assure all that had been recorded was correct. Differences would be adjusted that would reduce or eliminate variances between counts and records.

Where two scribes maintained independent inventory records, the first step would be to compare them and identify any differences and follow back to ascertain why such differences arose (e.g., an entry made into one record and not the other). Once they agreed or followed back and made adjustments to bring them into agreement, then procedures described earlier for only one record being maintained were implemented.

From an audit perspective, attest requires that something is compared with something (e.g., inventory with continuing record or one inventory with a second inventory). If agreement exists, then attestation or certification can be made. If disagreement exists, one of the following options must be adopted:

1. Identify differences between records, if two sets are independently prepared, and follow back to determine the cause after which adjustment(s) are made to bring them into agreement.

2. Identify differences between record(s) and inventory and determine *(a)* whether to accept inventory figures, making appropriate adjustment to record(s) if minor differences are identified or *(b)* whether a second inventory should be taken. If the two inventories taken are in agreement then normal practice is to adjust record(s) to inventory and attempt to determine causes for differences. If inventories indicate shortages, when

compared with records, a decision must be made as to what, if any, additional inventory controls are necessary, on a cost-justified basis, to assure better the integrity of the inventories. In some instances, if the two inventories differ, a decision may be made to take a third inventory. Normally this is only done when such differences are significant. Otherwise, the general rule-of-thumb, for practical purposes, is (1) accept the inventory which agrees with the records, thereby eliminating any need for adjustment of the records, or (2) accept the lower count, if both inventories differ from the records.

Why is attest considered a vertical review? Because a picture is worth a thousand words, the diagrams in Figure 2 will illustrate the vertical nature of such audit undertakings.

To put the preceding into perspective, now is the appropriate time to describe *vertical auditing.* It is not a single audit approach but a variety of auditing approaches and techniques which, by their nature, differ from those of *horizontal auditing,* which will be described in Chapter 3.

Vertical Auditing Under Various Audit Formats

Attest Reviews

This NOW concept compares a physical record to the items being recorded in such a record, in full or by specific classifications or category. Such reviews can be performed in either direction (e.g., record to item(s) or, the reverse, item(s) to record). (*Note:* The situation was just described in text.)

Financial Auditing

The trial balance approach to auditing the general ledger of a facility, division, department, area, region, product or service line, or entire company follows the account in their normal and logical order from beginning (top) to end (bottom) which sequentially list asset accounts, liability accounts, capital accounts, income accounts, and, finally, expense accounts at a specific date or for a specific audit period.

Operational Auditing

1. Systems Approach (utilized when there are *not* formal policy and procedure criteria to audit against, including criteria to

Figure 2
Vertical Aspect of Attest Audits

(A) Comparison of Inventory(ies) to Single Inventory Record

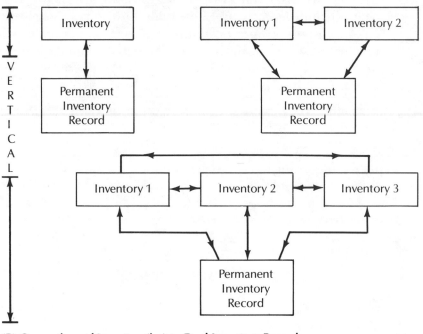

(B) Comparison of Inventory(ies) to Dual Inventory Records

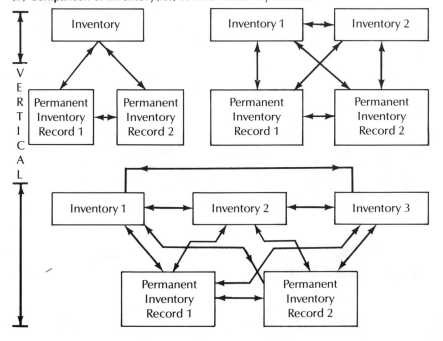

assure regulatory compliance). The auditor *(a)* develops flow charts and related information by actually following work processes and control requirements step by step and *(b)* then developing similar information, working with management, which is responsible for directing such work processes. The data developed under items *(a)* and *(b)* are then compared, and differences identified, discussed, and a decision made as to whether one or both should be revised to bring them into agreement. The operational environment agreed upon is then assessed by the auditor for efficiency, effectiveness, economy, and adequacy of internal controls and checks. Recommendations would be made to improve any of those factors, where and when appropriate.

2. Performance Approach (used when there is a formal policy or procedure to audit against, including criteria to assure regulatory compliance). The auditor must:

   (a) Evaluate the policy and procedure criteria to ascertain if they provide a work environment for the work processes that is efficient, effective, and economical, with adequate internal controls and checks, as well as assure compliance with all appropriate regulatory requirements. Deficiencies, if any are identified, would be reported to management with suggestions on how they could be eliminated.

   (b) Compare the actual work processes to determine whether they are in compliance with the policy and procedure criteria, as under item *(a)* above. If any deficiencies are identified, they would be reported to management with suggested changes required for compliance with the related policy and procedure criteria to assure full compliance with regulatory requirements.

Management-Oriented Auditing

1. Identifies variances such as "actual" against "budget" by cost-center, product or service line, activity, function, division, department, facility, or overall institution. Follow-up is needed to determine causes (e.g., timing difference, unrealistic budget objectives, ineffective marketing efforts, poor systems resulting in customer dissatisfaction).

2. Reviews and assesses organizational structure to assure that authority and responsibility are clearly defined so auditors can perform reviews on a "responsibility accounting" basis.

3. Determines that goals and objectives in strategic plan are the basis for forward management thinking or, if that has changed, the strategic plan has been revised accordingly and it has been communicated effectively to all management levels.

Financial Auditing

"A financial audit is a review of the assertions made on published financial statements. . . . This particular kind of audit must be made in accordance with generally accepted auditing standards. Although such an audit could be performed by internal or governmental auditors, a lesser degree of independence implicit in their relationship to the unit being audited may mitigate the reliability of their report. A financial audit is not a detailed review in any way. It is a test of accounting and other related records. The scope of these tests is determined by the auditors based on their own judgment and experience."[31]

U.S. external auditors determined "that the objective of external auditing changed" from the fraud-oriented approach of their U.K. counterparts "to a professional review of financial statements by an expert, so that a professional opinion indicating that financial condition and results of operations have been fairly presented can be given. The change in objective was effected because auditors recognized the importance of good internal control."[32] The basic logic was that internal control is "the plan or organization and all of the coordinate methods and measures adopted within a business to safeguard its assets, check the accuracy and reliability of its accounting data, promote operational efficiency, and encourage adherence to prescribed managerial policies."[33] "If the system of internal control is adequate, the probability that fraud or other errors exist in any magnitude is remote."[34]

"Independent auditors (private or governmental) must review the system of internal control in each engagement and based on its adequacy . . . develop the scope of their examination. Internal auditors are usually given the responsibility (among others) to design, implement, review, and revise the system of internal control in their company or agency."[35]

---

[31]Cashin, *op. cit.*, pp. 1-12.
[32]*Ibid.*, pp. 1-12.
[33]Howard F. Stetler. *Systems Based Independent Audits.* (Englewood Cliffs, N.J., 1967), p. 6.
[34]Cashin, *op. cit.*, pp. 1-12.
[35]*Ibid.*, pp. 1-12.

"The underlying assumption in auditing financial statements is that they will be used by different groups for different purposes. . . . For example, a general audit of a business may provide sufficient accounting information for a banker who is considering making a loan to the company, but a corporation considering a merger with that business may also wish to know the replacement cost of fixed assets and other information relevant to the decision. The corporation may use its own internal auditors "to get the information."[36] The internal auditor, when performing financial audits within his own institution, may be striving to determine (1) compliance with policies, procedures, and regulatory requirements; (2) proper use of accounts, particularly "suspense," or "interbranch clearing" types of accounts; and (3) adequacy of and compliance with required internal control and check criteria to provide reasonable comfort and confidence in the financial records to be audited.

In addition to internal and external auditors, a third classification is normally geared to financial audits, including compliance with applicable laws and regulations. That is governmental auditing. Before proceeding to the subject of financial auditing, readers should comprehend the function of governmental auditing, which is defined as:

> ". . . The most comprehensive of the three branches of auditing. Many governmental agencies have internal auditing departments which are expected to confine their investigations to the specific agency. Other governmental units such as the GAO (General Accounting Office) are set up' for the specific purpose of performing audits of other governmental units and of the private enterprises who do business with the government where the right of the governmental unit to perform such audits is a prerequisite for contract awards."[37]

Having commented on each of the three major classifications of auditing, it seems appropriate to note that "the similarities in the work of auditors in these several fields" of financial auditing "are far more important than the differences. All those engaged in auditing are concerned with audit evidence, collect it through application of the same basic techniques, and have similar problems of report writing and program planning. Certain essentials must receive first attention, therefore, regardless of which field of auditing constitutes the auditor's major interest."[38]

---

[36]Alvin A. Arens and James K. Loebbecke. *Auditing—An Integrated Approach*, 4th ed. (Englewood Cliffs, N.J.: Prentice-Hall, 1988), pp. 6, 258, 259.

[37]Cashin, *op. cit.*, pp. 1-12.

[38]"Philosophy of Auditing." Paper presented at American Accounting Assn. meeting in Chicago in 1961, p. 5.

19

Compliance Auditing

"Superior policies, procedures, or controls are of no value unless they are carefully followed in practice. Thus, once the internal auditor has evaluated the effectiveness of a given plan of organization and operation, he will endeavor to ascertain whether the planned program is actually being carried out in practice. The techniques range from inquiry and observation to examination of the records and reports prepared and proof of completed work to establish that the work has been properly performed. The compliance activities of the internal auditor are particularly important in companies with extensive branch operations. The procedures to be used in each branch will usually be carefully designed in the home office, and the internal auditor will thus concentrate on compliance and, of course, verification in making an examination of branch operations."[39]

"A compliance audit is one designed to determine if certain contractual agreements have been kept. For example, many contracts let by the federal government contain certain statements which tie the amount to be paid out under the contract to specific performance of the contractor. Quality of product and cost to produce are but two examples of many determinations governing the amount to be paid out in such contracts. A compliance audit seeks to determine if the terms of the contract have been kept. One agency of the federal government is set up for the express purpose of performing compliance audits—The Defense Contract Audit Agency."[40] In recent times, they have found violations by defense contractors resulting in fines up to nine figures and prohibiting guilty contractors from bidding for new government business until they have paid the fines and satisfied requirements on internal management, administration, accounting, and controls.

"The purpose of compliance tests is to provide evidence" that internal accounting controls and applicable administrative and operating controls, to a somewhat lesser degree "for the achievement of specific control objectives, are being applied as prescribed." Such tests "are usually performed only on those . . . controls that the auditor intends to rely on for . . . restricting substantive audit tests. This is true regardless of whether the controls are manually operated or carried out by computer programs to programmed procedures. The purpose of compliance testing dictates that all controls that the auditor intends to rely on as part of the overall audit strategy should be

---

[39]Howard F. Stettles. *Auditing Principles,* 4th ed. (Englewood Cliffs, N.J.: Prentice-Hall, 1977), p. 86.
[40]Cashin, *op. cit.,* pp. 1-12.

tested. The key to determining the appropriate compliance tests for audit purposes is to identify the internal accounting controls designed to achieve the specific control objectives applicable to a particular transaction cycle" supplemented by tests of administrative and operational control as appropriate." The compliance tests—which include examining records and documents for evidence, reperforming the controls by duplicating the actions of the "audited unit's" personnel, and observing how the controls are exercised. Such tests are designed to show whether the controls have operated satisfactorily throughout the period of intended reliance."[41]

"Compliance tests normally precede substantive tests because the evidence obtained from them provides the basis for determining the nature, extent, and timing of substantive tests. . . . Compliance tests' ordinarily involve examining evidence that a control was applied or reperforming the procedure constituting the control."[42]

Substantive Auditing

"Substantive tests consist of tests of the details of transactions and account balances, analytical review procedures, and other auditing procedures. The purpose of substantive tests is to provide the auditor with direct evidence of the validity of management's assertions that are implicit in the financial statements."[43] Another writer considers that "a substantive test is a procedure designed to test for dollar errors directly affecting the fair presentation of financial statement balances. Such errors (often termed monetary errors) are a clear indication of the misstatement of the accounts. The only question the auditor must resolve is whether the errors are sufficiently material to require adjustment or disclosure. Examples of substantive tests are comparing a sales invoice with a shipping document to determine whether the quantity shipped equals the quantity billed, footing the sales invoice for accuracy, and confirming the customers'"[44] accounts or loan balances. "The selection of substantive tests is based on the audit strategy and the degree of reliance placed on internal accounting controls"[45] as determined during the preceding compliance reviews. "Substantive tests generally fall into three broad categories: direct tests of the details of transactions and account balances, analytical review procedures, and 'other' auditing procedures. Substantive tests of details normally involve confirma-

[41]Sullivan, et al., *op. cit.*, pp. 187, 328, 329.
[42]*Ibid.*, pp. 187, 328, 329.
[43]*Ibid.*, pp. 187, 328, 329.
[44]Arens and Loebbecke, *op. cit.*, pp. 6, 258, 259.
[45]Sullivan, et al., *op. cit.*, pp. 187, 328, 329.

tion, vouching, and obtaining representations from the client. Analytical review procedures are tests of financial information made by a study and comparison of relationships among data. Examples of other auditing procedures include obtaining written and oral representations and reading minutes of meetings"[46] such as board of directors, credit committee, strategic planning committees, and audit committee of board.

Relationship Between Compliance and Substantive Tests

"To better understand the nature of compliance and substantive tests, an examination of their differences is useful. Compliance tests differ from substantive tests in that an error in a compliance test is only an indication of the likelihood of errors affecting the dollar value of the financial statements. Compliance errors are material only if they occur with sufficient frequency to cause the auditor to believe there may be material dollar errors in the statements. Substantive tests should then be performed to determine whether dollar errors have actually occurred. ..." A compliance audit procedure would be to examine a sample of loan disbursement invoices "for the initials of the person who verified" that all bank criteria had been met before disbursing funds. If there is a significant number of documents with a signature, the auditor should follow this up with substantive tests. ... There are two circumstances in which the auditor may decide not to perform compliance tests on a particular control in the system:

- "He concludes that the control procedure is not effective and the justification for not testing is that there is no reason to test a control the auditor considers too ineffective to reply upon."

- "When audit costs required to test for compliance is greater than the cost savings from reduced substantive tests that would result from relying upon the client's controls" ... and when such a situation is encountered "substantive tests would have to be increased accordingly."

"Even if the auditor's compliance tests yield good results, some substantive tests are necessary ..." "The audit procedures, sample size, selection of the items for testing, and timing of substantive tests

---

[46]*Ibid.*, pp. 187, 328, 329.

can be modified and reduced by compliance tests, but they cannot be eliminated."[47]

It is important not to forget that compliance and substantive tests are audit *techniques* whereas attest, financial auditing, and operational auditing are audit *methodologies*. While we have written up these techniques under financial auditing, they are applicable to all audit methodologies presented in this book with the exception of attest or attestation reviews, which by their limited scope prohibit effective use of the two techniques.

Summary

Simply stated, the vertical audit concept is:

1. Following a trial balance from beginning (asset) to end (expense), with the general ledger figures usually presented in a vertical format.

2. Separating the trial balance, as under item 1, and dealing with the two individual resulting statements, which are:

    (a) Balance Sheet; reflecting assets, liabilities, and net worth that are usually shown in a vertical format.

    (b) Income Statement; reflecting income and expenses that are usually shown in a vertical format.

3. Comparing a base item, which can be a primary or secondary record or the physical component recorded therein, with each maintained and controlled by different persons or authorities, one being of higher or lower rate than the other, thus creating the vertical environment under review.

Although compliance and substantive auditing are described in this chapter, you should recognize that as *techniques* not *methodologies* they are not limited to vertical reviews but can be used effectively in electronic data processing or horizontal reviews.

---

[47]*Ibid.,* pp. 187, 328, 329.

3

Electronic Data Processing Auditing

Objectives of a Sound EDP Organization

Basic objectives should serve the organization effectively by:

1. Promoting efficiency, effectiveness, and economy of operations.

2. Protecting the accuracy, integrity, and security of all data processed by or stored in the computer.

Some years ago, the primary emphasis was on point 1. However, in recent years, because of hackers, viruses, and internal manipulation of data to perpetrate fraud, the primary emphasis is now on the elements listed under point 2.

Three basic elements must be considered when analyzing the EDP organization. They are:

1. The reporting level of the function. This is critical as it indicates the lines of communication to management and other important related function in the organization.

2. The structure. This deals with the grouping and separation of functions in the EDP environment. Here, we are concerned with delegation of authority and responsibilities for reasons of balancing and ensurance of effective separation of duties.

3. The functional characteristics of each individual, unit, or group responsibilities. If the mission of each is adequately defined, this is referred to as the charter of responsibilities that assists in *(a)* avoiding misunderstandings as to duties, tasks, authority, and responsibility, and *(b)* enabling the establishment of effective internal controls, checks, and security throughout the EDP environment.

Now let us create hypothetical organizations for small, medium, and larger EDP administrative and operational environments:

1. One-Person EDP Organization
   Such an organization is obviously undesirable because it enables *(a)* no segregation of duties, and *(b)* virtually no internal controls or checks over the activities of the individual. That individual would perform all the data processing functions of systems, programming, machine operations, data preparation,

data control, and data security while acting as both worker and supervisor of the environment. Such organization looks like this:

Figure 3
One-Person EDP Organization (no separation of duties)

2. Organization for Small Installations

One simple organizational segregation of duties for small to medium-sized EDP installations would be as shown in Figure 4. It has the EDP manager, with three traditional separate functions of control, machine operations, and systems planning and development, including programming. The basic controls, with such segregation of duties, involves systems planning and development being responsible for new systems or revisions of current systems but never for their operation. On the other hand, operators do not have access to and do not change programs. The control function has the responsibility to coordinate and control the daily flow of work for the EDP organization. The manager is responsible for all key administrative functions in the environment.

Figure 4
Minimum Separation of Functions—Small/Medium EDP Organizations

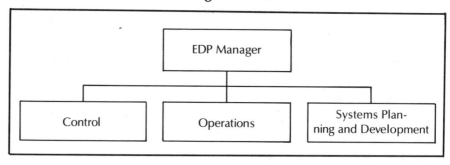

3. Organization and Separation of Function in a Large EDP Installation

In the development function, one can separate the systems

analysis and design function from the program design and programming function. The systems analysis and design personnel work towards the needs of the business or the user function and think in terms of what should or could be computerized versus what should not. They are the problem-definition and problem-solving personnel who must consider computer and noncomputer viable alternatives when dealing with specific problems. On the other hand, the programming function is oriented toward the machine-implementation phase. They determine how best to use the hardware/software capabilities.

As in any operating environment, the organization should be structured to provide maximum internal check by one function or activity over the actions of another. This is done while providing a clear mandate relative to each organizational segment, and with the environment structured so sound internal controls exist throughout in policies, procedures, and standards to the maximum degree. A sample organization is shown in Figure 5.

Figure 5 illustrates the importance of organization and separation of certain activities and functions in EDP. Consider the following:

(a) Development Function

The systems analysis and design functions, shown under "Systems," are oriented towards the needs of the business or specific *user* management. They think in terms of what should or should not be computerized. They constitute the problem-definition and problem-solving phase by considering options in the problem situation. They are responsible for assuring that sound controls end up in the adopted solution. On the other hand, program design and programming personnel, shown under "Programming," are oriented towards the machine-implementation phase. They strive to determine how best to use hardware/software capabilities relative to any problem situation.

If it is not organizationally feasible to have such a separation of duties, then recognize that the analyst/programmer should be responsible for the generation of detailed specifications for documentation purposes, even where that individual handles the programming. This assures proper future documentation.

(b) Operations Function

Sometimes referred to as the "machine operations func-

Figure 5
Organization and Separation of Functions—Large Installations

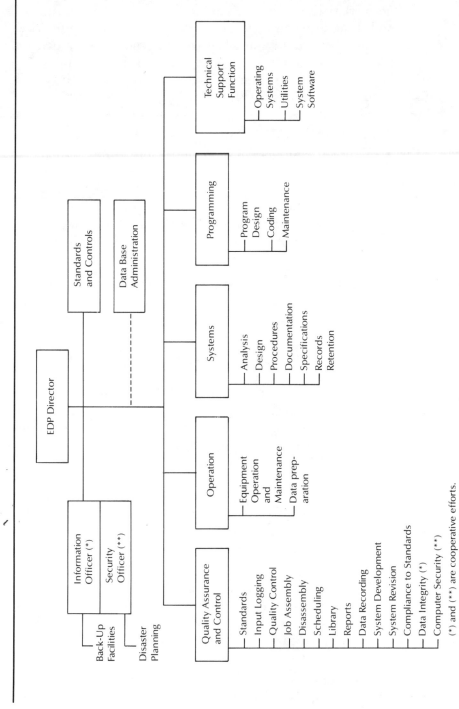

(*) and (**) are cooperative efforts.

tion," it should be responsible for only two functions, as shown, which are to operate the EDP equipment, and to maintain the equipment. They should be operating with a formalized set of operating standards and procedures.

(c) Data Preparation Function

In some organizations, this is combined with the other duties of the "machine operations function." Avoid this, if possible. Far better control exists when duties are separated. This separation requires effective communications between data preparation personnel and control function personnel who are responsible for delivering, scheduling, and receiving data. Where possible in this work environment, communications should not exist between data preparation personnel or (1) user (or data source) and (2) machine operations personnel. This separation reduces the risk of collusion involving irregular practices or activities.

(d) Technical Support Function

This function has to deal with the technical and administrative aspects of what can be referred to as "environmental" software that runs the computer hardware. The function also affects the application systems software. The personnel also have the ability to support the operating system, the data communications software, and the data base management systems. These three primary software packages are responsible for job and resource management or, if you prefer, the operating system. Usually, personnel in this area are the most technically skilled on the staff. It is a risk to become excessively dependent on their computer competency. They should operate within the framework of an adequate set of standards and controls to safeguard the integrity of the EDP systems.

(e) Data Base Administration

This program encompasses a series of functions and tasks vital to the design, operation, hardware and software maintenance, and security of the overall corporate data base. The function develops and coordinates standards and practices for data management. This function also is charged with managing key aspects of the data base systems management (DBMS) and data dictionary system (DDS), if one is used to assist in managing data.

(f) Data Security Administration Function

This function is charged with responsibility for the logical access security and the privacy and confidentiality of all data and computer security. Having an information officer and a security officer enables their duties to be separated. Together, they should be concerned with the selection, implementation, and administration of the data security access programs. Also, while data base administration focuses on developing ways to recover damage or loss of information in the data base, the security function will be more concerned with immediate and long-range contingency and recovery planning for the entire data center and related business systems.

(g) Quality Assurance and Control Function

Too often this function is understaffed and does not have the skill levels it needs in those carrying out the function. However, the function is an excellent source of control information that can be useful to EDP auditors. If properly structured and adequately staffed, this function could take on more control duties, releasing the EDP auditors for other duties. As shown in Figure 5, the duties of this function are varied and vital to effective control over all facets of EDP.

The following responsibilities of the function should be clearly understood:

(1) Input/output task is responsible for processing and/ or logging in all data, materials, documents, and reports that enter or leave the EDP department.

(2) Quality control and product monitoring are concerned with accuracy and timeliness of jobs processed in the data center.

(3) Job dispatching and (micro) scheduling units coordinate all EDP functions.

(4) File library function is responsible for all matters related to receipt, storage, retrieval, and custody of all files (e.g., magnetic media—tapes, disks, or other formats).

(5) Coordination and development of standards are critical. This function may either develop standards or coordinate their development and/or acquisition.

The other duties of this function are relatively self-explanatory.

4. Organizational Checklist for EDP Environment:

(a) Obtain organization chart of department.

(b) Review chart under item (a) and determine titles, authority and responsibility, and incumbents in each key position.

(c) Compare current staffing levels to budgeted level.

(d) Obtain current standards manual for department if available.

(e) Determine if manual under item (d) is current and effectively implemented throughout department.

(f) State who the EDP department manager reports to.

(g) Ask whether management provides adequate support and resources to EDP management.

(h) See whether the EDP department is independent of all operating units to whom it provides services.

(i) Ask whether job descriptions fit the organization chart and provide (1) adequate authority and responsibility to various management levels, and (2) segregated tasks and activities effectively for maximum built-in internal controls/checks.

(j) Set up surprise audits to verify adherence to established practices.

(k) Find out if the following administrative criteria exist:

(i) Systems and procedures manual.

(ii) Programming standards manual.

(iii) Program and console log books adequately documented.

(iv) File retention procedures established and adhered to.

(v) Master files kept under reasonable protective custody.

(l) Ask whether there is a periodic review, annual or more frequently, for evaluating and defining project priorities.

(m) Check whether a formal system exists for evaluating requests for computer services.

(n) Find out whether each accepted computer project undergoes a cost/benefit study before approval.

(o) Ask whether PERT and GANT chart is prepared on each approved computer project.

(p) See if EDP auditors effectively monitor each computer development or major modification of system project.

(q) Ask about periodic measure of the effectiveness of "internal" computer services made as against comparable "external" costs for similar work.

Note: Costs of control over the entire computer environment should be evaluated to assure "values received" exceed "costs incurred."

With a strong organizational structure, formalized standards, procedures, and practices, it is possible to begin assessing all of the following:

- EDP systems planning and development.

- EDP operations.

- EDP premises, including library.

- EDP back-up and disaster planning, which includes data integrity and computer security.

Importance of a Sound Internal Control in EDP Environment

"The system of internal controls or management controls is an essential aspect of running a successful business . . . to protect assets, control activities, and promote operational effectiveness at all levels of the organization."[48]

Most professional auditors and system reviewers may be familiar with how to test conventional and visible controls. However, with the sizable proliferation of computerized systems and the increase in the handling of business operations by computerized applications, the obvious need is for all concerned to become more intimately familiar with approaches, methodologies, and techniques for testing internal control in computerized applications."[49]

"The increased reliance on internal controls in computerized applications is causing auditors to shift audit emphasis. In manual systems, the emphasis was upon evaluating transactions, while in a computerized environment, the emphasis should be upon the evaluation of internal control. As a system reviewer, you have three basic questions on testing that should be answered prior to conducting the audit. These questions are:

1. "What tests should be performed?
2. "How much testing should occur?
3. "Which transactions should be tested?"[50]

The answers to those questions must be based on a value/time relationship by focusing on primary/major risks for each account. The above questions are answered below, in the same order:

1. What tests should be performed?

   By concentrating on the primary area of concern for each account, our testing approach would be designed to focus on these risks:

Category of Account	Primary Risk
Asset	That the accounts will be overstated.
Liability	That the accounts will be understated.
Capital/Equity	That the accounts will be overstated.
Income	That income will be overstated.
Expense	That expenses will be understated.

2. How much testing should occur?

   The degree of testing should be in direct proportion to the risks known or perceived in the area being audited. Risks can be identified and assessed by four general approaches, which are:

   - "Intuition/judgment—The auditor uses a combination of experience, guesswork, tips, and other heuristic criteria to pick areas where the auditor believes the risks exist.

   - "Application experience—The auditor knows where the errors and losses have been occurring and concentrates future tests in those areas.

---

[18] Javier F. Kuong, *Computer Auditing, Security and Internal Control Manual*. (Prentice Hall, 1987), p.6.
[19] *Ibid.*, p. 49.
[50] *Ibid.*, p. 9.

- "Common sense analysis—For example, if all the employees of an organization were paid the minimum wage and the latter multiplied by the number of employees equalled the actual gross payroll, then the auditor could assume minimal payroll risk.

- "Risk scenario—The auditor, in conjunction with other knowledgeable people, spends time identifying risks and then, working with individuals accountable for the application, assesses the severity of those risks."[51]

3. Which transactions should be tested?

- "Strength of internal control—The stronger the system of internal control the less the need for extensive testing.

- "Sampling audit risk—The auditor should make tests based on the sampling audit risk as opposed to the maximum audit risk. This follows the principles of "stratified" testing where the tests are split between amounts of transactions or nature of transactions.

- "Precision—The auditor must determine how much of an error can be tolerated in the audit area. This is the auditor's definition of audit materiality.

- "Reliability—This determines how certain the auditor wants to be that the results of testing are representative of the population. In statistics, this is expressed as confidence. For example, if the auditor wants to be 95 percent confident that the test is representative of the population being tested, an adequate sample to achieve that level of confidence can be developed."[52]

It is important to focus on "risks." They must be identified if anyone is to effectively test internal controls in a computerized environment. "Controls should not be considered a cost of doing business, but a cost-effective means of reducing risks to an acceptable level."[53] You must recognize that most analysts and programmers do not, by training or experience, have the awareness of the total importance of controls and checks that the auditors wish built into programs and systems. As an auditor, you must assume the worst on the part of the analyst or programmer because they are not control oriented but efficiency oriented. Accordingly, adding steps which provide controls and checks are avoided intu-

---

[51] *Ibid.*, p. 12.
[52] *Ibid.*, p. 16.
[53] *Ibid.*, p. 17.

itively unless they understand what should be incorporated into the program or system being developed.

"The following four types of risks need to be considered when reviewing systems of internal control:

- Product risk—The system does not do what the user wants it to do. This can also result from forcing a system to perform functions it was not designed to do.

- Technology risk—Problems in mastering the technology result in systems problems.

- User risk—The user does not understand the information and limitations in reports and/or makes faulty decisions based on that information. Violations of the boundaries of applicability of the system can lead to this.

- Security risk—Valuable information of the organization is stolen or compromised (the privacy and confidentiality implications)."[54]

A variety of techniques and approaches can be used to evaluate internal controls. "The five general methods that you can use to test systems of internal control are:

1. Checklist method—Using a series of questions to interrogate the adequacy of the system of internal control.

2. Static method—Examining the system of internal control from a policy and procedure perspective or on paper.

3. Test data—Developing test transactions to be processed through the application to test the system of internal control.

4. Live data method—Using live transactions as a means of testing the adequacy of internal control.

5. Parallel method—Running live data through the same application twice, or using two applications designed to achieve the same purpose to compare the results for consistency of control."[55]

The Audit Trail in an EDP System

Audit trail can be defined as those records that enable a transaction to be traced from its source forward to a summarized total

---

[54] *Ibid.*, pp. 227-229.
[55] *Ibid.*, pp. 244, 247.

in a financial statement or other document or to provide for tracing an amount in a summarized total back through the records to its source.... The audit trail is an aid to management in responding to questions from employees, customers, vendors, and government agencies as to the status of payments, shipments, and so forth. An EDP system can affect the audit trail in the following ways:

1. "Source documents, once transcribed onto a machine-readable input medium, may be filed in a manner that makes subsequent access difficult...

2. "In some systems, traditional source documents may be eliminated by the use of direct input devices.

3. "Ledger summaries may be replaced by master files that do not show the amounts leading up to the summarized values.

4. "The data processing cycle does not necessarily provide a transaction listing or journal. To provide such a listing may require a specific action at a recognized cost.

5. "It is sometimes unnecessary to prepare frequent printed output of historical records. Files can be maintained on computer media and reports prepared only for exceptions.

6. "Files maintained on a magnetic medium cannot be read except by use of the computer and a computer program.

7. "Sequence of records and processing activities is difficult to observe because much of the data and many of the activities are contained within the computer system."[56]

As indicated earlier, the effectiveness of persons auditing EDP systems planning and development and operations must recognize, from the beginning, that there are *no* shortcuts to performing a sound review of internal controls in the EDP environment, to enable a conclusion as to (1) areas of adequate controls, (2) areas of weak controls, and (3) areas of materially deficient or no controls. The areas under items (2) and (3) are invitations to perpetrate frauds and/or manipulate records. Even item (1), where collusion is involved, has the same risks.

Figures 6 and 7 attempt to put the preceding words into perspective through flow chart diagrams.

---

[56] Watne and Turney, *Auditing EDP Systems.* (Englewood Cliffs, NJ; Prentice-Hall, 1984), p. 98.

Figure 6
Logical Order of an EDP Internal Control System[57]*

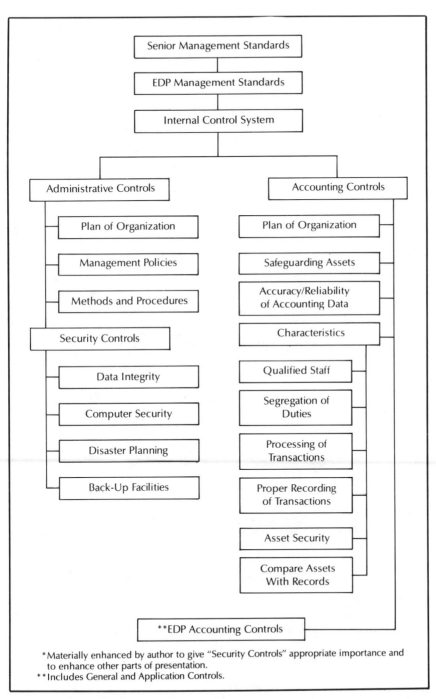

*Materially enhanced by author to give "Security Controls" appropriate importance and to enhance other parts of presentation.
**Includes General and Application Controls.

[57]*Ibid.*, p. 99.

Figure 7
Study and Evaluation of Internal Controls in EDP Systems[58]

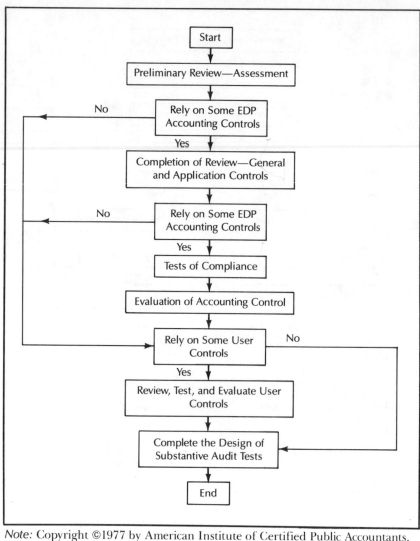

Note: Copyright ©1977 by American Institute of Certified Public Accountants, Inc. Adapted with permission.

EFT Systems

The basic systems should be designed to achieve the desired service, with risks being controlled at acceptable levels. Too often,

---

[58]*Ibid.*, p. 101, Chart adapted from *The Auditor's Study and Evaluation of Internal Control in EDP Systems* (New York: AICPA, 1977), pp. 21-24; not copied in detail for clearer presentation.

EFT systems are cost-ineffective before being put into service, because designers "seem to concentrate on trying to find all possible flaws or drawbacks in the systems, and on trying to force safeguards to be installed before the system even has a chance to operate. This process not only loads down a new system with a lot 'questionable value' safeguards and controls, but it imposes old values on new systems."[59] Remember that the end objective of a sound EFT system is to make it available to the maximum number of qualified users.

Real risks exist in such systems, proven by the fact that fraud on automatic teller machines (ATMs) have now exceeded those on credit cards. Some of the problems:

1. Misuse of Cards

    The biggest single problem seems to be that the cardholders insist on, no matter how hard the banks attempt to discourage this, keeping the personal identification number (PIN) with the cash card. Thus, if a wallet or pocketbook is lost or stolen, both elements needed to perpetrate a fraudulent transaction are there.

2. Privacy and Protection

    "Systems typically are protected as much by myth as by actual hardware procedures or legislation.... As such, they create useful expectations and concepts that make the systems seem satisfactory."[60]

As auditors, you have a responsibility to determine whether:

1. Educational efforts are undertaken continually by marketing to get cardholders to keep PIN numbers separated from the cards.

2. The bank actually prosecutes customers that are *grossly* negligent. The $50 loss limit by law assumes prudence on the part of the cardholder.

3. It is essential that, to the degree economically feasible, privacy and protection are not merely words but parts of the operational environment relative to EFT systems.

"The concern for the security of EFT systems is proper. Let us analyze security in payment systems to see its basic elements.

"First, it depends on the relationship between the financial institu-

[59]Colton and Kraemer. *Computers and Banking—Electronic Funds Transfer Systems.* (New York: Plenum Press, 1980), pp 150-152.
[60]*Ibid.*, pp. 150-152.

tion and its customers, and on an agreement on how orders-to-pay will be executed. It also depends on the uniqueness of this relationship or how easily it can be used by an outsider bent on fraud. The identification method...can literally be any signal that is mutually agreeable to the financial institution and the customer—a number, a signature, or several signatures. These signals have been standardized.... Since each institution and customer could work out their own signal combinations, it is conceivable that stolen checks, cards, or other entry devices would become quite worthless, since the proper signals could be maintained in encrypted form in the computer memory. Such private arrangements provide the possibility of making fraud more difficult in electronic systems than in paper systems, *if we utilize this latent capability.*"[61]

"Second, transfers between financial institutions depend upon the financial integrity of these institutions and the clarity with which their contractual funds transfer relations are spelled out. Here, too, within limits, full utilization of the capabilities of electronic information technology could make this communication more unique and more fraud proof."[62]

Unfortunately, marketing personnel are oriented to "making a deal" and, accordingly, even where they know of the safety features and controls which would reduce fraud potential, tend to make the deal that the customer wants. The auditor must perform reviews to assure that the bank's assets are protected to the maximum extent justified on a cost/value basis.

The EFT comments herein focus on (1) automated clearing house (ACH), (2) automated teller machines (ATMs), (3) point-of-sale (POS) systems, and (4) other direct institution-to-institution transfers, where such capability exists.

Data Protection

"The protection of EDP data stored on tape and disk forms and on other media and the need to protect the software and programs that operate on data is of paramount importance. There are two reasons for this: (1) the actual asset value or investment of the data in question or the cost of regenerating such data, and/or (2) the intrinsic value of the particular data to the firm."[63] Equipment can be replaced relatively easily, but "if data or information were lost, it may in

---

[61]*Ibid.,* pp. 150-152.
[62]*Ibid.,* pp. 150-152.
[63]Kuong, *op. cit.,* pp 227-229 and 244-247.

some cases, never be replaced, [and] its unavailability may spell disaster for the user organization."[64]

"Protection of software and programs is likewise very important for at least the following reasons:

- "They represent official policies and procedures of the organization which are encapsulated in the form of programs. They are often of a confidential nature.

- "They represent an asset of the organization in the sense that many years of effort may have gone into the development of these programs, They could be a target for theft by interested parties for various reasons, a common one being to save the development cost.

- "They can be subject to unauthorized alteration or fraudulent manipulation...to change assets, issue illicit payments, change contents of files, or even destroy someone's character by changing what is recorded [about them].

- "Once computerized, many businesses depend upon the availability of these programs to operate their businesses. If these programs were destroyed, and no backup provided, a major business disruption could result."[65]

Data are subject to any or all of the following risks, either accidental or intentional:

- Destruction, modification, or disclosure.

- Processing errors from improper procedures, program deficiencies, or human error.

- Hardware and/or software induced errors or data destruction.

Backup and Recovery Program

The intent of such programs is to bring the EDP environment back to normal operating conditions should the EDP equipment or computerized data be damaged temporarily or permanently and permit full recovery of files and restoration of operating capability in the data processing complex in the case of an accidental or deliberate disaster.

Too often backup and recovery are thought of only in the event of

---

[64]*Ibid.*, pp 227-229 and 244-247.
[65]*Ibid.*, pp 227-229 and 244-247.

a major disaster. In reality, backup and recovery must cover all of the following:

- "Provisions for short- and long-term interruptions of service.
- "Equipment and auxiliary equipment backup.
- "Data, file, and software backup and recovery (reconstruction) procedures.
- "Ancillary facilities, supplies, and procedures (know-how) backup.
- "Trained personnel backup."[66]

"The need for all these elements is predicated on the concept that 'the chain is no stronger than the weakest link.' It is hardly consolation to have provided for equipment alternatives and not have adequate file and software (programs) backup, or to have an alternate facility but lack the up-to-date procedures properly backed up [for use] when needed."[67]

Let us define the two elements:

BACKUP. "Pertaining to equipment or procedures that are available for use in the event of failure or overloading of normally used equipment or procedures. The provision of adequate back-up facilities is important to the design of all data processing systems, especially real time systems, where a system failure may bring the total operations of the business to a virtual standstill."[68]

RECOVERY. "Concentrates on the very process of initiating and conducting the recovery or reconstruction process. It is procedural in nature, or, at least, it is provided in the form of procedures."[69]

THE AUDITOR'S ROLE. The two basic roles of the auditor relative to backup and recovery are (1) He offers a useful service by playing the devil's advocate during the development phase of any catastrophe planning and recovery-program undertaking. He can review proposals and suggest ways to improve the end-program. (2) After the fact, he can help in the reconstruction program which may include a postmortem audit as to why events occurred or failed to occur, and help identify actions the firm should take to prevent or minimize possible recurrence.

The role under item (1) is the more important because it is done before a problem occurs and should be approached in a detailed and constructive way.

---

[66]*Ibid.*, pp. 227-229 and 244-247.
[67]*Ibid.*, pp. 227-229 and 244-247.
[68]Hutt, Bosworth and Hoyt. *Computer Security Handbook,* 2nd ed. (New York; Macmillan, 1988), p. 68.
[69]Kuong, *op. cit.*, pp. 244-247.

Difference in Approach for Data Security and Backup and Recovery Procedures

Simply stated:

1. Data Protection: "This is concerned with protection, access control, and preventive measures required to preserve the integrity of data. It also seeks to minimize the possibility of errors in data and any potential accidental or intentional destruction or modification of data."[70]

2. Backup and Recovery: These relate to the threat of data destruction and are concerned primarily with restoring operations to normalcy should a catastrophe occur.

Recovery from a potential fraud situation, under either situation defined, would be considered an administrative, audit, and legal problem.

Computer Security

"A process intended to control the people, physical plant, and equipment and the data involved in information processing so as to preserve and protect these valuable assets."[71]

A brief summation of Federal Information Processing Standards—Abstracts:

ABSTRACT-FIPS PUB 31: This provides guidelines to be used by federal organizations in structuring physical security programs for their ADP facilities.

ABSTRACT-FIPS PUB 39: This is a glossary which provides an alphabetic listing of about 170 terms and definitions pertaining to privacy and security related to data, information systems hardware, and software.

ABSTRACT-FIPS PUB 41: This provides guidelines for use by federal ADP organizations in implementing the computer security safeguards necessary for compliance with Public Law 93-579, and the Privacy Act of 1974.

ABSTRACT-FIPS PUB 46: This provides a standard to be used by federal organizations when the organizations specify that cryptographic protection is to be used for sensitive or valuable computer data.

---

[70]*Ibid.*, pp. 244-247.
[71]Hutt, et al., *op. cit.*, p. 385.

ABSTRACT-FIPS PUB 48: This provides a guideline to be used by federal organizations in the selection and evaluation of techniques for automatically verifying the identity of individuals seeking access to computer systems and networks by way of terminals, where controlled accessibility is required for security purposes.

ABSTRACT-FIPS PUB 65: This document presents a technique for conducting a risk analysis of an ADP facility and related assets.

ABSTRACT-FIPS PUB 73: This guideline describes the technical and managerial decisions that should be made to assure adequate controls are included in new and existing computer applications to protect them from natural and human-made hazards and to assure that critical functions are performed correctly and with no harmful side effects.

ABSTRACT-FIPS PUB 74: The Data Encryption Standard (DES) was published as *Federal Information Processing Standards* publication (FIPS PUB 46) on January 15, 1977. The DES specifies a cryptographic algorithm for protecting computer data.

ABSTRACT-FIPS PUB 81: This FIPS defines four modes of operation for the DES that may be used in a wide variety of applications.

ABSTRACT-FIPS PUB 83: This provides guideline information and guidance to federal agencies on techniques and practices that can be used to control computer resources by way of remote terminals and networks.

ABSTRACT-FIPS PUB 87: This provides guidelines to be used in the preparation of EDP contingency plans.

ABSTRACT-FIPS PUB 102: This has instructions intended for use by ADP managers and technical staff in establishing and carrying out a program and a technical process for computer security certification and accreditation of sensitive computer applications.

To avoid reinventing the wheel, instructions and standards in the reference documents should be considered and, where appropriate, used to provide your institution with the same level of safeguards considered adequate for governmental computer facilities.

Summary of Risks Relative to EDP Operations

1. The risks to data processing security may be categorized as follows:

   (a) Physical hazards.

   (b) Equipment malfunction.

   (c) Software malfunction.

    (d) Human error.

    (e) Misuse of data.

    (f) Loss of data.

    (g) Fire risks.

    (h) Water damage.

    (i) Power loss.

    (j) Vandalism and civil disorders.

2. Relative to all of the factors under item 1, each category of risk should be rated as to *(a)* probable frequency, and *(b)* impact on each instance, as to both human resources and monetary resources needed to become operational again.

Auditing General Computer Controls

"The auditor should obtain a preliminary understanding of computer applications and general computer controls as a basis for determining the audit strategy and completing the audit planning"[72] relative to a planned review of data processing computer environment. These are the auditing factors to be considered:

1. Strategy.

2. Planning.

3. Implementation controls.

4. Program security controls.

5. Computer operations controls.

6. Data-file security controls.

7. System software controls.

Remember, in today's environment "the auditor's ability to use the computer to examine [an] automated systems environment"[73] depends to a significant degree on the data available. A number of excellent software packages are available to assist the auditor in such undertakings. Most are inquiry and extract programs but others go beyond those limits. Some examples of such software are MASTERPLAN, developed by The Institute of Internal Auditors Inc., and PANAUDIT, developed by Pansophic Inc. However, others that are available are of comparable use and value.

---

[72]Sullivan, et al., *op. ct.,* p. 382.
[73]*Ibid.,* p. 392.

An effective EDP loss-control program is based on nine basic elements. Needed are: (1) full management support for such a program, (2) effective use of the risk management process effectively, (3) clear definition of control responsibilities, (4) development, implementation, and support of firm-wide control standards, (5) creation of an environment of effective interaction, relative to such controls, (6) encouragement of active cooperation between EDP and user management throughout the firm, (7) periodic program reviews, (8) establishment of a continuing program relative to new innovations in the EDP environment, and, finally, (9) establishment of a loss-control program, built on the foundation of the nine preceding elements.

Figure 8
Elements and Structure of an EDP Loss-Control Program

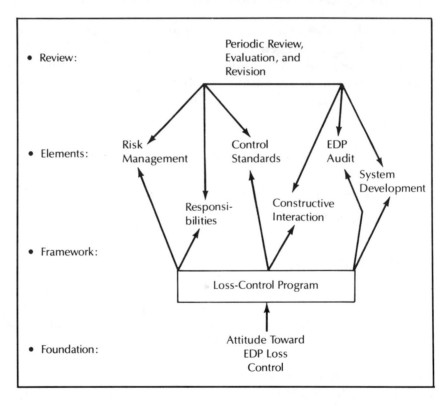

Summary

The preceding should confirm that EDP auditing is a *vertical* audit format, as shown below:

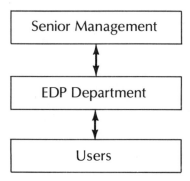

4

Administrative/Operational (Horizontal) Internal Audit Methodology

Definitions

1. AUDITING. "The relationship of auditing to accounting is close, yet their natures are very different; they are business associates, not parent and child. *Accounting* includes the collection, classification, summarization, and communication of financial data; it involves the measurement and communication of business events and conditions as they affect and represent a given enterprise or other entity. The task of accounting is to reduce a tremendous mass of detailed information to manageable and understandable proportions. *Auditing* must consider business events and conditions, too, but it does not have the task of measuring or communicating them. Its task is to review the measurements and communications of accounting for propriety. Auditing is analytical; it is critical, investigative, concerned with the basis for accounting measurements and assertions. Auditing emphasizes proof, the support for financial statements and data. Thus, auditing has its principal roots, not in accounting, which it reviews, but in logic on which it leans heavily for ideas and methods.[74]

"The purpose of any kind of audit is to add some degree of validity to the object of the review."[75]

"There are five 'primary concepts in auditing'"[76] which are:

(a) "Evidence.

(b) "Due audit care.

(c) "Fair presentation.

(d) "Independence.

(e) "Ethical conduct."

---

[74]Cashin, *op. cit.*, pp. 1-4. Based on *"The Philosophy of Auditing"* by R.K. Mautz and Hussein A. Sharof, from a publication of the American Accounting Assn. 1961, p. 14.

[75]*Ibid.*, pp. 1-4.

[76]*Ibid.*, pp. 1-4.

The five "primary concepts in auditing" apply equally to vertical and horizontal audit methodology, as described herein.

2. ACTIVITY. "An organizational unit for performing a specific function; also, its function or duties."[77]

3. FUNCTION. "The acts or operations expected. . . . Implies a definite end or purpose that the one in question serves or a particular kind of work it is intended to perform. . . . Applies to a task or responsibility."[78]

4. PRODUCT AND SERVICE. (1) Product: "The amount, quantity, or total produced."[79] (2) Service: "Useful labor that does not produce a tangible commodity" . . . "A facility supplying some public demand."[80]

5. ENTITY. "Independent, separate, or self-contained existence."[81]

6. PROJECT. "A planned undertaking."[82]

7. BUSINESS. "Purposeful activity. . . . An immediate task or objective. . . . A particular field of endeavor."[83]

8. CYCLE. "A course or series of events or operations that recur regularly."[84]

Each of the definitions from items 2 through 8 should be used together with the definition of auditing, as under item 1, to create a definition of each of these horizontal forms of auditing.

Horizontal auditing is used (1) when fundamentally all primary aspects of the audit are self-contained into one of the elements, as under items 2 through 8, (2) when looking at the whole of any of those elements against peer organizations, facilities, or comparable activity, function, product, or service, or (3) when comparing any of the elements against past and/or projected performance to determine when it may be (a) in its life-cycle or (b) relative to its economic viability.

Again, the familiarization phase of the planned audit is the most important single aspect of the overall review plan. Why? It will help you identify (1) risks, (2) areas of concern, (3) weaknesses in system

---

[77]*Webster's Ninth New Collegiate Dictionary, op. cit.*, p. 54.
[78]*Ibid.*, p. 190.
[79]*Ibid.*, p. 319.
[80]*Ibid.*, p. 416.
[81]*Ibid.*, p. 498.
[82]*Ibid.*, p. 938.
[83]*Ibid.*, p. 940.
[84]*Ibid.*, p. 1076.

of internal controls and checks, (4) noncompliance with requirements of policies, procedures, and practices, including those relative to internal controls and checks, (5) lack of adequate supervision, and (6) skills, in management and/or staff, not at the level necessary to handle effectively the tasks and duties relative to the subject environment.

Consider an example of each of the earlier definitions from items 2 through 8 relative to types of horizontal auditing:

2. Activity: The credit committee or the asset/liability committee of the institution that are established for a specific activity, as indicated by their title.

3. Function: Security section or risk management section of the institution that has been assigned specific functional responsibilities.

4. Product and Service:

    (a) Product: The card embossing section of the credit card department; which embosses cards being mailed to customers.

    (b) Service: The night depository of an institution, which is a service accommodating businesses that do not wish to retain the day's receipts overnight at their facilities.

5. Entity: A subsidiary (e.g., brokerage, real estate, international organization—banking, commercial or merchant, or trust, Edge Act bank. (*Note:* Some would add "facility" under this category, such as a single office of a subsidiary, such as an Edge Act bank, as above, or a loan production office).

6. Project: Such as constructing a new separate computer center or building to house credit card operations.

7. Business: This could be any of the following:

    (a) Peer analysis, to determine how your institution is doing against others of the same size and scope of activities (e.g., geographic, types of business activities).

    (b) Merger and acquisition analysis, to evaluate whether (i) the business being appraised meets the standards established by management when considering an acquisition or (ii) determining whether the price asked is reasonable based on your assessment of the business, as under point (i), or based on return on investment during a defined period.

    (c) An analysis of your institution to determine (i) how it can be more cost efficient (e.g., adopting a profit-improvement program, or organizationally restructuring it to obtain better information for each product or service) or (ii) how it can establish better "responsibility accounting" by converting from traditional pyramid organization to matrix organization, or vice versa.

8. Cycle: This is based on an approach developed and used by a number of the larger public accounting firms. It is an "approach to studying and evaluating internal controls," which provides a "recognition that the economic events that impact" a depository institution "and the resultant web of transactions, systems, processing procedures, interfaces, and data bases can be broken down logically into a limited number of groups." The term used to describe such "groups is cycles. Cycles are based on what is accomplished."[85] "Each function is made up of one or more functions." They describe function as "a major processing task or a segment of a system that processes logically related transactions. As with systems, there is no uniform definition of functions."[86]

Each institution's "functions are unique.... With one exception" one of the cycles established by the public accountants, "every function" is "involved in processing transactions or preparing financial statements.... The exception is financial planning and control, which consists of management's supervision, control and review of the cycles."[87] The cycles identified are:

1. Deposit.

2. Treasury.

3. Loans.

4. Investment.

5. Payroll Disbursements.

6. Nonpayroll Disbursements.

7. Trust.

8. Financial Planning and Control.

---

[85]*A Guide for Studying and Evaluating Internal Accounting Controls—Banking.* (Chicago: Arthur Andersen & Co., 1980), p. 10.
[86]*A Guide for Studying and Evaluating Internal Accounting Controls—Savings and Loan Associations.* (Arthur Andersen & Co., 1982), p. 9.
[87]*A Guide for Studying and Evaluating Internal Accounting Controls—Banking, op. cit.,* p. 10.

Internal Control/Check Audits

Other definitions

1. INTERNAL CONTROL. "The general methodology by which management is carried on within an organization; also, any of the numerous devices for supervising and directing an operation or operations generally. . . . Internal control, a management function, is a basic factor operating in one form or another in the administration of every organization, business or otherwise.

"Although sometimes identified with the administrative organism itself, it is often characterized as the nervous system that activates overall operating policies and keeps them within practical performance ranges. . . . In a corporation, internal control commences with the institution and enforcement of top policies established by the board of directors and continues down through the organizational structure, taking form in the development and operation of management policies, administrative regulations, manuals, directives, and decisions; internal auditing; internal check; reporting; employee training and participation. . . . An important element in maintaining internal control is provided in the work of the internal auditor. Although his presence may, and often does, act as a deterrent to departures from required practices, his aim is neither to deter nor to enforce but to investigate and comment. . . . Internal control does not end with the testing of conformance to policies and operating standards but extends to practical operations involving individuals or group decisions or actions that, intentionally or otherwise, are within the discretion of the individual and are covered neither by role nor convention . . ."[88]

2. Internal Check. "The design of transaction flows that provide effective organization and operation and protection against fraud. A principal feature is the allocation of organizational responsibility in such a manner that no single individual or group has exclusive control over any one transaction or group of transactions. . . . Effective internal check is so devised that a transaction can be consummated only through prescribed operating procedures, of which the mechanism of internal check is invariably an integral part. The term should not be confused with the post-transaction, staff function of internal auditing, or with overall internal control, of which internal check is but an element."[89]

---

[88]Kohler, *op. cit.*, pp. 240-242.
[89]*Ibid.*, pp. 240-242.

The key factors in planning the scope of any audit, vertical or horizontal, is, during the familiarization phase, determining (1) the inherent risks in the environment; (2) the existence of compliance with and effectiveness of policies and procedures; (3) whether adequate internal control and internal check exists relative to the factors under items (1) and (2); and (4) competency of the management and staff in the environment to be audited to fulfill the duties, tasks, authority, and responsibility assigned by senior management.

Keep in mind that the concepts of *(a)* compliance auditing, and *(b)* substantive auditing, as described in Chapter 2 are equally applicable to horizontal audits as they are to vertical audits.

Two key factors used throughout this book will be:

1. *Risks,* relative to the nature of the activity or function.

2. Adequacy or inadequacy of *internal controls* and *internal checks,* both as conceived and as functioning, relative to the risks determined under item 1.

The type of audit does not matter as to (1) methodology (e.g., attest, financial, operational, (2) format (e.g., vertical or horizontal), or (3) environment (e.g., financial auditing, or activity, functional, product, or entity auditing). The preceding two *risk-oriented* factors are the foundation on which sound audit scope is determined and where specific focus will apply relative to any audit undertaking.

Example

While all three of the approaches to horizontal auditing, as described earlier in this chapter, have value, surprisingly (at least to the author) they were the findings resulting from similar activities or functions at different operating units of the institution. For example:

1. I once selected and reviewed the audit work papers from five recently completed audits of the foreign exchange (FX) section operations at *(a)* the head office, and *(b)* four branches, throughout the world.

2. All of them had been cited for minor exceptions but generally were deemed to be functioning adequately. Most of the minor exceptions were differences between practice and the procedure requirements of the international banking department procedures manual.

3. When viewing the five sets of work papers side by side, it was quite obvious that three of the procedures were being inter-

preted quite differently by each FX section. The conclusion was drawn, *only* from this comparative horizontal audit (e.g., like entities, relatively same period, same procedure instructions) that they were not adequate and should be revised. They were so broad in interpretation that it was, when viewed horizontally, sufficiently loose so that they could be implemented and *appear* to be in compliance, or relatively so. The internal checks as set forth in the procedure could be bypassed, creating a possible fraud situation.

4. Unfortunately, before the procedures could be revised, a fraud was perpetrated at one of the five FX sections by the failure to implement effectively the internal control and internal check requirements of the instructions. When the fraud was identified, it was simple to determine how it had come about. Obviously, the procedure instruction was revised to preclude any repetition.

Example

The following is an illustration of the situation just described:

All Audit Reviews Cover Approximately Same Time Period

	FX Unit 1	FX Unit 2	FX Unit 3	FX Unit 4	FX Unit 5
Variance Code Used: Exact Compliance Code Used:	———	– – –	oooooo	******	......
Foreign Exchange (FX) *(A)* Procedure	...... ****** ———	...... ******	......	– – – ooooo	– – – ———
Variance from *(B)* Compliance:	– – – ooooo	——— ––	oooooo ****** oooooo	******	oooooo ...... ******

(A) = Noncompliance with procedure requirements.

(B) = Overly strict compliance resulting in inefficiency and uneconomical administrative, financial, and operational performance.

Gross variance is *maximum* on *(A)* side, plus maximum on *(B)* side, providing totally different perspective than when viewing variance of a single FX unit.

Follow the variance code used for each of the five foreign exchange units reviewed on a horizontal basis and you can readily identify how most had implemented each of the five procedures (used for our example purposes) differently. Yet in following the performance of each FX unit you can note inconsistent interpretations by each of the FX units. Note that each has adopted some procedures as under item *(A)* and others as under item *(B)*. Either the instructions are not well written and clear or the managers have attempted to take some liberties, which are *risks* in fulfilling bank standards, in the five procedures. The variance analysis indicated can only be identified by a horizontal audit.

Unique Aspects of Described Horizontal Internal Audit Methodologies

1. Activity auditing enables the auditor to review an activity (*Note:* see earlier definition), such as the bank's asset/liability committee, activity auditing assures that activity is performing all of the requirements and fulfilling the duties stipulated by management, as well as by reference to what is considered "good practice" for the activity in various reference sources. Activity auditing also can compare changes in requirements and duties resulting from internal decisions or criteria that have become accepted as "good practice" for the activity and can evaluate how accurately the decisions and conclusions of this activity have been and what actions can be taken to improve the prospects of it being more on target.

2. Functional auditing enables the auditor to focus on a specific work phase or control responsibility (e.g., settlement unit relative to controlling the efforts undertaken by foreign exchange and/or futures trading relative to "gap" or total currency position limits). Functional auditing enables the review of the unit on compliance *(a)* right now to policies, procedures, practices, standards, and regulations; *(b)* over two to five audit periods in the same perspective as in item *(a)* to determine whether a weakness has occurred in compliance in any way; or *(c)* between the unit and two or more other units that have the same responsibilities and duties.

3. Product and service auditing permits the same review environments, as under items 2(a) through 2(c), for any selected environment. Primary focus is on compliance, costs, and risks relative to same, as well as noncompliance with relative criteria.

4. Entity auditing also enables review formats, as under items 2(a) through 2(c), for any selected entity, and, as appropriate, comparable entities (e.g., branches, loan production offices).

5. Project auditing has the same options as under items 2(a) through 2(c) but also adds the additional burden of comparing performance against contract time-schedules and costs, for both the general contractor as well as subcontractors. Project auditing also requires monitoring authority and impact on time to complete performance and costs for approved changes to original plans. If an internal engineering unit is charged with the basic responsibilities, as indicated, then a functional audit of such unit can be made, seeing how it has performed in controlling costs and "time to complete" for other projects they have supervised. If that engineering unit also is charged with monitoring efforts of borrowers, where the funds are designated for a specific project, that also can be audited.

6. The business audit is difficult, as it is broad based as under definition 7(a) through 7(c) of this chapter. The auditor can make comparative reviews relative to any of the three classifications indicated.

7. Cycle auditing is defined earlier in this chapter.

8. Internal control/check was broadly defined earlier in this chapter. The control/check is essential to the flow chart or in preparing written descriptions of the processing stages for each work phase or to control responsibility for assuring controls and checks are functioning as intended to controls risks in the area under review.

5

Situation/Condition Internal Audit Methodology

Definitions

1. SITUATION. "The way in which something is placed in relation to its surroundings....Position or place of employment....Critical, trying, or unusual state of affairs."[90]

2. CONDITION. "Something essential to the appearance or occurrence of something else....A restricting or modifying factor....A premise upon which the fulfillment of an agreement depends."[91]

3. OPERATIONAL AUDITING. The concept is an "organized search for ways of improving efficiency and effectiveness. Although popularized by internal auditors and the federal government's General Accounting Office, operational auditing is increasingly being performed by independent auditors and management consultants....An operational audit is a nonfinancial audit whose purpose is to appraise the managerial organization and efficiency of a company or part of a company. It can be considered a form of constructive criticism....Known by many names, it appears in the literature as operations auditing, management auditing, performance auditing, systems auditing, efficiency auditing, expanded scope auditing among others."[92]
   My personal favorite definitions are:

   (a) "A systematic review and evaluation of an organization, or subunit thereof, made with the purpose of determining whether the organization is operating efficiently. It is, in effect, an organized search for efficiency-related problems within the organizations."[93]

   (b) "Operational auditing is using common sense, or logical audit techniques, with management perspective, and applying them to company objectives, operations, controls, communications, and information systems. The auditor is

---

[90]*Webster's Ninth New Collegiate Dictionary, op. cit.,* p. 273.
[91]*Ibid.,* p. 1102.
[92]Flesher and Siewert, *op. cit.,* p. vii.
[93]*Ibid.,* p. 3.

59

more concerned with the who, what, when, where, why, and how of running an efficient and profitable business than just the accounting and financial aspects of the business functions.:[94]

4. SYSTEMS AUDITING.
   (a) Manual Systems:
      (1) System: "A collection of objects or events conforming to a plan; the plan itself."[95]

      (2) System Design: "The specification for a particular organization of a classification of accounts, the form and use of bookkeeping and records, methods of internal check and control, and the character and frequency of internal report..."[96]

   (b) Computer Systems.
      (1) System: "When applied to information processing, any combination of people, procedures, hardware, and software necessary to perform specific processing or other activities."[97]

      (2) System Design: "The specification for a computer system. System design includes determining the following information: (a) What are the functions to be performed? (b) What hardware, software, and personnel resources are required? (c) What interactions are involved?"[98]

5. MANGEMENT-ORIENTED AUDITING (repeated from Chapter 2).
   (a) Identification of variances, actual against budget, by cost-center, product or service line, activity, function, division, department, facility, or overall institution. Follow up to determine cause (e.g., timing difference, unrealistic budget objectives, ineffective marketing efforts, poor systems resulting in customer dissatisfaction).

   (b) Review and assessment of organizational structure to assure that authority and responsibility are clearly defined so

---

[94]*Ibid.*
[95]Kohler, *op. cit.*, p. 423.
[96]*Ibid.*, p. 423.
[97]Robert A. Edmunds. *The Prentice-Hall Glossary of Computer Terminology*, 4th ed. (Englewood Cliffs, N.J.: Prentice-Hall, 1985), p. 429.
[98]*Ibid.*, p. 432.

that the auditors can perform reviews on a "responsibility accounting" basis.

(c) Determine that goals and objectives in the strategic plan are the basis for forward management thinking or, if that has changed, the strategic plan has been revised accordingly and that information must be communicated effectively through all levels of management.

A supplement to the preceding definition is that of management audit, being used herein as synonymous with management-oriented auditing. "Management audit [is] an independent examination of objective evidence, performed by trained personnel, to determine whether integrated management systems, which are required to fulfill the contractual and legal obligations of the company to its customer and the community, are being effectively implemented and [are] the true and fair presentation of the results of such examination."[99]

6. SOCIAL AUDITING. "The role of business in society has been a source of public concern since the days of Hammurabi. Particularly since the 1970s, consumerist demands for increased accountability by all institutions have been characterized as a social revolution. The broad aim of social measurement and reporting is to provide adequate measures of progress toward social goals and to evaluate and regulate resource commitments with those goals in mind." (*Note:* Companies such as ARCO, Philip Morris, and Ford Motor Co. inaugurated social reporting nearly two decades ago.) "Social measurement and reporting can be helpful to management in two areas: First, if management believes certain rules are about to be promulgated . . ." and "second, if new requirements can be forecast, and the management information system can be modified to produce the requisite data . . ." (*Note:* The AICPA published several works on social measurement that still serve as useful and concise guides.)[100] Some have referred to a social audit as measuring what a business has put back into the geographic environment in which it operates, indicating its social responsibility.

7. PREEMPTIVE AUDITING. Such audits involve "a review of business actions before they are concluded; it is not limited to fi-

---

[99] Allan J. Sayle. *Management Audits—The Assessment of Quality Management Systems.* (New York: McGraw-Hill Book Co. (U.K.) Ltd., 1981), p. 4.
[100] Sullivan, et al., *op. cit.,* p. 1005.

nancial data, but concerns all information that can be quantified and verified. The raw material of a preemptive audit consists of contracts being drawn, budgets being developed and systems being designed.... A preemptive audit focuses on determining that planning and budgeting controls are in place and that exception-type controls flag departures from plans and targets before economy and efficiency of operations can be impaired.... Preemptive audits often involve several special techniques..." as follows:

- Careful attention is given to be sure that all parties to an agreement receive pertinent information, and systems are coordinated.

- Risk management identifies potential threats and risks to projects (e.g., inflation and shortage of materials).

- Organization effectiveness over projects involves outside organizations (e.g., architects, engineers, contractors).

8. STRATEGIC AUDITS. Such audits deal with strategic planning and "attempt to match environmental threats such as loss of supplies, changing consumer demand, regulatory legislation, and emerging social mandates with corporate resources, talents, and other capabilities, on a relatively long-range basis." Audits may "contribute to strategic planning in the following ways"[101]:

   (a) Defining data requirements.

   (b) Improving handling and end reporting of information.

   (c) Establishing and evaluating strategic scenarios.

   (d) Encouraging adoption of strategic plans developed.

9. LOAN REVIEW EXAMINATIONS. "The loan review function is designed to provide a continuing evaluation of the bank's loan portfolio. It helps identify potential problem loans before they reach a critical stage. It involves classifying loans when they are initially made (as well as at periodic intervals) on a scale from the most to the least risky. It is important to keep this function independent of the banking department, since objectivity is essential." (*Note:* This objectivity is the reason some banks include this function as a full-time segment of their internal auditing function while other banks have it totally inde-

---

[101]*Ibid.*, p. 1008.

pendent, in which case the internal audit function must test the work done by loan review, just as any other activity or function, to assure it is fulfilling its mandate independently, objectively, and with effective follow-up on risks and problems it has reported.) "It is the responsibility of the loan review officer to monitor compliance with internal lending policies, to classify loans, used by management to assess overall loan quality and adequacy of loan loss reserves and capital. . . . Monitoring compliance with laws and regulations imposed by external agencies is a necessary and important function" that should be part of the scope of the loan review function, wherever positioned organizationally.[102]

10. CONSULTING SUPPLEMENTAL INTERNAL REVIEWS. "I see the internal auditor as an internal consultant, not as an internal adversary; not a cop on the beat but a guest in the house; not merely a searcher for errors, large or small, but a guide to improved operations. [I see him] not a second-guesser dedicated to putting people down, but a counselor who lifts people up to do better and be better; not only concerned with whether things are being done right but also with whether the right things are being done . . . "[103]

Based on the preceding definition, Lawrence Sawyer developed "The Ten Commandments of Internal Auditing,"[104] which are:

1. "Know the objectives.

2. "Know the controls.

3. "Know the standards.

4. "Know the population.

5. "Know the facts.

6. "Know the causes.

7. "Know the effect.

8. "Know the people.

9. "Know when and how to communicate.

10. "Know the modern methods."

---

[102]Herbert V. Prochnow, ed. *Bank Credit*. (New York: Harper & Row, 1981), p. 75.
[103]Lawrence B. Sawyer. *Elements of Management-Oriented Auditing*. (Altamonte Springs, Fla.: The Institute of Internal Auditors, 1983), pp. 1-2.
[104]*Ibid.*, pp. 4-7.

I would like to supplement Sawyer's Ten Commandments by adding regulatory requirements to item 4 and by transposing items 6 and 7. The latter change would be made on the basis of the traditional audit concept that:

(a) In audit reviews, you identify "effects" of noncompliance with policies, procedures, practices, and standards and the impact of those conditions on internal control and internal check.

(b) On the basis of "effects" identified, as under item (a), the internal auditor would seek out and identify why the causes for them occurred.

(c) With the information under items (a) and (b), internal auditors can, within the limits of their competency, recommend solutions, and, beyond the limits of their competency, indicate other skills that should be called on to help develop solutions. The auditors can then assess those solutions to indicate whether such actions would accomplish the desired effect.

Using the principles indicated, properly trained and skilled internal auditors are qualified to perform numerous internal consulting types of review undertakings. Some of these could be:

(1) Merger and acquisition studies.

(2) Profit-improvement program implementation.

(3) Organizational evaluations (e.g., total, department, division, section, facility).

(4) Economic feasibility studies relative to possible new or broadened products and services.

(5) Operational capabilities and risks relative to the studies under item (4).

(6) Economic viability studies relative to any current product, service, activity, function or facility.

(7) Review and evaluation of job descriptions against actual tasks and duties, as well as authority and responsibility, of any person, section, division within the organization.

(8) Performance of risk assessment reviews in areas of high risk where management has concern about adequacy of administration, accounting, operational and security environment, but not in the role of an auditor but as a consultant looking for ways to improve controls, reduce

risks, and enhance efficiency, effectiveness, and economy.

(9) Problem loan and work-out situations to determine ways to better protect interests of the institution and could involve functioning as a management or control official while the institution determines its forward course of action.

It is not possible to list all of the ways that internal auditors can function as internal consultants, but it is a broad-based environment, limited only by their skills and management's confidence in them.

Explanation

Each of the audit methodologies as defined in this chapter focuses on a review of one or more of the following:

1. Organization.

2. Job descriptions.

3. Designation of authority and responsibility.

4. Responsibility accounting.

5. Effective use of cost centers or equivalent.

6. Policies, procedures, practices, standards, and regulatory environment.

7. Efficiency, effectiveness, and economy.

8. Internal control and internal check.

9. Risk assessment and determination of level of each risk acceptable to management, which is then accomplished by items (6) and (8) and (10).

10. Risk management, making determinations as to (a) risks to be retained in full, (b) risks to be co-insured with an insurance firm and level of deductible, and (c) risks to be transferred to an insurance firm fully.

Unique Aspects of Situation/Condition Internal Audit Methodology

1. Operational auditing has changed the whole perspective of internal auditing from the limitations of attest and financial

review to, within the limits of their mandates from management, being able to review administrative and operational performance in the environment being audited, relative to *(a)* compliance with policies, procedures, practices, standards, and regulations, *(b)* adequacy of internal control and check procedures to hold risks at the levels acceptable to management; and *(c)* attempt to identify ways to achieve efficiency, effectiveness, and economy without reducing the level of risk control, as under item *(b)*.

2. Systems auditing, manual and computer, are approaches under operational auditing. They are described adequately in the definitions provided earlier.

3. Management-oriented auditing formally accepts internal auditing as truly a management function and the internal auditor as part of management. As such, the mandate given the function must be broadened to enable it to review various management activities, following the same objectives as under items 1*(a)* through 1*(c)*.

4. Social auditing is relatively new and, if not already adopted by a bank, is certainly something that will become increasingly standard in the future, as communities want the banks to put something back into the geographic area they service. This is spelled out clearly in the definition given earlier.

5. Preemptive auditing also is a relatively new approach, using both financial and mostly operational auditing techniques and approaches. The definition provided earlier is adequate in identifying its scope and purpose.

6. Strategic auditing also is a relatively new approach with comments under preemptive auditing being applicable here.

7. Loan review examinations are historical-audit reviews in banking but often have been poorly performed by persons with inadequate credit experience to make sound judgments relative to specific loans. Persons performing loan reviews must have the same relative skills and credit knowledge as those who made the loans. Also, they certainly must know the bank's policies, procedures, practices, and standards and all regulatory and filing requirements to protect the bank's interests. They must watch for conditions of *(a)* overload in a given credit category (e.g., oil and gas—Continental Illinois National Bank & Trust Co.; real estate—Texas banks and Chase Manhattan; and REITs, as a special area of real estate, Chase Manhattan)

and *(b)* a management's breach of its own controls (e.g., National Bank of San Diego, where C. A. Smith made loans to his own companies, which at the time, were not creditworthy enough for an extension of credit).

8. Consulting supplemental internal reviews are virtually unlimited except by the skills within the audit function. To maintain its integrity, internal audit must never try to do reviews beyond its skills. It can engage outsiders or use insiders, as needed, to enable it to perform such reviews.

Summary

One of the seven "attributes of a good internal auditor" is salesmanship. The internal auditor must prove by performance and broadening capabilities within the competency of its personnel. However, it need not be limited to only operational, systems, or management (oriented) auditing, of the various situation/condition internal audit methodologies described in this chapter. Management must be sold on the internal auditor's value to perform all of the other reviews indicated, through and including a variety of internal consulting services to supplement internal audit efforts.

6

Reactive Internal Audit Methodology

Definitions

1. REACTION: "The act or process or an instance of reacting."[105]

2. REACTIVE: "Relating to, or marked by reaction or reactance.... Readily responsive to a stimulus."[106]

3. ANTICIPATORY: "Characterized by anticipation: Anticipating."[107]

4. ANTICIPATORY AUDITING: "Today's auditor must continuously monitor the condition of the bank ... to be assured that assets are protected. This dynamic approach is referred to as anticipatory auditing. Central to this approach is the development and monitoring of key indicators. The continuous monitoring of key indicators provides an effective way to improve overall coverage and control audit costs."[108]

5. KEY INDICATORS: "A key indicator is information extracted from reports, data or statistics of a financial, operational, or managerial nature; highlights potential problems, unfavorable trends, and abnormal fluctuations; enables both the auditor and line management to anticipate, prevent, and resolve potential problems.

   "In addition to its anticipatory function, key indicators improve audit's ability to manage audit scopes; monitor audit risk in interim periods between audits, increase the auditor's knowledge and understanding of the bank's operations; and thus, enhance the audit department's service to management."[109]

6. EXCEPTION: "A case to which a rule does not apply."[110]

---

[105]*Webster's Ninth New Collegiate Dictionary, op. cit.,* p. 979.
[106]*Ibid.,* p. 979.
[107]*Ibid.,* p. 91.
[108]First National Bank of Chicago. *Anticipatory Auditing Seminar,* reference manual. Promoted in seminars by Bank Administration Institute, Rolling Meadows, Ill., p. 4.
[109]*Ibid.,* p. 4.
[110]*Webster's, op. cit.,* p. 432.

7. REPORT: "To describe as being in a specified state.... To announce or relate as the result of investigation."[111]

8. EARLY: "Before the usual process, or series.... Before the usual time.... Occurring before the usual time."[112]

9. WARNING: "The act of warning; the state of being warned."[113]

10. INFORMATION: "The communication or reception of knowledge or intelligence.... A formal accusation of a crime...."[114]

11. RECEIVED: "To accept as authoritative, true, or accurate."[115]

12. RESPONSE: "Something constituting a reply or a reaction."[116]

Unique Aspects of Reactive Internal Audit Methodology

All of these methodologies, as the name indicates, *react* to information that alerts the internal audit staff that something may be wrong. Some feel these are new concepts. Not true! About three decades ago, a major chemical company initiated the key indicator concept. Unfortunately, that was in the era of electronic accounting machines (EAM), which preceded computers and were very limited in what they could do and what information they could provide, particularly when comparing an *actual* situation to a *plan* or some preestablished *standard*. As a result, it was necessary to perform most calculations manually within the internal audit function, working with data provided by the EAMs against other information (e.g., budgets and standard costs). As more key indicators were identified, the clerical burden grew until the concept, identified herein as anticipatory auditing, had to be dropped because internal auditors could not perform the necessary calculations and follow up on data developed and maintain the normal audit schedule expected of them by management.

Since electronic data processing/computers replaced EAM, a variety of techniques and approaches have come into existence, all trying to provide information to internal audit so it can move quickly and decisively in any environment being monitored under any of the *reactive* approaches. The writer strongly supports these concepts if (1) limited to specific high-risk environments and (2) the reactive approach adopted is part of an overall internal audit program as a

---

[111]*Ibid.*, p. 999.
[112-116]*Ibid.*

supplement to and not a replacement of the various vertical or horizontal internal audit approaches that management has accepted as criteria to be used by internal auditing to fulfill the mandate of management.

Description of Each Reactive Internal Audit Methodology

1. Anticipatory Auditing: This concept consists of three primary elements, which are:

   (a) Key Indicators defined earlier in this chapter: A key indicator contains information extracted from reports, data, or statistics. This can be administrative, accounting, finance, operational, or managerial data. The indicators are intended to highlight potential problems, unfavorable trends, bypassing control limits (e.g., currency position long or short), or sufficiently abnormal fluctuations to focus attention on the situation. They allow line management and internal auditors to detemine whether a problem or potential problem exists and take appropriate actions to either bring the problem under control or prevent one from occurring.

   (b) Call Program: This concept is designed to establish effective lines of communication between line or staff management in any area and the internal auditors. By this interchange, internal auditors are made aware of new products and services, banking trends, and new systems or programs being put into use. This information can result in (1) establishing new key indicators, (2) dropping modifying existing key indicators, or (3) modifying the audit scope of an area or environment.

   (c) Traditional Auditing: This will be in the mode used by the institution, either the vertical or horizontal types indicated earlier in the book. However, because of the reliance placed on reviews reacting to key indicators, traditional auditing is reduced, and, unfortunately, possibly discontinued in some environments of the institution.

   Anticipatory auditing has many merits when it is used to supplement a normal audit program, in whatever mode of vertical or horizontal internal auditing is being used. However, it is not, in the author's opinion, broad enough to justify the use of only key indicators to audit any product, service, task, duty, activity, function, entity, or facility. Obviously, with anticipatory auditing in place, and functioning as intended, it often can reduce the scope and/or frequency of various normal vertical or horizontal internal audit reviews which in the past had been done by internal auditing. Anticipatory auditing should never be used to even reduce the scope and/or frequency of other internal audit reviews on any new product, service, task, duty, activity, function, entity, or facility. Why? Because, a reasonable period of time is needed for the strengths and weaknesses of the systems/programs and management/other personnel to be identified. This history indicates where key indicators can be used; where the risks are higher than originally projected; and where problems are actually occurring.

2. Exception Report Auditing. This concept is similar to anticipatory auditing because data is developed between line/staff management and the internal auditors and both determine what factors warrant an exception report being put out by the computer system. Such reports can cover simple matters (e.g., a nominal overdraft in a consumer DDA) or focus on complex matters (e.g., a sufficiently unusual or irregular accounting entry that the computer flags it—a debit to an equity account from some location other than the comptroller's department; a long or short foreign exchange or futures position exceeding established limits). This information is meaningful to both line/staff management of the environment and the internal auditors. The basic difference to anticipatory auditing is that, under that concept, internal auditors always react immediately. Under the exception report auditing concept, the internal auditors wait for action by management, relative to *most* situations. They monitor how management has acted promptly and prudently regarding the exception reports they receive. If the exception report deals with a clearly or potentially serious situation, however, the internal auditors would respond immediately, just as they would do in anticipatory auditing.

   This concept does not affect the normal audit review requirements of the internal audit function. While accomplishing much of the values of anticipatory auditing, exception report auditing never tends to reduce the overall internal audit review scope. Exception reporting, therefore, is truly an early-warning approach and nothing more.

3. Early Warning Signal Auditing. This is fundamentally the same concept as under item 2, in the sense that the auditors establish the exception reports they want and specify the condi-

tions when such reports should be received from the computer system. They respond to each of the reports. This is not a cooperative or joint effort with the line/staff management. However, it does add dimension, in that, using both manual- and computer-prepared trial balances, listings, and other reports, personnel in internal audit seek out certain questionable conditions or situations manually, which they follow up promptly when appropriate. The value of this second aspect is that they, and only they, know what circumstances, situations, or balances trigger a prompt reaction from the internal audit function. This is important in that no one outside of internal audit knows what will trigger a review by personnel of that function. Why is that important? Because persons who are planning to perpetrate a fraud or hide violations of policies, procedures, practices, standards, and/or regulations, can over time identify *(a)* anticipatory auditing key indicators, *(b)* things that internal audit responds to in the exception reports or early warning signals, usually in the form of exception reports. Accordingly, they will deliberately design their wrongdoing so it will bypass the warning signals and the normal reactive auditing efforts of the internal audit function. Internal audit should have such calculations set up within the function, manually or on an off-line microcomputer. Where such an approach is used, periodic reviews should be made to determine *(a)* new factors they wish to monitor, *(b)* previously monitored factors they no longer wish to monitor, or *(c)* revisions in approach, details or information desired relative to factors being monitored.

4. Information Received Auditing. Internal auditors should establish a reputation of being *(a)* constructive, and *(b)* consistent in how they react to problems, and *(c)* consistent in how they deal with those being audited, both management and staff. Why? Because, if those requirements are fulfilled, internal audit personnel will likely receive information from both management and staff personnel relative to *(a)* questionable conduct or actions by an associate, *(b)* specific actions taken to hide problem conducts, *(c)* breaches of policy, procedure, practices, standards, and/or regulations, or *(d)* ineffective internal control and/or check applications, either because the systems or personnel indicate they did something they have not done as the documents improperly show (e.g., authorization to process made without actually checking documents; initials, indicating internal check as to mathematical accuracy, when such confirmation was not actually performed).

While an audit is under way, such information, whether from management or staff, others in the company's environment not being audited, or outsiders should be followed up promptly and to the degree appropriate to determine whether controls broke down, a deficiency was hidden, assets were stolen, or balances in liability accounts were altered. Based on the follow-up findings, appropriate actions should be initiated as promptly and thoroughly as necessary.

How important is the information from whistle blowers, frustrated employees, and unhappy clients? Remember that from 20 to 25 percent of fraud is discovered by auditors; about the same percentage is found through the effectiveness of the systems of internal control and check; and more than 50 percent is found out by accident or intentional tips or unintentional leads.

Personally, I have been involved in more than 200 fraud situations as an internal auditor; as a senior internal audit official; as a corporate officer—controller, treasurer, and vice president in charge of line or staff functions for a major bank; or as an outside consultant. It is fair to say that more than 50 percent of the fraud was uncovered by leads from nonaudit employees. That same percentage would hold true in cases of negligence, gross negligence, or records manipulations to hide something.

Therefore, opening up communications so that unsolicited information will be directed to the internal audit personnel should be encouraged. Obviously, you will receive some false leads or inaccurate data (e.g., frustrated employees or resigned former employees). However, all tip-offs should be assessed and followed up to some degree unless senior internal audit personnel decides the situation does not warrant action at that time but will be checked out at the next audit.

Summary

Reactive internal audit methodology has many values. The overall internal audit approach must determine how much reliance should be placed on one or more of the methodologies described in this chapter. My preferences are anticipatory auditing, exception report auditing, and early warning signal auditing. All should be used to supplement normal audit reviews to the degree that they are *early warning* sources.

Information received response auditing should be used to the extent that it can support data or a condition that warrants (1) an immediate follow-up review, or (2) a review when the next regular audit takes place.

Part II
Risk-Oriented Internal Auditing

7

Concepts and Principles of Risk-Oriented Internal Auditing

Introduction

This chapter sets the stage for all of the chapters in Part II. It is important that (1) depository institutions, (2) risk, and (3) the concepts and principles of risk-oriented internal auditing, for the institutions described, are in perspective so the merits and potential values of adopting this method will be understood.

Depository Institutions

Definitions:

1. BANK. "The term 'bank' in its broadest sense may be applied to any organization engaged in any or all of the various functions of 'banking', i.e., receiving, collecting, transferring, paying, lending, investing, dealing, exchanging and servicing (safe deposit, custodianship, agency, trusteeship), money and claims to money, both domestically and internationally. Under this broad concept, the title 'bank' is found in the American financial system applied to such institutions as Banks for Cooperatives, Central Bank for Cooperatives, Export-Import Bank, Federal Intermediate Credit Banks, Federal Land Banks, Investment Bankers, and Mortgage Bankers. . . . In its more specific sense, however, the term 'bank' refers to institutions providing deposit facilities for the general public. Such institutions in turn may be classified into two broad groups: *(a)* commercial banks and their central banks; and *(b)* noncommercial banking institutions."[117]

2. COMMERCIAL BANKS. Such institutions "are unique in not only being banks of deposit but in also providing the most important means of payment, 'checkbook money' or demand deposits subject to check, which may be expanded or contracted by commercial banks by their lending and investing."[118]

---

[117]F.L. Garcia. *Encyclopedia of Banking and Finance*, 7th ed., revised and enlarged. (*Boston:* Bankers Publishing, 1973), pp. 64, 65.
[118]*Ibid.*, p. 65.

3. NONCOMMERCIAL BANKS. Such institutions are "engaged in deposit banking, including the mutual savings, stock savings banks, and credit unions which in addition to receiving savings of members in payment for 'shares' also receive savings deposits from the public at large. By contrast, mutual savings and loan associations (or building associations, building and loan associations, homestead associations, and cooperative banks) do not specifically accept deposits but members of such institutions provide savings capital and are technically shareholders. On the other hand, stock savings and loan associations in various states accept savings accounts, which are entitled to payment in full before any payment may be made to stockholders in liquidations."[119]

4. CREDIT UNIONS. "The Federal Credit Union Act was passed" in 1934 "to establish a Federal Credit Union System, to establish a further market for securities of the United States, and to make more available to people of small means credit for provident purposes..." The National Credit Union Administration was established in 1970, taking over administrative responsibility for the credit unions. The law permitting establishment of that organization "authorizes the administrator to insure credit union member accounts.... The insurance is mandatory for federal credit unions, and available to state-chartered credit unions on an optional basis provided they meet certain standards set forth in the Act" of 1970. Such insurance is normally at the same level... offered by the FDIC or FSLIC. In the federal credit unions, "money saved by members is normally placed in a 'share account.' Earnings of the credit union are divided and paid back as 'dividends' on each share (usually in $5 units)."[120]

5. SAVINGS AND LOAN ASSOCIATIONS. "Savings and home financing institutions [are] mostly mutual organizations having no capital stock. Also known as 'savings associations', 'building and loan associations', 'building associations' or 'building societies', 'cooperative banks', and 'homestead associations.'"[121]

6. DEPOSITORY INSTITUTIONS. The "Depository Institutions and Monetary Control Act of 1980," known hereafter as "the Act," is an omnibus act consisting of nine distinct segments. "Deposi-

---

[119]*Ibid.*, p. 65.
[120]*Ibid.*, p. 243.
[121]*Ibid.*, p. 813.

tory Institutions," as defined in "the Act" consists of *(a)* commercial banks; *(b)* credit unions; and *(c)* savings and loan associations. "The Act" permits the three categories of organizations to compete in many respects where law previously had prevented the current degree of competition.

Depository institutions as used in the title of this book and hereafter, will be the three categories of organizations explained in definition 6.

Risks

Definitions

1. RISK. "Chance of loss. . . . Degree of probability of loss."[122]

2. MEASUREMENT OF RISK. "Risk is measured in terms of probabilities, reflecting relative chances in the occurrence of possible outcomes. . . . Because probabilities are ratios or relative numbers, it follows that when probabilities of all possible outcomes are summed, the sum equals 1. . . . No matter how the probabilities are determined, it is clear that the larger the probabilities of an outcome, the more certain the occurrence of the outcome. The extreme values are 1 and 0. When an outcome is certain, the probability of its occurrence is 1. When the outcome is impossible, its probability is 0. This being so, it is reasonable to weigh each uncertain outcome with the associated probability—to discount, so to speak, the uncertainty contained in the outcome. When all possible outcomes are thus adjusted with their associated probabilities and summed, the resulting number is defined as the expected value, or mean. Because the expected value represents a discount for certainty, it often is a reasonable practice to compare two decision alternatives in terms of the expected value of the possible outcomes and regard as superior the alternative with a higher expected value. . . . A manager who is ignorant of or unwilling to make subjective estimates of probabilities still can make decisions in a systematic way. The theory of games described two such ways: the minimax or . . . the maximax principle. . . . Under the minimax principle, the decision maker will choose the alternative that has the smallest worst loss. . . . Under the maximax principle, he will choose the deci-

---

[122]Kohler, *op. cit.*, p. 377.

sion alternative that has the maximum most favorable outcome."[123]

3. BUSINESSMAN'S RISK. "A risk such as is involved in a business or security, the income from which is uncertain, but which promises large returns under favorable management; a risk which a businessman is warranted in taking because of his concern in which the investment is made, and his ability to protect himself in case of unfavorable developments, but . . . an unwise risk for others not familiar with these facts."[124]

4. BUSINESS RISK. "An expression used by credit men in contradistinction to moral risk and property risk. The business risk is that element of a credit risk which depends upon the business ability of the managers of the concern under consideration. The chief test of this risk is capacity to produce profits over a period of time. In measuring or testing a business risk, the credit man investigates the following points: (a) Is the business sound, well established and stable, or relatively new and risky? (b) Is the volume of business declining, advancing, or stationary? (c) Are modern production and sales methods being used? (d) What reputation does the product of the concern enjoy in the trade? (e) What has been the ratio of profits to invested capital for, say, the past five years? (f) What is the (1) range of fluctuation of gross profits, (2) percentage of operating expenses to gross profits, (3) range of fluctuation of this percentage, (4) margin of profits above operating expenses, and its range of fluctuation?"[125]

5. CREDIT RISK. "A term applied by bankers and credit men to an individual, firm, or corporation to whom money is loaned or to whom merchandise or service is delivered on a credit basis. Wherever credit is extended it is attended with the risk of nonpayment varying from practically zero to a large percentage. The degree of risk involved is determined by the credit department, and when too high, credit is refused. By extension, therefore, the term is used to refer to anyone to whom credit is given."[126] "Those who deal regularly with the credit decision are familiar with the three Cs of credit. They

[123]Lester R. Bittle and Jackson E. Ramsey. *Handbook for Professional Managers.* (New York: McGraw-Hill, 1985), p. 806.

[124]Garcia, *op. cit.*, p. 157.

[125]*Ibid.*, p. 157.

[126]*Ibid.*, p. 243.

are character, capacity, and capital.... Character, combining integrity with fortitude, is placed by many at the head of the line.... Character is an inner quality and not something worn as a visible garment.... Capacity is the ability of those who manage a business to manage it successfully."[127]

6. DISTRIBUTION OF RISK. "This is a well-known investment principle popularly expressed in the maxim, 'Don't put all your eggs in one basket.' The principle, usually applied to conservative investors and speculators, and enforced upon the banks by the banking laws, implies the spreading of investment funds over a number of media, instead of a single medium."[128]

7. INVESTMENT RISKS. "The basic risks in investment are: financial risk (risk of nonpayment by the obligor or issuer), also known as credit risk; interest rate risk (risk of open market price depreciation should interest rates rise, applicable to high-grade bonds and obligations), also known as money risk; and purchasing power risk (risk of decline in purchasing power of principal and income because of rise in the price level), also known as inflation risk. Investment ratings (quality ratings) reflect primarily financial risk.... Other risks include: governmental and political risk; foreign exchange and expropriation risk; risk of institutional change (in social and economic system); risk of war and international tension."[129]

8. MORAL RISK. "That part of the risk involved in loaning money which depends upon the integrity or honesty of the borrower or prospective borrower."[130]

9. PROPERTY RISK. "That risk involved in lending money which varies according to, and therefore is determined by, the value of the net assets or net worth of the borrower. If a loan is well protected, the borrower should possess sufficient unpledged net tangible assets which if converted into cash would be sufficient to cover amount of loan, whether secured or unsecured. ... The property risk is distinguished from moral and business risk. Together they constitute the classical three-fold divisions of a credit risk. Property risk is usually regarded as less important than the moral or business risk."[131] (*Note:* Refer

---

[127]Prochnow, *op. cit.*, p. 2.
[128]Garcia, *op. cit.*, p. 275.
[129]*Ibid.*, p. 498.
[130]*Ibid.*, p. 585.
[131]*Ibid.*, p. 756.

to 5 and the three Cs of credit, which are, in principle, the same for the three above named risks).

10. SPECULATION. "In its broadest sense, speculation is risk-taking, i.e., taking investment risks with the anticipation of profit but incurring the chances of loss."[132] Some other examples would be:

    (a) Lending long and funding short, which can create serious liquidity problems (e.g., incurred by the S&L industry in the early 1980s).

    (b) Funding long and lending short, which can result in rates dropping, and subsequent rolling over of debt at reduced returns to the extent of negative spreads impacting on capital.

    (c) Excessive positions, long or short, in one or more foreign currencies, when they move against the institution resulting in substantial losses that can impact negatively on capital, create problems of liquidity, and damage the image of the institution if the information becomes public knowledge, resulting in loss of depositors or sources of future borrowings.

11. OFF-BALANCE-SHEET RISKS. Such "activities are contingent claims or financial services that generate income and create portfolio risk. A contingent claim involves a commitment or guarantee to lend that does not create an item on the balance sheet. The most familiar forms of bank contingent claims include such traditional activities as loan commitments, lines of credit, letters of credit.... forward contracts in foreign exchanges.... and more recently, "futures contracts and lease agreements."[133] Figure 9 provides a listing of a number of the off-balance-sheet activities of various institutions.

Business Perspective

Business is defined as "the carrying on of trade or commerce, involving the use of capital and having as a major objective, income derived from sales or services..."[134]

---

[132]*Ibid.*, p. 855

[133]Richard C. Aspenwall and Robert A. Eisenbeis. *Handbook for Banking Strategy.* (New York: Wiley-Interscience, 1985), p. 357.

[134]Kohler, *op. cit.,* p. 69.

Figure 9
Some Standard Off-Balance-Sheet Activities

Contingent Claims	Financial Services
Bank loan commitments, including unused portions of:	Mortgage (1st and 2nd) servicing Student loan servicing.
• Loan commitments made.	Loan pass-throughs, such as:
• Revolving credits extended.	• Mortgages (GNMA, FNMA).
• Lines of credit extended.	• Student loans (SLMA).
• Fed funds arrangements.	• Construction loans to corporations.
• Eurodollar line-of-credit extensions.	Trust-related services, such as:
• Commercial paper backup lines of credit.	• Portfolio management.
Letters of credit:	• Customer stock, bond, and money market brokerage.
• Standby.	• Investment advisory services.
• Commercial.	• Security exchange and processing.
• Import/Export.	• Trust management.
Bankers' acceptances.	• Estate management.
Futures and forward contracts:	Payment services, such as:
• Foreign exchange.	• Transaction processing.
• Financial.	• Overdraft banking (ready-reserve use).
Agreements to provide financial support to joint ventures, bank affiliates, or subsidiaries.	• Credit/debit cards.
	• Cash management.
Loan participations:	• Wire/money transfers (SWIFT).
• Direct use of funds.	• ATMs.
• Risk participations.	• POS.
• Take position and sell off part or all of same, with servicing fee.	• Home banking.
	• Network arrangements.
	Loan participation (down-stream).
	• Fund generation.
	Correspondent banking services.
	Other:
	• Export/import consulting.
	• Trade financing.
	• Insurance services.

Activities Having Elements of Both Contingent Claim and Financial Services

Merchant banking:	Customer leasing:
• Private placements.	• Tax leasing.
• Securities lending (repos).	• Lease brokering.
• Equity participations.	• Fleet leasing.
• Corporate finance consulting.	
• Foreign exchange advisory services.	
• Tax shelters.	
• Precious metals trading.	
• Other commodities trading.	

The following on business are from *The Forbes Scrapbook of Thoughts on the Business of Life,* Fourth Edition, two volumes, published by Forbes in 1976:

- "All business proceeds on beliefs, or judgments of probabilities, and not on certainties."—Charles W. Eliot

- "Contrary to the commonly accepted belief, it is the risk element in our capitalistic system which produces an economy of security. Risk brings out the ingenuity and resourcefulness which insure the success of enough ventures to keep the economy growing and secure."—Robert Rawls

Note that the definition of business indicates a *major objective* is to generate *income,* but the *risk* always exists that it will not be achieved. Of the two quotations shown, note that the first refers to "judgments of probabilities, and not on certainties," which is another way of referring to *risk;* while the second focuses on the *risk* element in doing business.

Risk-taking is a requirement of all business but probably no industries face the day-to-day level of *risk* as do depository institutions. That is why internal auditing, in both preparing for and performing its reviews, must consider seriously the merits of *risk-oriented* audit principles, standards, techniques, procedures, and concepts. These criteria have been described thusly:

1. "Auditing principles are the basic premises of auditing which indicate the purpose and objectives of auditing.

2. "Auditing standards are criteria or measures of performance. Principles define objectives; standards set up criteria to be observed in accomplishing these objectives.

3. "Auditing techniques are the devices or methods available to the auditor for obtaining competent evidential matter. They are the working tools of the auditor.

4. "Auditing procedures are ways of applying techniques to particular phases of a particular audit. The procedures adopted in different engagements result from the judicious application of the available techniques."[135]

5. The five "primary concepts in auditing" are:

   (a) "Evidence.

   (b) "Due audit care.

---

[135]Cashin, *op. cit.,* pp. 1-12. Based on article by C.A. Mayer in *Journal of Accountancy,* published by *AICPA,* December, 1952.

(c) "Fair presentation.

(d) "Independence.

(e) "Ethical conduct.[136]

"Audit techniques and audit procedures are as closely related as
principles and standards. Audit techniques are tools which can be
used on specific audit engagements. . . . Audit procedures are the
specific means used to carry out a specific audit technique. For example, on a specific engagement, positive-type confirmation requests instead of negative type of requests could be used to implement the technique of confirmation. A physical examination could
be carried out in one situation if the auditor merely viewed certain
items, but in another situation, the auditor might deem it necessary
to view and handle certain items."[137] Some standard "audit techniques [are]:

1. Physical examination and count.

2. Confirmation.

3. Examination of authoritative documents and comparison
   with the record.

4. Recomputation.

5. Retracing bookkeeping procedures.

6. Scanning.

7. Inquiry.

8. Examination of subsidiary records.

9. Correlation with related information.

10. Observation of pertinent activities and conditions."[137]

Overview of Risk-Oriented Auditing

As Figure 10 indicates, all of the four groupings of various internal
audit formats (e.g., vertical, horizontal, situation/condition, and reactive) have the same keystone, which is *risk*. While each deals with
risk in varying ways, all internal audit methodologies are concerned
with:

1. Identification of risk.

---

[136]*Ibid.*, pp. 1-12. From *The Philosophy of Accounting* by Mautz and Hussein.
[137]*Ibid.*, pp. 1-12.

Figure 10
Risk as an Auditing Keystone

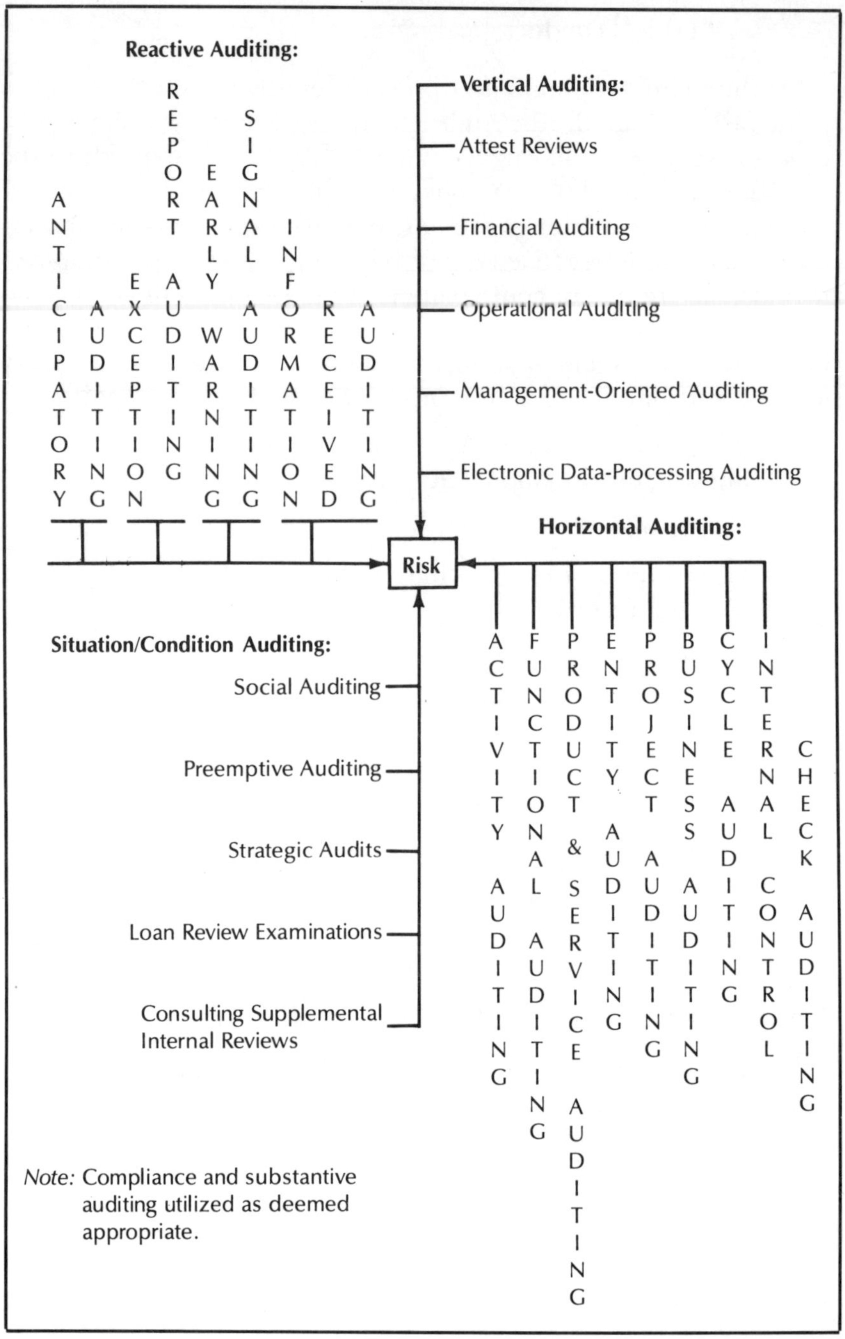

Reactive Auditing:

Vertical Auditing:

— Attest Reviews

— Financial Auditing

— Operational Auditing

— Management-Oriented Auditing

— Electronic Data-Processing Auditing

Horizontal Auditing:

```
        R       S
        E       I
        P   E   G
        O   A   N
A       R   A   N
N       T   R   I
T           L   L   I
I           L   Y   N
I   E   A       F
C   A   X   U   A   O   R   A
I   U   C   D   W   U   R   E   U
P   D   E   I   A   D   M   C   D
A   I   P   T   R   I   A   E   I
T   T   T   I   N   T   T   I   T
O   I   I   N   I   I   I   V   I
R   N   O   G   N   N   O   E   N
Y   G   N       G   G   N   D   G
```

Situation/Condition Auditing:

Social Auditing —

Preemptive Auditing —

Strategic Audits —

Loan Review Examinations —

Consulting Supplemental
Internal Reviews —

Risk

```
A   F   P   E   P   B   C   I
C   U   R   N   R   U   Y   N
T   N   O   T   O   S   C   T
I   C   D   I   J   I   L   E
V   T   U   T   E   N   E   R
I   I   C   Y   C   E       N
T   O   T       T   S   A   A
Y   N   A       A       U   L
    A   &   A   U   S   D
A       S   D   U   A   I   C
U       E   I   D   U   T   O
D   A   R   T   I   D   I   N
I   U   V   I   T   I   N   T
T   D   I   N   I   T   G   R
I   I   C   G   N   I       O
N   T   E       G   N       L
G   I               G
    N   A
    G   U
        D
        I
        T
        I
        N
        G
```

Note: Compliance and substantive
auditing utilized as deemed
appropriate.

2. Determination of level of exposure of each identified risk, as to probable incidents in a specified period and the average amount per incident to enable stratification (e.g., primary, secondary, tertiary, and quaternary).

3. Appropriate analysis to determine various probable scenarios on how best to deal with each risk, so that the risk can be eliminated or reduced to a level acceptable by risk management, internal auditors, and senior management.

4. Actions to accomplish the risk reductions under item 3 to bring each identified risk to a level satisfactory to the three management groups indicated.

5. Follow-up to ascertain whether the actions taken under item 4 have, in fact, achieved the desired level of risk reduction and, if not, what further actions are needed within what time frame to accomplish the control risk objectives desired.

The most effective audit approach to identifying risks is a thorough and diligent review and assessment of internal controls and checks as built into the accounting (finance), administrative and operational policies, procedures, practices, standards, and systems. Not only will this identify risks but the review of the systems and procedures provides confirmation that all laws and regulatory requirements are being complied with or, if not, the degree of noncompliance so that appropriate actions can be taken to bring the institution into full compliance. The 12 building blocks of effective internal controls and checks are indicated in Figure 11.

The traditional internal or external audit phases are:

1. Familiarization.

2. Examination.

3. Evaluation (of examination findings).

4. Report.

For risk-oriented auditing, the number of internal audit phases are increased, as follows:

1. Familiarization (*Note:* The scope is broadened to cover all of the twelve internal control and check building blocks, as shown in Figure 11).

2. Determination of audit methodology to be followed (*Note:* vertical, horizontal, situation/condition, or reactive auditing, as shown in Figure 10 or fraud auditing, which is commented upon later in this chapter and is covered extensively in Chapter 8).

Figure 11
The 12 Building Blocks of Effective Internal Controls/Checks

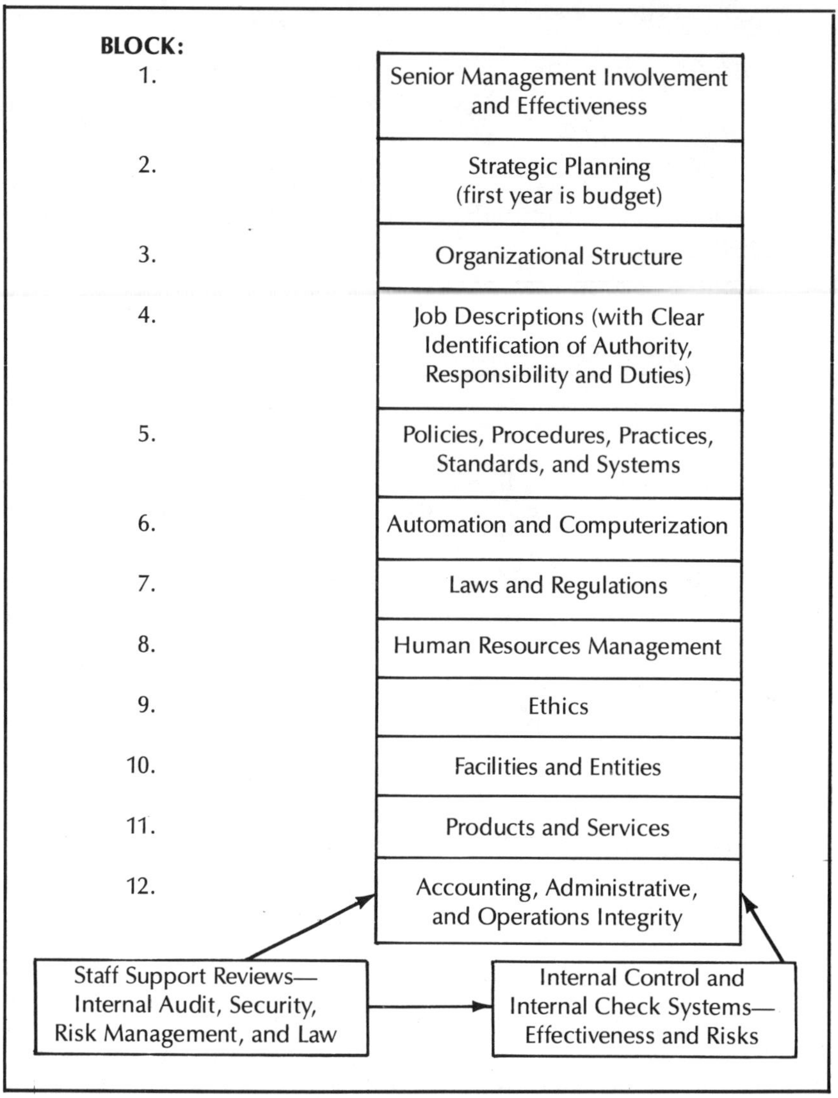

BLOCK:	
1.	Senior Management Involvement and Effectiveness
2.	Strategic Planning (first year is budget)
3.	Organizational Structure
4.	Job Descriptions (with Clear Identification of Authority, Responsibility and Duties)
5.	Policies, Procedures, Practices, Standards, and Systems
6.	Automation and Computerization
7.	Laws and Regulations
8.	Human Resources Management
9.	Ethics
10.	Facilities and Entities
11.	Products and Services
12.	Accounting, Administrative, and Operations Integrity

Staff Support Reviews— Internal Audit, Security, Risk Management, and Law	→	Internal Control and Internal Check Systems— Effectiveness and Risks

3. Development in scope of initial reviews, after giving priority to risks identified during the familiarization phase, under item 1, (an approach detailed later in this chapter).

4. Examination.

5. Evaluation of findings.

6. Additional examinations, as deemed warranted, based on phase 4 findings.

7. Evaluation of total findings under phases 4 and 6.

8. Implementation of corrective actions, working with management at environment being audited under methodology determined under phase 2.

9. Reports, with appropriate reference to actions agreed to under phase 8.

10. Follow-up for assuring that appropriate actions have been taken under phases 8 and 9 and that those actions have dealt with the identified risks and other deficiencies (e.g., unqualified personnel, failing to comply with procedures, as intended).

Phases 6, 7, and 10 in the preceding list may be repeated with the scope modified as seen necessary. This is illustrated in Figure 12, which shows the seven stages of audit; from 1, a standard (initial) audit scope, through 7, an audit scope where fraud is known or virtually certain.

Some years ago, a fraud involving a retail organization in a major midwestern city was headline news. A reporter asked a partner of a

Figure 12
The Seven Stages of Audit

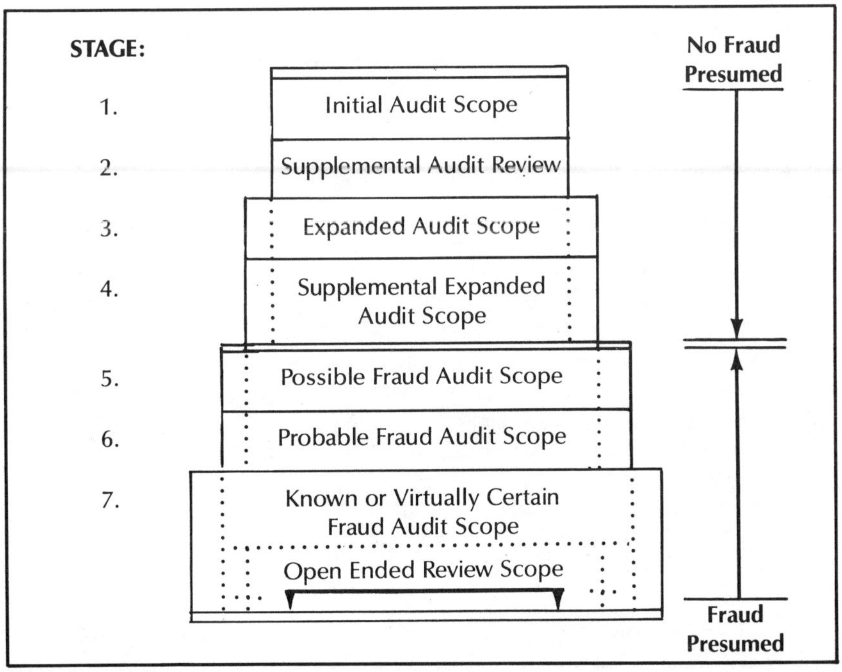

"Big 8" firm, "Why don't you auditors find more of these frauds earlier?" The partner responded: "If my firm contracted to do an audit of your newspaper for 'X' dollars, with both expecting that a clean audit certification would be issued but the audit review findings indicated that a *fraud audit* was warranted, I would advise that the cost would be '20X' dollars [at a] minimum and, potentially, two or three times that amount!"

Let me put that into perspective in Figure 13.

In some instances, the auditors must work through each stage, developing increased evidence, until reaching and operating in the open-ended principle of Stage 7. In other instances, such as a con-

Figure 13
Approach to Seven Stages of Audit (Figure 12)

Stage	Nature of Scope	Cost to "X"	
1.	Initial Audit Scope (Based on Familiarization efforts to determine strengths and weaknesses):	1.0	
2.	Supplemental Audit Review (Where the auditor feels some further tests are needed to draw a conclusion):	0.5	
3.	Expanded Audit Scope (Involves more detail checking of both Compliance and Substantive nature, and broadening out to observe more work-tasks and processes):	2.0	
4.	Supplemental Expanded Audit Review (Same in principle relative to Stage 3 as Stage 2 is to Stage 1, meaning there are still some concerns as to integrity of financial, administrative, or operational data):	1.0	
—	Total (No Fraud Presumed):	4.5	
5.	Possible fraud audit scope (First stage where "presumed fraud" is the attitude taken by the auditors, based on reviews in Stages 1 through 4):	3.75	
6.	Probable Fraud Audit Scope (Where findings under Stage 5 have increased concern about fraud but have not yet proven it without doubt):	3.75	
7.	Known or Virtually Certain Fraud Audit Scope (Where findings of all preceding stages prove or make it virtually certain fraud exists so this stage wants to determine extent as to nature of activities, amounts involved, and period of wrongdoing):	8.0	(+ or −)
—	Total (Presumed Fraud):	15.5	(+ or −)
—	Total Review Effort	20.0	(+ or −)

fession of fraud, when following up on a matter in Stage 1, the auditor proceeds directly to Stage 7. Using the seven stage concept, in Figures 12 and 13, the auditor (1) can stop the review at any stage, when the findings until then do not justify further reviews; or (2) can bypass one or more stages, when the findings to that point do justify such a move. The facts disclosed or implications of review findings dictate when to continue any audit review beyond the stage being reviewed.

The auditor may proceed into fraud auditing from any of the four audit groupings, as indicated in Figure 10, which are (1) vertical, (2) horizontal, (3) situation/condition, and (4) reactive. The auditor also may proceed directly into a fraud auditing from risk-oriented auditing. A broader discussion of fraud auditing is in Chapter 8.

Concepts of Risk-Oriented Auditing

1. Definition of Risk-Oriented Auditing

   An audit concept based on thorough review of each of the twelve building blocks of effective internal controls/checks (*Note:* detailed in Figure 11) and such other information or factors, relative to a specific audit examination to ascertain *(a)* risks, *(b)* deficiencies in internal control and check procedures and practices, as implemented, *(c)* deviations from criteria of the institution as well as laws and regulations, and *(d)* situations of accounting, administrative, and operational practices that are considered ineffective, inefficient, and uneconomical. Findings under items *(a)* through *(d)* should be evaluated and priorities set for corrective actions to (1) accomplish compliance, (2) improve productivity, (3) improve internal controls/checks, and (4) ascertain actions necessary to eliminate risks or bring them down to a level satisfactory to management, based on risk management criteria established for the institution.

2. Objectives of a Risk-Oriented Audit

   (a) Identification of and classification of all risks (i.e. primary, secondary, tertiary, and quaternary) based on (1) probable frequency of occurrence during the review period or like future period; (2) impact in dollars per predicted occurrence (e.g., reduced productivity, accidental or deliberate clerical inefficiencies and noncompliance with criteria of the institution as well as laws and regulations, which will arrive at (3) aggregate effect of item (1) multiplied by item (2).

(b) Evaluation of systems of internal controls and checks for strengths and weaknesses and situations of noncompliance.

(c) Ascertaining integrity of records, manual or computer, as well as security of same to determine vulnerability of (a) accidental distortion, (b) deliberate distortion/manipulation, or (c) loss of data.

(d) Adequacy of policies, procedures, practices, standards to achieve intended purpose and level of compliance with them.

(e) Compliance with all laws and regulations or determination of instances of noncompliance (effect) and reason for same (cause) so that appropriate actions (solutions) can be taken to achieve required compliance.

(f) Qualifications of personnel relative to (1) authority and responsibilities assigned them and/or (2) duties and tasks they are to perform as well as effectiveness of management in fulfilling the full requirements of all aspects of their job descriptions.

(g) Identification of (1) corrective actions on deficiencies identified relative to objectives (a) through (f), and/or (2) revision of methods, approaches, or technology to improve efficiency, effectiveness, and/or economy of any aspect of work performed without, in any way, reacting negatively on the internal controls and checks so that all objectives are accomplished with emphasis on objectives (a) and (b).

The seven indicated objectives are described in broad terms. The objectives may (1) be revised to meet specific situations, known before or identified during the familiarization phase of the audit work to be performed, or (2) be supplemented by additional objectives, where found appropriate by audit management in any specific review. Note, however, that *none* of the seven objectives may be dropped if the intent is to perform a risk-oriented audit, as all of the indicated information must be known before the initial audit scope determinations can be made relative to the examination phase of the review. Obviously, where appropriate, the auditor may change the priority of the objectives but, as stated earlier, data in segments 1 and 2 are the driving concept behind risk-oriented auditing.

3. Standards for the Professional Practice of Internal Auditing

All of the criteria stated in the pamphlet issued with the preceding title by The Institute of Internal Auditors, Inc. are required for effective and properly conducted risk-oriented audits. The emphasis, as always, remains on the PIO factors, which are P = professionalism; I = independence; and O = objectivity. Detailed criteria are given in Appendix A.

4. Knowledge Base Required of the Auditor

The auditor must have a good understanding of any environment to be audited so communications with the company management and staff will enable the auditor to learn details of the audit environment, such as *(a)* terminology, *(b)* authority and responsibilities, *(c)* unique aspects or requirements, and *(d)* fundamental risk inherent in the subject environment. This information should be developed by the auditor doing a review before starting the familiarization phase. And subordinates should be indoctrinated before the examination work begins. The primary sources of such information are:

(1) Continuing audit file (CAF) of previous audits of the environment, if any.

(2) Best possible reference source on audit environment. For example, if preparing to audit the institution's letter-of-credit operations, then some reference source such as *Letters of Credit Guidebook,* written by Dominick J. Policano, and published by Executive Education Press, should provide an understanding of the audit environment. The first five chapters of most such references provide a general overview. That is required reading for all auditors of senior rank or higher. Additional parts of such text should be read, as required, or used as a reference to check information provided to the auditors by those being audited.

(3) On rare occasions, data should be sought from an outside consultant who specializes in the environment being audited.

5. Audit Scope for Stage One

This should be based on:

(a) Accomplishing objectives of a risk-oriented audit, as under segment 2.

(b) Meeting the standards in the conduct of the audit, as under segment 3.

(c) Using compliance and substantive audit techniques, as appropriate.

(d) Focusing on the "show me" and "interview" aspects of the audit, as appropriate.

(e) Having the knowledge base of the environment being audited, as under segment 4.

Allocation of total time determined as applicable to audit stages between familiarization and report aspects of review should be:

(1) Risk focused auditing: 20 to 30 percent of time allotted.

(2) Evaluation of internal control and check systems, implementation of same, and effectiveness of same: 20 to 30 percent.

(3) Fulfillment of audit objectives 3 through 6: 10 to 20 percent.

(4) Traditioinal compliance and substantive reviews: 10 to 20 percent.

(5) Specific evaluation of all accounting, administrative, and operational procedures and practices to ascertain:

(i) Integrity of data and security of data: 10 to 15 percent.

(ii) Whether practices achieve maximum efficiency, effectiveness, and economy: 10 to 15 percent.

The total time under items (1) through (5) are minimum of 80 percent and maximum of 130 percent. Obviously, time assignments must be adjusted, as appropriate by auditor-in-charge to a 100 percent total. That time must be supplemented by time assigned to (a) familiarization phase, (b) efforts to develop mutually agreed solutions with the audited management, (c) report writing, editing, and, if appropriate, explanation, and (d) follow-up.

Principles of Risk-Oriented Auditing

Risk-oriented auditing principles are as follows:

1. Approach each audit assignment with the joint perspective of management and auditing; thereby, in most instances, creating a "constructive approach" perception by the function being audited and its senior management.

2. Focus on (a) risk identification, (b) risk assessment, (c) risk stratification, and (d) risk management, by recommending actions to (1) eliminate specific risks or (2) reduce the probability

factor of specific risks to a level in line with the institution's risk management program.

3. Review and evaluate the effectiveness of the systems of internal controls and checks that support the accounting, administrative, and operational aspects of the audited environment.

4. Confirm that selected officers and other personnel know of the code of ethics of the institution and the authority, responsibility, duties, and tasks set forth in their specific job descriptions.

5. Supplement item 3 by assuring that all of the Twelve Building Blocks of Effective Internal Control and Check, as detailed earlier, are functioning and providing the safeguards for assets and activities.

6. Provide the institution with the highest possible return on investment for each dollar spent on auditing, whether it is the head office or individual entity or facility (local) audit personnel.

7. Key principles of risk-oriented auditing are:

   (a) Proactive Aspects

      (1) The internal auditors must sell management on the "constructive approach" of their efforts and the fact that they are associates working in the best interests of the organization, and not adversaries. Unfortunately, many internal audit groups have managers believing them to be antagonists.

      (2) The internal auditors must establish good communications with each key activity, function, product, service, facility, and staff management, and work at maintaining those contacts with managerial personnel. This will encourage managerial personnel to come to internal auditing with both real and possible problems that concern them, rather than trying to determine the full situation of the real or possible problem and letting it ride until the next scheduled audit review. If internal auditing will respond with assistance in the form of functional audits on real or possible problems, management will feel more comfortable by identifying such conditions quickly. Why? Because, unless they are overstaffed, most managers, in-line or staff functions, do *not* have surplus skilled and capable people to perform

thorough reviews of areas of real or potential problems and then implement the corrective actions found warranted.

(b) Traditional Aspects

This requires some education of the management in each key activity, function, product, service, facility, and staff function to understand:

(1) The management mandate given to internal auditing.

(2) How internal auditing, in effect, monitors the code of ethics of the institution and assures that (a) authority and responsibility, as stipulated in job descriptions, are being fulfilled properly and within reasonable time, (b) policies, procedures, practices, and standards are being complied with, and (c) all aspects of internal controls and internal checks on items (a) and (b) are functioning as intended and are controlling risks efficiently, effectively, and economically.

(3) How internal audit has the primary responsibility of assuring that all management is fulfilling its responsibilities relative to:

(i) Having properly trained competent personnel in all positions.

(ii) Monitoring, or having designates monitoring, the work of all persons under them (*Note:* Most managerial personnel are usually sufficiently busy that this most important monitoring of day-to-day efforts is the lowest thing on their priority list and, as a result, is rarely done with the frequency and scope required to assure risks in accounting, operations, administration, and controls are held to a minimum or below what management considers acceptable).

(c) Reactive Aspects

The four types of "reactive" auditing, as indicated in Figure 10., in this chapter, and described earlier, must be used as determined by internal audit management, so there is quick response to any "red flag" of potential problems. Three of the four types (e.g., anticipatory auditing, exception report auditing, and early warning signal auditing) do not require any input from management as the information is provided in another manner. The fourth "reactive" auditing format may or may not involve management but will involve input from an internal officer or staff member or, on occasion, input from an outsider, identifying the existence of a possible or real problem. This "information-received auditing" is quite important. This may come by (i) telephone, where the callers may or may not identify themselves; (ii) note or memo, under same conditions as for item (i); (iii) through a special whistle-blower program, which must provide appropriate production for the informant; or (iv) "suggestion programs," worked in conjunction with human resources department, encouraging personnel to try for cash or other awards for making suggestions on how controls can be improved, how work processes can be simplified, and/or how improved productivity can be accomplished. Surprisingly, these "suggestions" will often identify risks that the auditor should respond to by conducting an appropriate review. The management mandate, as under segment 7(b)(1) should be known by all officers and staff and clearly indicate the "constructive" nature of the function to minimize fears of identifying problems to internal auditing.

(d) Follow-Up Requirement

Regarding any reviews performed under 7(a) through 7(c), the internal audit function must make it quite clear during the closing review with management that a "follow-up" will be scheduled by internal audit personnel on any actions recommended to reduce risk, ensure compliance with policies, procedures, practices, and standards, where noncompliance was identified; and, evaluate whether all corrective actions have produced the desired result as to risk, compliance, productivity, or internal control/check.

Types of Risk-Oriented Internal Auditing

1. Risk Analysis/Appraisal Auditing

The term "risk" has been adequately defined earlier in this book, which should be referred to by the reader. Let us, therefore, focus on:

(a) Risk Analysis

(1) Definitions

    (i) ANALYSIS. Separation of a whole into its complex elements and their relationships.

    (ii) ANALYZE. "To interpret or draw conclusions from a financial statement or statements . . . to determine or examine the composition of an item, account, or amount . . ."[138]

(2) "Risk Analysis"

    (i) Most auditors limit their reviews relative to the indicated subject to accounting, administration, financial statements, and operational performance. That is not enough, as indicated by item (2) (ii).

    (ii) The scope must also include policies, procedures, practices, and standards on compliance and whether, when implemented, they accomplish what management set out to do regarding productivity and risks.

    (iii) The scope also must include compliance with laws and regulations and adequate controls for achieving such compliance.

Variance analysis (e.g., actual to budget) is valuable but not enough. All risk analysis is focused on controls of risks relative to the levels acceptable by management and whether such controls are cost-efficient relative to risk constraint. If limited to two figures of the same period (e.g., actual to budget) that is known as "comparative analysis." Comparison of figures from the current period with the previous corresponding period, or any two comparable periods, also is known as "comparative analysis." As a norm, variances of some predetermined percentage, or less, require no further review to ascertain causes. Variances that exceed such predetermined percentages do require follow-up analysis to identify why?

When analysis is done on three or more consecutive periods of like duration and the same accounts, that is known as "trend" analysis. I believe that if only three periods are used they only indicate a possible trend and do not provide

---

[138]Kohler, *op. cit.*, p. 27.

a firm enough base for a judgment. The value in comparing either three or more periods is to focus not only on percentage changes, from the oldest period used, which is "trend" analysis, but, more importantly, the variances of budget to actual for each period. Why? Because that indicates whether the budget reacts to the realities of previous performance or has placed more emphasis on "hopes and aspirations." Often you will find budget to actual variances remain the same or even increase, either favorably or unfavorably, working from the oldest period to the most current period. To develop "trend" analysis with a firm base, in my opinion, requires five or more comparable periods and/or accounts. Such analysis not only provides the above indicated benefits but also assists in focusing on the causes for variances.

(b) Appraisal Auditing

   (1) Definitions

      (i) ANALYZE. "To interpret or draw conclusions . . . determine or examine the composition of an item, account, or amount."[139]

      (ii) APPRAISAL. "The act of appraising; the result of appraising; an appraisal report."[140]

      (iii) APPRAISE. "To establish cost or value" or risk "by systematic procedures that include physical examination . . ."[141]

   (2) Appraisal

      The objective of this internal audit approach is to determine why certain conditions exist, which should not, or do not exist but should. It is not enough to compare actual to budget and identify a variance. Why does such variance exist? Were the budget figures too optimistic or too pessimistic? Is the variance merely a timing thing (e.g., a new product introduction being deferred two months later than planned)?

      Once some basic information has been established, through appraisal, the auditors then have the respon-

---

[139]*Ibid.*, p. 27.
[140]*Ibid.*, p. 19.
[141]*Ibid.*, p. 29.

sibility to go out and talk to personnel involved to see whether they can make suggestions for improved controls or more efficient operations or "walk through" selected transactions to make their own assessments. Sound analysis can not be accomplished merely through figures. Facts behind the figures are also needed. When those facts have been developed, the auditors should be able to recommend appropriate changes in the criteria of the organization, improvement in the quality of personnel performing sensitive or high-risk duties, or stronger controls.

This is an area where the internal auditor may need the expertise of other internal personnel, if reliance can be placed on their professional integrity, or outside expertise. Let me emphasize again that the internal auditor should not try to be all things or assume that the ability to audit financial data is adequate to perform appraisal or evaluate worth in all instances. Therefore, as the function charged with protecting the assets of the organization, the internal auditor can dictate the scenario on when professional expertise, with the skills needed in any situation, is to be used. Under segment 1(c) below, a number of situations are identified where auditors called in professional skills from outside the internal audit function.

(c) Situations Where Nonaudit Expertise Was Utilized by Auditors

(1) Major Building Complex in Canada

The building complex consisted of three high-rise apartment buildings of about 340 units each; one high-rise office building, with one million square feet of space; one hotel of about 300 rooms; and one parking building having several floors above ground and several floors below ground. All of the buildings were connected underground by a two-floor shopping mall complex with a multicinema theater, grocery store, drugstore, and a variety of specialty stores.

An American bank was the lead institution in a 10-figure consortium loan to the contractor. The loan officer on the assignment had hired an independent engineering appraiser in the Canadian city where the project was being built. Because the loan officer was not an engineer, he believed that hiring the outside engineer was all he had to do to fulfill his obligation. He relied totally on reports from that consulting engineer who confirmed progress reports from the contractor, with only minor deficiencies identified, all of which were corrected promptly by the contractor. An officer from the loan review division of the audit department was sent to examine the project because the bank group was only providing the construction financing. The end financing, while arranged with a U.K. pension fund (superannuation fund), had set a date after which it would not accept the project under the long-term financing agreement with the contractor. The funds from the end-financing organization would pay off all of the construction loans from the American and Canadian bank group.

By phone, the loan review officer advised the general auditor that (i) the project was not as far along as the contractor's progress reports indicated but which had been confirmed as accurate by the project's consulting engineer hired by the bank's loan officer; and (ii) the city building inspectors, monitoring progress on the project, had filed 32 complaints, but only 21 had been corrected, none of which had been reported to the bank by the consulting engineer hired by the bank's loan officer. It also was his opinion that unless a second shift started working immediately, the project would not be completed and turned over to the organization, which agreed to provide end-financing within the time limits of its commitment. He also indicated that though he was not an engineer he had no confidence in the consulting engineer hired by the loan officer. The loan review officer also suggested that another consulting engineering firm should be hired to review the project and advised what should be done to get the project completed and turned over to the end-financing firm before its commitment expired.

A senior audit officer, assisted by two staff members, monitored the project to completion. He immediately hired an engineering consulting firm with an outstanding reputation. The three learned all they could from the consulting engineer and then he was discharged. (*Note:* He was a one-man consulting firm and was on his first major project. The loan officer had hired him on the recommendation of the contractor.) Because the loan officer had not acted "prudently" in monitoring the project, the general auditor recommended he be replaced. The general auditor requested the in-house law department to advise on the bank's contingent liability for failing to keep the other banks in the loan group informed of the problems on the project and that the end financing was in jeopardy because the project was running behind schedule. (*Note:* Periodic reports issued by the original loan officer relied on the progress reports of the contractor and confirmation by the consulting engineer he had recommended for the project.) The law department advised that the bank's contingent liability as the lead bank, for which it received a handsome fee, could be (i) as much as the amount of "cost overrun" if the project were completed on time and turned over to the end-financing organization lined up for that purpose and (ii) the amount of item (i) plus as much as 10 percent of the $1.5 billion project, because the consortium of banks would have to carry the project until another end-financing organization could be found and the project sold to them.

The head of the bank's commercial loan department assigned the real estate division chief as the contact officer to the project until its completion. He immediately assigned two of the engineers in the engineering section of that division to work full time on the project. They were to be on-site to assist the bank's internal auditors; also on-site were the outside consulting engineers and the contractor.

Through their combined efforts, the project came in on time with a cost overrun of $35 million. This total was less than 3 percent, a contingent figure in the consortium loan agreement and the same figure in the end-financing agreement. Thus, the British pension fund took title to the project and the banks in the consortium loan were paid off on time. The cost of the second consulting engineers were treated as part of the project's cost. The services of the bank's on-site engineering and audit personnel, as well as that of the new loan officer, and other senior management of the bank were absorbed as part of the lead bank's costs, which, fortunately, were less than the fee paid to the lead bank for monitoring the project.

(2) Resort Development on South Carolina Island

Two major U.S. banks had provided lines of credit of about $30 million each to construct the development's infrastructure (e.g., road, sewers, electric and telephone lines, sewerage treatment facility, golf course and clubhouse, tennis courts, pool, restaurant, sales office, and maintenance shed and equipment). Over a five-year period virtually all the lines of credit were used, but the development, which exceeded 4,000 acres, had sold only 200 lots, and less than 100 houses had been built by purchasers. The credit exposure, at both institutions, had been reclassified to be "cash basis" loans, on which no further interest accruals were made. Other developments on the island seemed to be selling out much faster, and the loan officer servicing the account could not explain why the project, which had extensive waterfront property, was not moving equally well. For that reason, management decided to have a senior audit officer, working alone, review the records, facilities, and meet with real estate agencies to find out why the project was so unsuccessful.

The audit officer found out the following, not disclosed in any reports issued on the project:

(i) The company that owned the project was a subsidiary of a holding company, which also owned the largest and most developed project on the island.

(ii) The parent company had assigned its personnel to manage the lingering project.

(iii) A visit to selected independent realtors and sales offices of two other development sales offices disclosed that:

- Only the parent organization's sales office or the sales office of the unsuccessful project site, staffed by personnel of the parent, could sell property in the development.

- Several mentioned that the parent organization was using a "bait and switch" approach on prospective buyers. They would be offered a package consisting of a free lunch at the restaurant at the project, a round of golf on the one completed golf course, or two hours of tennis or swimming. The costs for the packages were charged to the unsuccessful project.

Based on those findings, the audit officer, yet unknown to anyone at the project or parent organization, went to the sales office of the parent and heard a sales presentation on both projects. He indicated an interest in the unsuccessful project and was given the "visitor package." He visited the project and came back to the sales office on the premises. When he expressed an interest in buying property, to his surprise, he was directed to return to the sales office of the parent, which he did. When he repeated his interest in property at the unsuccessful project, they immediately tried to switch him to buy property or sell used condominiums or houses at the primary project. He was given a tour of the property and some of the used condominiums or homes. When he mentioned the other project, he was told, "Why buy there when it is a dying project." With this information, he proceeded to the nearest major city in eastern Georgia and engaged an independent real estate appraiser that was recommended by a correspondent bank of his institution. They returned to the project and the appraiser indicated that the project "was as good as any on the island, with sound infrastructure in place." He indicated that "it just needed proper marketing," and should be using as many realtors as possible to draw attention to the project.

With that information, he introduced himself and exercised the bank's right to audit the books. While doing so, he noted that all costs were incurred and paid by the parent who, in turn, charged the unsuccessful project with the direct cost of personnel, depreciation on equipment, and supplies used at the project. In addition, they charged the project with a management fee equal to 10 percent of all other costs. The management agreement, as approved by the banks, provided that the parent could only charge the project management overhead at the rate of 2 percent of all other costs. So the actual charges were 5 times that allowed in the agreements. The auditor traced it back and found this had been going on since the lines of credit were extended by the two banks for the project. The practice had never been uncovered, reported, or objected to by the loan officers of the two banks.

On the basis of what he had seen, heard, and been advised, the audit officer wrote a report to bank and real estate division management indicating that:

- The banks should take possession of the project through a "deed in lieu of foreclosure," a procedure he had used before, in somewhat similar situations, as advised by the bank's law department.

- All personnel of the parent organization should be replaced or resign from that organization and come to work for the banks, which would take over management of the project.

- An experienced major project manager should be hired. He suggested one finishing up a major project in another state, who had family ties to South Carolina, and pay him on a performance basis (e.g., beat budget as to sales, with a stipulated required ratio of income to expenses). A major developer interested in the project, but not financially capable of buying it, had provided the name and location of the manager.

- The project should be placed in the multiple listing service on the island to generate interest in the site.

- A new loan officer should be assigned to the project.

- An internal auditor should monitor the project, using outside appraisal expertise when appropriate on a continuing basis.

All of the foregoing recommendations were adopted, and the project which had been written down to $5 million from $28 million by both banks was sold out in six years. Both banks recovered fully, not only their principal but all of the interest on the loans. That could not have been achieved without an appraisal audit, whether done by an internal auditor or other qualified person.

2. Risk Minimization (Control) Audits

They perform a detailed familiarization review of the audited environment (e.g., activity, function, product, service, facility, or staff function) on the following:

- Each of the 12 Building Blocks of Internal Control shown in Figure 11 earlier in this chapter.

- Assessment of the effectiveness of the internal controls in the policies, procedures, practices, and standards relative to each task, duty, or other responsibility of the audited environment. This must identify all risks and the degree of control thereof, if any, or whether such risks are controlled to the level acceptable to management.

- Review of all risks identified with the risk management, security, and law functions of the CHARLES team and give priority to it as to (i) the real risk involved (e.g., probable occurrences in a year and the potential loss average for each occurrence—the mean is determined by averaging projected maximum and minimum loss figures; and (ii) the fact that the average embezzlement goes on more than three years before discovery and the average computer fraud has gone on for about a year before discovery; and (iii) an estimated amount for the unusual "hit and run" risk abuse, that are one-time fraud or mismanagement situations, which, on average, are smaller than those under item (i) and are discovered only by accident or generally because of information from someone in the organization.

- Stratification of the risks and determination of what level in each case management considers acceptable.

On the basis of the foregoing, the organization should establish new or improved controls to hold each identified risk to the level of occurrence and amount acceptable to management. This is the basis on which risk management will obtain outside insurance protection for the institution.

The normal familiarization reviews, for an internal or external audit, do not totally fulfill the requirements of such effort performed for a risk minimization (control) audit. That scope must be expanded by a thorough study, before starting the familiarization review, of:

- Authority and responsibilities of the head of the environment being reviewed.

- Historical problems of the environment being reviewed.

- Problems in the environment being reviewed, which other

institutions have encountered in the last 12 months (minimum) or 36 months (maximum).

- Turnover rate of personnel in the environment being reviewed.

- Whether personnel in key positions have the education and/or experience to perform assigned duties fully and properly to assure that risks are kept at the acceptable level.

- New automated/computerized procedures and practices and their impact on transaction and audit trails.

- Safeguards in the automated/computerized procedures, in the preceding review step.

- All tasks and duties being performed within the environment under review and assess the adequacy (in theory) of the policies, procedures, practices, and standards, relative thereto, to provide the desired level of internal controls and checks to contain risks or identify abuses.

Based on the broader familiarization scope, an adequate understanding of the environment under review can be determined to ascertain which risks appear to be potentially higher than acceptable. On that basis, the internal auditor can recommend enhancements to procedures and practices and internal controls and checks to reduce those risks appropriately.

3. Probable Deficient Performance Audits

   (a) Mismanagement Auditing

   The prefix "mis" refers to something being done badly or wrongly. Therefore, *mismanagement* refers to someone with authority and responsibility fulfilling their duties badly or wrongly. Because a manager's authority and responsibilities involve accounting, administration, operations, integrity of records, compliance with policies, procedures, practices, and standards and fulfilling all legel and regulatory requirements, an audit in this environment involves:

   (1) Financial auditing in the vertical auditing grouping shown in Figure 10 in this chapter, and explained earlier.

   (2) The applicable types of horizontal auditing (also in Figure 10) as described earlier. This could be one or more of the following: activity auditing, functional auditing,

product or service auditing, entity auditing, and always internal control/check audit.

(3) Operational auditing, in the same group as the audit approach under item (1) above.

(4) Whichever type of reactive auditing that prompts the auditors, on their own or at the request of senior management, to undertake a mismanagement audit.

All four audit approaches must be incorporated appropriately when performing this audit, as it must deal with all areas of authority and responsibility that the person being audited has been assigned. It is very much a hands-on type of auditing, requiring interviews with supervisors and subordinate staff to (i) ascertain what they are doing, (ii) determine whether they are doing what they are supposed to be doing, and (iii) evaluate what the person being audited is doing properly or improperly so a conclusion can be reached.

The reasoning behind such auditing can be the result of:

- Observations and findings when performing other audit reviews that make it appear warranted to undertake such an audit.

- High variances from budget and/or far higher than normal staff turnover and poor morale as identified during other audit reviews.

- Signs of stress burnout noted by auditors when performing other reviews.

- Types of irregular, inconsistent, or deliberate violation of policies, procedures, practices, and standards, which may be found during an audit or come from a tip-off.

Sufficient justification is necessary to undertake such a review that would begin at Stage 3 of the seven levels of audits, presented in Figure 12, plus supporting comments. The review findings at that level normally result in:

- Stopping the review at that stage, as the facts do not indicate justification in proceeding to Stage 4 or higher.

- Moving right to Stage 5 or 6, because "mismanagement" can sometimes be used as a means to hide a fraud or direct the auditors away from the fraud by having them focus on mismanagement factors.

(b) Gross Negligence Auditing

    (1) Definitions of Negligence

        (i) Basic. "Failure to exercise due care."

        (ii) Ordinary. "Arises from errors of judgment...and from oversights and mistakes that might be committed by anyone but never with willful deceit."[142]

        (iii) Gross. "Adds the element of recklessness and an extreme disregard of common standards.... The deliberate concealment or intentional misrepresentation of a material fact, event, or condition constitutes fraud."[143]

The reasoning that warrants a review in this environment is the same as for mismanagement auditing, described earlier. Also involved are all of the four audit approaches set forth under mismanagement auditing. If only "ordinary" negligence is assumed as the audit begins, it would be based on an audit scope appropriate to starting the reviews at Stage 3 of the seven stages of auditing in Figure 10 and would proceed further or stop at that stage.

However, if the review is begun assuming gross negligence, it would start at Stage 4 of the seven stages of auditing in Figure 10. It would stop at that stage or proceed to Stage 5, 6, or 7, as warranted, based on findings in the Stage review. Remember, fraud is not an expected conclusion where gross negligence is concerned.

Reviews of ordinary and gross negligence require a hands-on approach with interviews to supplement the normal compliance and substantive auditing approaches called for in the initial audit program.

(c) "Security Breach" Audits

The word security, as used here, refers to being secure, having freedom from danger, having protection. Security does *not* mean documents indicating evidence of indebtedness or surety. The unit within the organization designated by management (e.g., security section or security division) has the task of providing security.

---

[142]*Ibid.*, p. 289.
[143]*Ibid.*, p. 289.

The word "breach," as used here, refers to infraction or violation of laws and regulations, failing to comply with policies, procedures, practices, standards, and/or security standards established to protect the assets, documentation, records, or integrity of financial information, or creating a risk from failing to protect adequately those items or personnel.

With such a broad scope, as provided in the definitions of the audit type, the source of information justifying a security breach audit could be:

- Deficiencies in one or more of the indicated environments under the breach definition as identified during a regular audit.

- Exception reports indicating irregular conditions or situations with the environment to be audited.

- Tips, from whatever source, indicating that one or more security breach situations exist in a specific activity, function, product, service, entity, staff function, or facility.

Because this is more an audit to determine violations of normal criteria, which could result in reduced or ineffective controls, and higher resulting risks, such reviews, when undertaken, start at Stage 2 of the seven stages of audit, as shown in Figure 10. As described earlier, the scope of Stage 2 is less than Stages 1 or 3 but remember that, at this point, we are merely trying to determine whether a security breach does exist. When the limited review is completed, it becomes necessary to decide whether the act is (i) done with malice, or (ii) because of incompetence, unqualified personnel, or inept supervision. If item (i) is the cause, then proceed immediately to Stage 5 to initiate efforts to identify whether the security breach was done to hide fraud. If the findings warrant action, proceed through Stage 6 on to Stage 7. If the Stage 2 review indicates incompetence, unqualified personnel, or inept supervision, move to Stage 3 to see how serious the situation is, and conclude the review at Stage 3. At that point, make recommendations, which could be as serious as (1) replacing a manager and/or supervisor, (2) replacing from one to all personnel, with persons of higher education and experience who are qualified to perform the duties and tasks of the area being audited, or (3) modifying systems and procedures so that more internal checks strengthen the probability that compliance with policies, procedures, practices, standards, laws, and regulations will be accomplished through improved internal controls.

(d) Fraud Audits

This is another class of probable deficient performance audits and so important that all of Chapter 8 is devoted to it.

Summary

In reviewing the concepts, principles, and overall approach of risk-oriented auditing, remember, it draws on all other auditing methodologies. It also adopts those aspects that provide the greatest value to the institution in controlling risks, strengthening internal controls and checks, and assuring that accounting, administration, and operations are as efficient as they can be considered in all aspects of the business under audit. Properly implemented, risk-oriented auditing should, on an informal basis, contribute more to the organization than it costs while assuring the board of directors and senior management that all audit environments are functioning satisfactorily with business risks controlled adequately and effectively.

8

Overview of Fraud Auditing

Definitions

FRAUD. "The successful practice of deception or artifice with the intention of cheating or injuring another. Ordinarily, fraud involves willful misrepresentation, the deliberate concealment of a material fact for the purpose of inducing another person to do or to refrain from doing something to his detriment, or the failure to disclose a material fact..."[144]

FRAUD. According to the Michigan Criminal Law, Chapter 86, Section 1529, "Fraud is a generic term, and embraces all the multifarious means which human ingenuity can devise, which are resorted to by one individual, to get an advantage over another by false representations. No definite and invariable rule can be laid down as a general proposition in defining fraud; as it includes all surprise, trick, cunning, and unfair ways by which another is cheated. The only boundaries defining it are those which limit human knavery."[145]

CORPORATE FRAUD. "This is any fraud perpetrated by, for, or against a business corporation. Corporate fraud can be internally generated (perpetrated by agents, employees, and executives of a corporation, for or against it, or against others) and externally generated (by others against the corporation, i.e., suppliers, vendors, customers)."[146]

MANAGEMENT FRAUD. "This is the intentional overstatement of corporate or unit profits, perpetrated, or induced by employees servicing in management roles who seek to benefit from such frauds in terms of coveted promotions, job stability, larger bonuses, or other economic incentives and status symbols."[147]

FINANCIAL FRAUD. "Material misrepresentation of a financial fact intended to deceive another to his economic detriment."[148]

DECEIT. "A fraudulent and cheating misrepresentation, artifice, or device, used by one or more persons to deceive and trick another who is ignorant of the [truth] to the prejudice and damage of the party imposed upon."[149]

---

[144]Kohler., *op. cit.*, p. 201.
[145]Jack Bologna. *Corporate Fraud—The Basics of Prevention and Detection.* (Stoneham, Mass: Butterworth, 1984), p. 18.
[146]*Ibid.*, p. 18.
[147]*Ibid.*, p. 18.
[148]*Ibid.*, p. 18.
[149]*Black's Law Dictionary.* (St. Paul: West, 1957), 493.

DEFALCATION. "The act of a defaulter; misappropriation of trust funds or money held in any fiduciary capacity; failure to properly account for such funds . . ."[150]

EMBEZZLEMENT. "Fraudulent misappropriation of property by a person to whom it has been entrusted, or to whose hands it has lawfully come."[151]

FALSE ENTRY. "An entry in books of a bank or trust company which is intentionally made to represent what is not true or does not exist, with intent either to deceive its officers or a bank examiner or to defraud the bank or trust company."[152]

FALSE REPRESENTATION. "A representation which is untrue, willfully made to deceive another to his injury."[153]

FALSE STATEMENT. "Under statutory provision, making it unlawful for officer or director of corporation to make any false statement in regard to corporation's financial condition, the phrase means something more than merely untrue or erroneous, but implies that statement is designed untrue and deceitful and made with intention to deceive persons to whom false statement is made or exhibited."[154]

FALSE TOKEN. "In criminal law, a false document or sign of the existence of a fact—in general used for the purpose of fraud"[155] (Example: counterfeit money).

FALSIFY. "To counterfeit or forge; to make something false; to give a false appearance to anything. To make false by mutilation or addition; to tamper with, as to falsify a record or document."[156]

FORGERY. "The false making or material altering with intent to defraud, of anything in writing which if genuine, might apparently be of legal efficiency or the foundation of a legal liability."[157]

FRAUDULENT CONCEALMENT. "The hiding or suppression of a material fact or circumstance which the party is legally or morally bound to disclose."[158]

FRAUDULENT CONVERSION. "Receiving into possession money or property of another and fraudulently withholding, converting, or applying the same to or for one's own use and benefit, or to use and benefit of any person other than the one to whom the money or property belongs."[159]

---

[150]*Ibid.*, p. 504.
[151]*Ibid.*, p. 614.
[152]*Ibid.*, p. 722.
[153]*Ibid.*, p. 724.
[154]*Ibid.*, p. 725.
[155]*Ibid.*, p. 725.
[156]*Ibid.*, p. 726.
[157]*Ibid.*, p. 779.
[158]*Ibid.*, p. 790.
[159]*Ibid.*, p. 790.

FRAUDULENT REPRESENTATION. "A false statement as to material fact, made with intent that another rely thereon, which is believed by other party and on which he relies and by which he is induced to act and does act to his injury, and statement is fraudulent if speaker knows the statement to be false or if it is made with utter disregard of its truth or falsity."[160]

LARCENY. "Wrongful taking and carrying away of the personal property of another with intent to convert it or to deprive the owner of its use and possession."[161] (*Note:* Usually includes theft and stealing).

MALFEASANCE. "Evil doing; ill conduct; the commission of some act which is positively unlawful.... [U]njust performance of some act which the party had no right or which he had contracted not to do."[162]

MISAPPROPRIATION. "The act of misappropriating or turning to a wrong purpose; wrong appropriation; a term which does not necessarily mean peculation, although it may mean that."[163]

NEGLIGENCE. "Failure to exercise due care.... Ordinary negligence arises from errors of judgment attributable, for example, to a lack of seasoned experience, and from oversights and mistakes that might be committed by anyone, but never from willful deceit.... "Gross negligence adds the element of recklessness and an extreme disregard of common standards—for example, of auditing and reporting. The deliberate concealment or intentional misrepresentation of a material fact, event, or condition constitutes fraud."[164]

PECULATION. "The fraudulent misappropriation by one to his own use of money or goods entrusted to his care."[165]

Description of Fraud Audits

1. Fraud Audits

   "Independent auditors may be engaged to perform an examination specifically for the purpose of determining whether irregularities have occurred and, if so, their magnitude. Such an examination performed either as an adjunct to, or separately from, an audit of financial statements is informally referred to

---

[160]*Ibid.*, p. 790.
[161]*Ibid.*, p. 1023.
[162]*Ibid.*, p. 1109.
[163]*Ibid.*, p. 1149.
[164]Eric L. Kohler, *A Dictionary for Accountants.* (Englewood Cliffs, N.J.: Prentice-Hall, Inc., 1970), p. 289).
[165]Kohler, *op. cit.*, p. 289.

as a 'fraud audit.' There are no professional standards with respect to fraud audits, and generally such an audit consists of an extension of ordinary audit procedures, as proposed by the auditor and, in some instances, agreed to by the client. Fraud audits are not considered to be an economic method of either detecting or preventing irregularities, since the client incurs a great deal of expense, and there is relatively little assurance of success. It is generally more cost effective to employ the methods of deterrence" as routinely used in performing regular audit reviews "to prevent fraud than to contract for a fraud audit with the hope of detecting fraud."[166]

While written for external auditors, the statements in the preceding quotation are totally applicable to internal auditors if they are operating in a financial auditing mode. The potential for discovering fraud increases in the audit methodologies that deal with accounting, administration, and operations (e.g., operational auditing, management-oriented auditing, and risk-oriented auditing). Because risk-oriented auditing puts increased emphasis on *(a)* risk identification, evaluation, and corrective actions to bring risk to a level acceptable to management, and *(b)* all 12 of the building blocks of internal auditing (meaning it is broader based than the other two methodologies named), the risk-oriented method is the best from the probability of identifying a fraud at a lower cost. The use of the seven stages of auditing helps to hold down costs as the auditor cuts off those avenues of review that do not appear fruitful, at any stage, and focuses on avenues where the evidence being developed indicates the potential for wrongdoing.

Although the AICPA has recently put out a series of SASs focusing more on the fraud responsibilities of the external auditor, including broader reliance on competent internal auditors, no formal professional standards exist for fraud audits. The disciplines of risk-oriented auditing, as set forth in the preceding chapter, go beyond the statements and limited doctrines of the AICPA in permitting the internal auditor to concentrate on *(a)* risks, and *(b)* internal controls, augmented by other review efforts as necessary to fulfill the seven stated objectives of risk-oriented auditing. Another unique thing is that the methodology for a fraud audit does not change but merely broadens its scope from the levels considered acceptable for a standard audit review.

---

[166]Sullivan, et al., *op. cit.,* p. 127.

2. What Is Fraud Auditing?

"Fraud auditing is the creation of an environment that encourages the detecting and preventing of frauds in commercial transactions. The main thrust . . . is to provide auditors and investigators with further knowledge and insight into fraud as an economic, social, and organizational phenomenon. . . . Investigating fraud in books of account and commercial transactions requires the combined skills of a well-trained auditor and criminal investigator. However, the combination of these skills in one person is rare", making it a requirement "to better acquaint auditors with criminal-investigative rules, principles, techniques, and methods and to provide criminal investigators with some knowledge of accounting and auditing rules, principles, techniques, and methods. . . . Fraud auditing cannot be reduced to a simple checklist. It is an awareness in the broadest sense of many components such as the human element, organizational behavior, knowledge of fraud, evidence and standards of proof, an awareness as to the potentiality for fraud, and an appreciation of the so-called red flags."[167]

Recognition that two distinct skills are required in conducting a fraud audit is important. Each skill requirement should be fulfilled at suitable professional levels, whether this is one individual or two, or an audit team supplemented by one or more qualified criminal investigators. They are qualified persons with both areas of skill. Recently, they have been recognized by issuance of the certified fraud examiner (CFE) title, which is issued by the National Association of Certified Fraud Examiners, in Austin, Tex. If an individual is more skilled in one area than the other, they are not reluctant to bring in more skilled persons to assist in a fraud audit. Two distinct skills are required to do a fraud audit properly. Such a review is a *complex* matter and not just a simple audit review broadened to deal with suspicion of wrongdoing.

Red Flags of Fraud

There are a number of listings of red flags of fraud but probably none from such an authoritative source as the one selected for this book. First, what are red flags of fraud? They are warning signs of possible fraud and insider abuse. This list, adopted by Chairman L.

---

[167]Bologna and Lindquist. *Fraud Auditing and Forensic Accounting—New Tools and Techniques.* (New York: Wiley, 1987), p. 27.

William Seidman of the Federal Deposit Insurance Corp., indicates "they are designed to alert examiners to potential problem areas involving insider transactions and to provide guidance on follow-up procedures." They were published as a special section of *Bank Fraud,* a monthly publication of Bank Administration Institute and cover 12 critical areas. They are:

1. Corporate Culture/Ethics

    (a) Absence of a code of ethics.

    (b) Absence of a clear policy on conflict of interest.

    (c) Lack of oversight by the bank's board of directors, particularly outside directors.

    (d) Absence of planning, training, hiring, and organizational policies.

    (e) Absence of clearly defined authorities and lack of definition of responsibilities that go along with the authorities.

    (f) Lack of independence of management in acting on recommended corrections.

2. Loan Participations

    (a) Excessive participation of loans between closely related banks, correspondent banks, and branches or departments of the lending bank.

    (b) Absence of formal participation agreement.

    (c) Poor or incomplete loan documentation.

    (d) Investing in out-of-territory participations.

    (e) Reliance on third-party guaranties.

    (f) Large paydown or payoff of previously classified loans.

    (g) Some indication that there may be informal repurchase agreements on some participations.

    (h) Lack of independent credit analysis.

    (i) Volume of loan participations sold is high in relation to the size of the bank's own loan portfolio.

    (j) Evidence of lapping of loan participations. For example, sale of a loan participation in an amount equal to or greater than, and at or about the same time as, a participation that has matured or is about to mature.

    (k) Disputes between participating banks over documenta-

tion, payments, or any other aspect of the loan participation transaction.

3. Insider Transactions

   (a) Financing the sale of insider assets to third parties.

   (b) Evidence that an insider is lending his/her own funds to others from a review of personal financial statements.

   (c) Improper fees to major shareholders.

   (d) Frequent changes of auditors or legal counsel.

   (e) Unusual or unjustified fluctuations in insiders' or officers' personal financial statements or statements of their interests.

   (f) Frequent appearance of suspense items relating to accounts of insiders, officers, and employees.

   (g) An insider borrowing money from someone who borrows from the bank.

   (h) Purchase of bank assets by an insider.

   (i) A review of the bank's fixed assets or other asset accounts reveals that the bank owns expensive art works, expensive automobiles, yachts, airplanes, or other unusual items that are out of character for a bank of its size and in its location.

   (j) A review of the bank's expense accounts reveals expenditures for attorney's fees, accountant's fees, broker's fees, etc., that do not appear to correspond to services rendered to the bank or that appear unusually high for services rendered.

   (k) Heavy lending to the bank's shareholders, particularly in conjunction with recent capital injections.

   (l) A large part of the insider's bank stock has been pledged to secure debts to other financial institutions.

   (m) An insider has past due obligations at other financial institutions.

   (n) An insider is receiving all or a part of the proceeds of loans granted to others.

   (o) An insider is receiving special considerations or favors from bank customers. For example, an insider may receive favorable lease terms or favorable purchase terms on an automobile obtained from a bank customer.

4. Real Estate Lending—Secured Lending

(a) Lack of independent appraisals.

(b) Out-of-territory loans.

(c) Evidence of land flips.

(d) Loans with unusual terms and conditions.

(e) Poor or incomplete documentation.

(f) Loans that are unusual considering the size of the bank and the level of expertise of its lending officers.

(g) Heavy concentration of loans to a single project or to individuals related to the project.

(h) Concentrations of loans to local borrowers with the same or similar collateral that is located outside the bank's trade area.

(i) Asset swaps [which are sales] of . . . real estate or other distressed assets to a broker at an inflated price in return for favorable terms and conditions on a new loan to a borrower introduced to the bank by the broker. The new loan is usually secured by property of questionable value and the borrower is in weak financial condition. Borrower and collateral are often outside the bank's normal trade area.

(j) Failure to consider the risk of decline in collateral value.

5. Lending to Buy Tax Shelter Investments

(a) Block loans to individuals to buy tax shelters arranged by the tax shelter promoter.

(b) Shelters promise tax deductions that would not appear to withstand the scrutiny of the IRS.

(c) Specific use of the invested funds cannot be ascertained.

(d) Loan payments to be made by a servicing company.

(e) Investments reflect no economic purpose except to generate tax write-offs.

(f) Financial no-cash deals where transactions are structured to avoid any cash flow. For example, a long-term certificate of deposit is matched against a loan payable from the proceeds of the CD at its maturity. Interest accumulates on the CD in an amount equal to or greater than the compounded interest owed on the corresponding loan. The depositor/borrower never provides or receives any cash but still gets the tax write-off.

6. Money Laundering

    (a) Increase in cash shipments that is not accompanied by a corresponding increase in number of accounts.

    (b) Cash on hand frequently exceeds limits established in security programs and/or blanket bond coverage.

    (c) Large volume of cashier's checks and/or money orders sold for cash to noncustomers. Amounts may range from $1,000 each to just under $10,000 each.

    (d) Large volume of wire transfers to and from offshore banks.

    (e) Large volume of wire transfers for noncustomers.

    (f) Accounts that have a large number of small deposits and a small number of large checks with the balance of the account remaining relatively low and constant. The account has many of the same characteristics as an account used for check kiting.

    (g) A large volume of deposits to several different accounts with frequent transfer of major portions of the balances to a single account at the same bank or at another bank.

    (h) Loans to offshore companies.

    (i) A large volume of cashier's checks or money orders deposited to an account where the nature of the account holder's business would not appear to justify such activity.

    (j) Large volume of cash deposits from a business not normally cash intensive, such as a wholesaler.

    (k) Cash deposits to a correspondent bank account by any means other than through an armored carrier.

    (l) Large turnover in large bills that would appear uncharacteristic for the bank's location.

    (m) Cash shipments that appear large in comparison to the dollar volume of currency transaction reports filed.

    (n) Dollar limits on the list of bank customers exempt from currency transaction reporting requirements that appear unreasonably high considering the type and location of the business. No information is in the bank's files to support the limits.

    (o) Currency transaction reports, when filed, are often incorrect or lack important information.

(*p*) List of exempted customers appears unusually long.

7. Third-Party Obligations

(*a*) Incomplete documentation on guaranties.

(*b*) Loans secured by obligations of offshore banks.

(*c*) Lack of credit information on third-party obligor.

(*d*) Financial statements reflect concentrations of closely held companies or businesses that lack audited financial statements to support their value.

8. Linked Financing/Brokered Transactions

(*a*) Out-of-territory lending.

(*b*) Loan production used as a basis for officer bonuses.

(*c*) Evidence of unsolicited attempts to buy or recapitalize the bank where there is evidence of a request for large loans at or about the same time by persons previously unknown to the bank. Promise of large dollar deposits also may be involved.

(*d*) Promise of large dollar deposits in consideration for favorable treatment on loan requests. (Deposits are not pledged as collateral for the loans).

(*e*) Brokered deposit transactions where the broker's fees are paid from the proceeds of related loans.

(*f*) Any time a bank seriously considers a loan request where the bank would have to obtain brokered deposits to be able to fund the loan should be viewed with suspicion.

(*g*) Solicitations by persons who purportedly have access to multimillions of dollars from a confidential source, readily available for loans and/or deposits in U.S. financial institutions. Rates and terms quoted are usually more favorable than funds available through normal sources. A substantial fee may be requested in advance or the solicitor may suggest that the fee be paid at closing but demand compensation for expenses, often exceeding $50,000.

(*h*) Prepayment of interest on deposit accounts where such deposit accounts are used as collateral for loans.

9. Offshore Transactions

(*a*) Loans made on the strength of a borrower's financial statement when the statement reflects major investment in and income from businesses incorporated in bank secrecy-haven countries such as Panama and the Netherlands Antilles.

(b) Loans to offshore companies.

(c) Loans secured by obligations of offshore banks.

(d) Transactions involving an offshore "shell" bank whose name may be similar to the name of a major legitimate institution.

(e) Frequent wire transfers of funds to and from bank secrecy-haven countries such as Panama, Cayman Islands, and the Netherlands Antilles.

(f) Offers of multimillion dollar deposits at below market rates from a confidential source to be sent from an offshore bank or somehow guaranteed by an offshore bank through a letter, telex, or other "official" communication.

(g) Presence of telex or facsimile equipment in a bank where the unusual and customary business activity would not appear to justify the need for such equipment.

10. Wire Transfers

(a) Indications of frequent overrides of established approval authority and other internal controls.

(b) Intentional circumvention of approval authority by splitting transactions.

(c) Wire transfer to and from bank secrecy haven countries.

(d) Frequent or large wire transfers for persons who have no account relationship with the bank.

(e) In a linked financing situation, a borrower's request for immediate wire transfer of loan proceeds to one or more of the banks where the funds for the brokered deposits originated.

(f) Large or frequent wire transfers against uncollected funds.

(g) Wire transfers involving cash where the amount exceeds $10,000.

(h) Inadequate control of password access.

(i) Customer complaints and/or frequent error conditions.

11. Credit Cards and Electronic Funds Transfer

(a) Lack of separation of duties between the card-issuing

function and issuance of personal identification number (PIN).

   (b) Poor control of unissued cards and PINs.

   (c) Poor control of returned mail.

   (d) Customer complaints.

   (e) Poor control of credit limit increases.

   (f) Poor control of name and address changes.

   (g) Frequent malfunction of payment authorization system.

   (h) Unusual delays in receipt of cards and PINs by the customers.

   (i) Bank does not limit amount of cash that a customer can extract from an ATM in a given day.

   (j) Evidence that customer credit card purchases have been intentionally structured by a merchant to keep individual amounts below the "floor limit" to avoid the need for transaction approval.

12. Miscellaneous

   (a) Indications of frequent overrides of internal controls or intentional circumvention of bank policy.

   (b) Unresolved exceptions or frequently recurring exceptions on exception reports.

   (c) Out-of-balance conditions.

   (d) Purpose of loan not recorded.

   (e) Proceeds of loan used for a purpose other than the purpose recorded.

   (f) A review of checks paid against uncollected funds indicates that a customer is offsetting checks with deposits of the same or similar amount and maintains a relatively constant account balance, usually small in relation to the amount of activity and size of the transactions.

If you are working with a basic list of red flags of fraud it must be flexible so additional flags can be added to the list whenever (1) concern arises on specific transactions or practices, or (2) policies, and procedures seem deficient, in any specific area, so they result in "excessive risks" relative to any transactions or work activities. Although the red flags of fraud listing that is provided is excellent, here are examples of additional flags, for each of the twelve listed categories:

1. Corporate Culture/Ethics

    (a) Where an institution does have a code of ethics, are all new employees given training relative to the code and do all employees receive periodic "refresher" training on the code with emphasis on the possible penalties for violations (e.g., suspension, demotion, discharge, arrest, and prosecution)?

    (b) Where an institution does have a clear policy on conflict of interest, are the criteria under training and refresher courses on the code followed according to this policy?

2. Loan Participations

    (a) Where the institution is the leader or co-leader of a major loan participation, involving a number of institutions, is it properly fulfilling its responsibilities as the "lead" or "co-lead" concerning the loan? (*Note:* If not, the institution could be subject to lawsuits for negligence or gross negligence for failing to perform duties paid for by the other participating institutions.)

    (b) Have the loan participations taken, when added to the institution's own loans in the same industry or industry grouping, resulted in excessive risk in that industry or industry grouping? (*Note:* Remember, the excess position of Continental Illinois Bank relative to its oil and natural gas industry exposure resulting from dealings with Penn Square Bank of Oklahoma as well as loans its officers had made directly to firms in the oil and gas industry.)

3. Insider Transactions

    (a) Frequent changes of internal audit, loan review, risk management, in-house legal, and security personnel.

    (b) Restriction of authority relative to reviewing or monitoring insider transactions of any of the staff functions indicated under item 3(a).

4. Real Estate Lending—Secured Lending

    (a) Use of one or more independent appraisers on a routine basis, with no second opinions obtained, could indicate collusion between loan officer and customer to overvalue collateral and make a loan on the property appear to be more collateralized than it really is because of an appraisal overstating value of the real estate.

(b) Ineffective monitoring of progress of construction and quality of materials used by qualified personnel supporting the loan officer on construction financing loans.

5. Lending to Buy Tax Shelter Investments

(a) Accept evidence of title on collateral without verification of actual existence, as the basis for making loans or financing deals in tax shelter environment. (*Note:* A major midwestern bank suffered losses in the tax shelter environment of an offshore island of the United Kingdom by financing nonexistent yachts while accepting titles on those vessels without verifying whether the yachts existed.)

6. Money Laundering

(a) Review work processed in bank locations where it is thought money is being laundered to see whether any deposit slips have amounts printed on them, with date and account number written in. Where identified, a "desk check" of the platform officers is warranted as it may disclose their helping certain customers use the facility to launder money (e.g., you find a supply of deposit slips with $9,000 printed in under "Cash," "Subtotal," and "Net Deposit").

7. Third-Party Obligations

(a) Failure to check whether prior liens have been filed on collateral provided.

8. Linked Financing/Brokered Transactions

(a) High activity with specific brokers indicating possible collusion between such persons and loan officers, with the possibility of kickbacks to the latter.

9. Offshore Transactions

(a) Accepting unaudited statements to support loan decision.

(b) Accepting financial statements from foreign countries, without converting figures to the equivalent of U.S. standards (e.g., GAAP, GAAS, SEC, and IRS) so proper assessment can be made.

10. Wire Transfers

(a) Passwords not changed as frequently as warranted by the inherent risks in such transactions.

11. Credit Cards and Electronic Funds Transfer

    (a) Issuance of cards to persons whose credit bureau reports indicate that they already have an excessive number of cards from other institutions relative to their income, clearly indicating the possibility of kiting, with the customer using cash obtained from one institution to pay off minimum repayment amounts due on other cards.

12. Miscellaneous

    (a) Loans being rewritten just before they would become delinquent, deferring amounts due, when financial statements of borrower indicate current cash-flow problems, without additional collateral to reduce net exposure of institution.

The auditor operating in a risk-oriented mode must attempt to ascertain "what can go wrong?" Then ask himself, "Have I devoted enough time to a specific audit area, work-task, activity, or function?" And "do I know the risks remaining after evaluation of the system of internal controls and checks?" The risk-oriented auditor must be proactive in thinking about what can go wrong and determine whether the risks warrant a review or a broadened review, if already covered in the related audit program. The risk-oriented auditor also must be reactive in prudently following up on deficiencies found during the audit or identified during audits.

The auditor who becomes aware of a possible irregularity (e.g., noncompliance with policies, procedures, standards, practices, and internal control/check requirements) or a possible illegal act must exercise judgment relative to the potential impact of same and adjust his work program accordingly. While working with the definition of "What is Fraud Auditing?" covered earlier in this chapter, understand that fraud auditing involves a variety of pertinent components that must be considered and, as appropriate, incorporated in the fraud audit scope. They include (1) the human element, (2) organizational integrity, (3) organizational behavior (e.g., Do senior officials set a proper example as to ethics and conduct for subordinates?). Others are: (4) knowledge of fraud, (5) knowledge of auditing, (6) knowledge of what constitutes evidences and legal standards to prove fraud or intent to defraud, and (7) an awareness of the risks relative to every environment within the institution. Still others are: (8) what other staff skills are available inside or outside of the institution that can be drawn on for assistance in a fraud examination (e.g., the other parts of the CHARLES team, which are *(a)* C = controller/chief financial officer; *(b)* H = human resources/

personnel; (c) A = audit personnel, other than those with the special competency to handle fraud matters; (d) R = risk management/insurance; (e) L = law/legal; (f) E = electronic data processing/MIS; and (g) S = security). And finally: (9) an awareness of the strengths and weaknesses in the accounting, administrative, and operational systems as regards (i) efficiency, effectiveness, and economy, and (ii) strengths and weaknesses in related internal control and check systems as well as risks, mentioned earlier under item (7).

The Fraud Auditor

If there were a perfect fraud auditor, that person would have the:

1. Wisdom of Einstein.

2. Patience of Job.

3. Philosophy (ethics) of Socrates.

4. Curiosity of Edison.

5. Deductive reasoning of Sherlock Holmes.

6. Detailed knowledge of the audit environment of a skilled and experienced internal auditor.

7. Tenacity of a qualified criminal investigator.

8. Ability to communicate (interview and interrogate) like a psychiatrist or psychologist.

9. Imagination and forward planning capabilities of a chess master (so as (a) to put all of the facts, findings, and implications into perspective, and (b) to bring all of the pieces in the (fraud) puzzle together to focus on completing the matter (checkmate).

A competent fraud auditor needs each of the following:

1. A broad knowledge of all the 12 building blocks of internal control/check, and the related risks as presented earlier herein.

2. A historical record, developed from (a) prior audits; (b) prior frauds at the institution; and (c) general fraud information of the type perceived to have occurred from reliable sources involving other institutions (e.g., FBI, regulators).

3. Competency to fulfill the seven general objectives of a sound fraud audit as discussed earlier.

4. Knowledge of the sociological factors causing human behavior.

5. Ability to draw out information during interviews and inter-

rogations, and ability to put the findings together with review facts to indicate the directions that the fraud audit should take.

6. Information relative to economic and competitive factors currently or projected to affect the institution.

7. The ability to discern, detect, and document fraud audit review findings so they can be of value to any *(a)* legal; *(b)* regulatory; and/or *(c)* evidential requirements connected with the fraud audit.

The required skills relative to items 1 and 3 have been covered earlier. Any well-run internal audit function normally would have the information specified under item 2 or it can be obtained, relative to outside fraud involving other institutions. The following comments focus on the pertinent aspects of items 4 through 7, in that order:

4. The sociological factors causing human behavior
   The following are theories but can provide insight into why persons commit fraud:

   (a) Differential Association Theory (Sutherland and Cressey, 1978):

   (1) Criminal behavior is learned not inherited.

   (2) Criminal behavior is normally learned through interaction with other people (e.g., verbal communication).

   (3) Criminal behavior is learned within intimate personal groups where such conduct is acceptable.

   (4) Criminal learning includes the techniques of committing the type of crime, including fraud, as well as the motives, drives, attitudes, and even the rationalizations that accompany it.

   (5) Individuals will perpetrate a crime, including fraud, when their psychological perception makes the crime appear acceptable, as opposed to following normal conduct, including the law.

   (b) Nonshareable Need (Cressey, 1953)
   This theory assumes a "violation of a position of financial trust" that the person originally took in good faith. Cressey wrote that "trust persons become trust violators when they conceive of themselves as having a financial problem which is nonshareable, are aware that this problem can be secretly resolved by violation of the position of financial trust, and are able to apply to their conduct in that situation verbaliza-

tions which enable them to adjust their concepts of themselves as users of the entrusted funds or property." Under this theory, there must be a (1) nonshareable problem, (2) an opportunity for trust violation, and (3) a set of rationalizations that define the behavior as appropriate in a given situation. For the person to perpetrate a fraud, all three elements are usually present.

(c) Sociological theories explaining fraud can be causes for such action(s) as:

(1) Situational Pressures Contributing to Management Fraud

- Heavy investments or losses.
- Insufficient working capital.
- High debt.
- Inability or reduced ability to acquire credit.
- Profit squeeze.
- Restrictive loan agreements.
- Erosion in quality of earnings.
- Urgent need for favorable earnings.
- Unmarketable securities.
- Excessive dependence on one or two (i) products or services or (ii) customers.
- Too rapid expansion.
- Unfavorable economic conditions within the industry.
- Heavy and growing competition.
- Significant litigation.
- Validation of liquidity deficiency, capital adequacy shortfall, or significant potential loss write-offs or write-downs affecting profitability.

(2) Opportunities that Allow or Encourage Management Fraud

- Related-party transactions.
- Use of multiple auditing firms.
- Reluctance to give auditors requested or needed data.

- Use of multiple legal counsel.
- Continuous problems with regulatory agencies and examiners.
- Lack of an effective internal audit staff.
- Loose controls in computer management and operations areas.
- Inadequate internal controls and checks overall.
- High turnover of key personnel.
- Large year-end and/or unusual adjustments or transactions.
- Failure to have appropriate red flags, early warning signals, and exception reports for management action relative to accounting, administration, and operations.

(3) Personal Characteristics That Lead to Fraud

- Low moral character.
- Rationalization of erratic or contradictory behavior.
- Lack of a personal code of ethics.
- A wheeler-dealer.
- Instability.
- Desire to beat the system (e.g., computer hackers).
- Criminal or questionable background.
- Poor credit rating and/or financial status.

(4) Situational Pressures on Employees That Could Lead to Fraud

- High personal debts or financial losses.
- Inadequate income.
- Living beyond one's means.
- Stock market or other speculative undertakings.
- Excessive gambling.
- Improper involvements with persons other than spouses of similar sexual persuasion.
- Excessive use of drugs or alcohol.
- Undue family, community, or social expectations.

- Perceived inequities in the organization.

- Corporate or peer-group pressures.

- Environment or sociological pressures or feelings of having been wrongly treated in the past.

5. Interviewing and Interrogation

   (a) Definitions:

   INTERVIEW: "A meeting at which information is obtained."[168]

   INTERROGATE: "To question formally and systematically."[169]

   (b) Interviewing:

   The art of effective interviewing is to make interviewees comfortable and place them in a position where they feel free to leave (e.g., the person being interviewed should be closer to the door than the interviewer). Try to have the interview in a location where interruptions are minimized, and, ordinarily, interview the person one on one. The principles of such meeting follow:

   (1) The interviewer asks questions, trying to take up no more than 15-25 percent of the meeting time, but keeping the objectives open so as to pick up on what may be meaningful and unexpected comments from the interviewee. If the interviewee permits, and your legal advisors approve, tape the meeting. If not, minimize note-taking (e.g., taking down "key" words or "phrases" only) so eye contact can be maximized.

   (2) The interviewee should do 75-85 percent of the talking during the meeting, with the interviewer listening to pick up on unexpected statements or leads, and encourage further conversation on such matters. Keep the meeting casual and relaxed.

   (3) The interviewer not only must be careful in listening and reacting to statements of the interviewee, but also should be observant of the body movements of the interviewee. Certain behavior may be a tip-off that the interviewee is being deceptive. Here are things to watch for:

---

[168]*Webster's Ninth New Collegiate Dictionary, op. cit.,* p. 633.
[169]*Ibid.,* p. 633.

- Any extreme departure from a relaxed and upright seated position, either an exaggerated slouch or a superrigid pose.

- Nonfrontal alignment, with the interviewee facing off to one side of you rather than directly at you.

- Closed or obstructive body language (e.g., folded arms, crossed legs, or staring intently at the floor).

- Other signals such as erratic, jerky, unnatural-looking changes of posture or pushing the chair further away from you or fiddling and fidgeting of hands (e.g., scratching, pulling nose or earlobes, twiddling hair, cracking knuckles, doing hand exercises, playing with coins or keys in hand or pocket, rubbing the forehead, winding watch, picking lint from clothes, tying shoestrings).

- Not only is the body language of the interviewees something to watch but you also should note their overall mental attitude. Are they on time for the meeting? Do they appear composed and attentive to what you say? Are they visibly hostile? Are their answers responsive, given relatively quickly? Do they appear overanxious? Are they giving nonanswers? Are the answers delayed, as though they have to think about them? Are their answers aggressive, not too polite, or conciliatory? If you are called to perform such interviews, be prepared. Obtain a book on "body english" and learn the positive and negative signs you can read from an interviewee's conduct. This approach is known as behavioral analysis interviews. You can learn a lot from behavior as well as statements of interviewees.

(c) Interrogate

This is the stage you move into when you have singled out a person or persons, through interviewing or other investigative steps, who seem to be covering up guilt of themselves or others. Interrogation is confrontational and accusatory. In an interrogation, unlike interviewing, the interrogator does most of the talking. Good interrogation technique is a sort of psychological *tour de force*. It calls for the use of extremely subtle, subliminal ploys. The objective is to *deny* suspects any feeling of having the advantage. *Never* con-

133

duct the interrogation "on their turf." It can be in your office, a neutral office, a neutral conference room, or, on some occasions, your home. Always address them by first name. Such techniques are calculated to keep the persons being interrogated from feeling they are in control of the confrontation. Wherever the meeting takes place, position yourself between the interviewees and the nearest door. Try to use a one-door room. Try to be in a location where you are face-to-face with nothing between you (e.g., desk, table). This tends to make the interrogated persons feel hemmed in, almost as though the only way for them to get out of the room or have the interrogation stop is their confession. Your objective is to ensure complete concentration of the persons being interviewed. The ideal environment is a room without windows, only one door, and as stark as possible (e.g., no pictures), with no telephone. If appropriate, have an associate outside the door to prevent anyone interrupting the interrogation. Always begin the interrogation with a direct accusation of guilt (e.g., "Our investigation shows that you deliberately turned your back, failing to perform your control duties, enabling the fraud to occur"). Give specific details, if appropriate. Your observation during the interrogation focuses again on body language as well as the words of the person being interrogated. Body behavior may signal that you are on the right track. If the person is innocent, often the response will be swift and angry (e.g., "I did not!"). If the denials are persistent and vehement, you may not have the right person. In that case, reduce the level of accusations (e.g., "Then maybe you have suspicions you haven't told me about regarding what others are doing!"). Psychologists say that a strong opening accusation normally will result in weak or evasive responses, if you have someone involved in or aware of the fraud (e.g., "Who me?" [or] "How could I have done that?") Guilt-oriented responses, such as those, are green lights for proceeding with your current line of questioning.

It is important for you to remember:

- You may *imply* to suspects things that may help to get them to confess or identify others they believe may be involved in the wrongdoing.

- You must *not* state the ideas as facts unless they are totally supportable.

Here is a summary of the nine basic steps in interrogation:

(1) Direct positive confrontation (i.e., based on fraud situation).

(2) Theme development (i.e., based on data developed to date).

(3) Have a Plan "B" if denials by the interrogated person convince you your approach is in error.

(4) Be prepared to overcome objections to (i) your strong approach, and (ii) the implied wrongdoing.

(5) Keep the interrogated person on the defensive, moving from wrongdoing to possible punishment and back as appropriate.

(6) If the suspect turns passive or breaks down and cries, focus on getting a confession or identification of others involved in the fraud. However, don't let up, but show understanding.

(7) If the interviewee offers two incriminating choices on some aspect of the crime, choose (i) the primary one and follow it through and (ii) move to the secondary one only after you believe you have gotten all you can from the first.

(8) As a follow-up to items (6) and/or (7), use a statement of reinforcement (e.g., "Bill, we were confident that was the situation all along").

(9) Once a verbal confession has been obtained, have it converted to a written confession. In doing this, always have an associate (e.g., another auditor, member of the institution's internal or external legal counsel, or a member of its security function) present to affirm that the confession was not given under duress and statements were made by the person under questioning. Move as quickly as possible to have it signed by that person and witnessed. Do *not* be surprised if the person being questioned is reluctant to sign the confession after seeing it in writing. If your legal advisers will allow it, tape the confession while it is being dictated to the typist. Then you and the typist are witnesses to the taped confession. Also, the taped confession reduces the suspect's resistance to signing the confession.

6. Economic and Competitive Factors

Obtain this information from staff support personnel (e.g., economics department, marketing department, and strategic planning committee) if they do not appear to be involved in the wrongdoing under fraud audit review. Use outside statistical development sources (e.g., regulators or Bank Administration Institute) to replace insiders, if possibly involved, or to supplement their data, if the insiders do not appear to be involved. If making an audit at the management level (e.g., branch manager, area or zone manager, product manager), obtain budgets for last three years and current year to see whether "books have been cooked" to make it appear they made or almost made their budgetary expectations when, in fact, they missed the target badly.

7. Discern, Detect, and Document Fraud Audit Efforts

This is a standard audit or investigatory requirement. It must be more detailed and its accuracy assured, because, at some time in the future, some or all of the documents may be used as evidence against the wrongdoers. Follow the traditional rule of having another person review the work done by any team member. All data should be placed under this review standard.

Summary

It can be concluded that the skills of an experienced auditor and those of an experienced criminal investigator are, in some ways, similar as both strive to seek the truth. The auditor focuses on the accounting, administrative, operational, and internal control/check criteria. The criminal investigator just wants the facts, as Jack Webb used to say on TV's "Dragnet." There are people with both skills. Often, however, it is necessary to use an audit team concept, consisting of both auditors and criminal investigators, who must coordinate their activities to avoid redundancy while working toward the same objective. Who makes the break-through in identifying the wrongdoers and the impact on the institution is not important. What's important is that the crime is solved and appropriate actions are taken (1) against those involved, and (2) to improve procedures and controls to eliminate or reduce the risk's recurrence to a level acceptable to management. During a review, all involved should be looking for other risk factors not identified or, if previously identified, not acted upon, based on the real rather than the perceived level of risk.

The objective of a fraud audit, probably the most difficult of all audit approaches, must be based on a risk orientation. The risk-oriented methodology, properly used in such circumstances, will be (1) far more effective in determining the nature and scope of the problem; (2) quicker in identifying the persons involved, once item (1) has been accomplished; and (3) far more effective in taking appropriate actions to eliminate or reduce the risks to acceptable levels.

Some writers contend fraud auditing is much more heuristic (a good-bet strategy) as against normal audit approaches that are algorithmic (fixed procedures). That is true of financial auditing but less so with operational auditing or management-oriented auditing, to the point that either of these approaches is a good beginning for a fraud audit and then, based on findings, make good-chance decisions as avenues to review further the techniques to be applied to scope. The concept of risk-oriented auditing, which combines both fixed procedures as well as trial and error, must determine the total risk potential as to possible frequency and amount per incident of each risk identified. By far risk-oriented auditing is the most logical audit concept to use when you are trying to determine: (1) what went wrong? (2) who is involved? (3) how much is involved? (4) when did the wrongdoing begin?, and (5) what will be the final cost to the institution if not fully disclosed and appropriate actions aren't taken? Also, how can the risk be held to a level acceptable to management in the future?

Here is an analysis of fraud:

	Annual Loss (Billions)	Percent of Total Frauds
1. Bankruptcy frauds	$ 0.2	0.2
2. Bribery, kickbacks	5.0	7.2
3. Computer related fraud*	5.0	1.0
4. Consumer fraud (all categories but credit cards)	28.0	51.0
5. Credit cards	2.0	3.0
6. Embezzlement	4.0	8.0
7. Pilferage	5.0	10.0
8. Securities fraud and forgery	6.0	10.0
9. All others.	4.8	9.6
TOTALS	$ 60.0	100.0

*15 percent or less is discovered and only 20 percent of that reported; average fraud exceeds $500,000.

A recent study indicated that "potentially 25 percent of employees are "totally dishonest whenever possible;" 25 percent are "totally honest at all times;" and 50 percent are "as honest as controls and personal motivation dictates."[170]

---

[170]Michael J. Comer. *Corporate Fraud*, 2d ed. (New York: McGraw-Hill, 1985), p. 5.

The *ABA Banking Journal* of April 1989, reported, under "Washington Briefs," that the FDIC "has formed a special 'fraud squad' to conduct investigations at thrifts [under] the agency's new authority [of] the Administration's thrift rescue plan. . . . [T]he examiner's job will be to 'get back misappropriated thrift assets and help send those responsible to jail, when appropriate.'" The author had one serious problem with the above which is that a similar *fraud squad* is needed for banking! Need I remind you of (1) National Bank of San Diego and C.A. Smith lending to his own companies, which were not creditworthy, (2) the two brothers with banks in Tennessee and Kentucky who stole from their institutions (e.g., drums of pre-1974 quarters and dimes buried behind a barn on a farm of one of them), and (3) Continental Illinois Bank and the poorly documented and/or unsupported loans it purchased from Penn Square Bank, in Oklahoma, with awareness of senior management and probable collusion of the contact officer of the purchasing bank, because the selling bank made large signature loans to him. It would be possible to extend this listing for pages.

For some years I have been frustrated by the fact that (1) many banks do not report frauds unless the *proven amount* exceeds "X" number of dollars, with the bank itself determining the "X" amount; and (2) the regulators and law enforcement personnel, in many instances, not taking proper follow-up actions to have a criminal prosecution placed on the record of the identified fraud perpetrator.

The best information available to me indicates the following:

1. Only about a third of noncomputer frauds over $1,000 are discovered, with less than a fifth of those under $1,000 being found. The reported frauds to the regulatory and law enforcement authorities depends on the amount as discussed in the preceding paragraph, as determined by the specific institution.

2. Somewhere between 2 and 15 percent of computer frauds are discovered, with the average amount of those identified now running more than $500,000. Unfortunately, only about one of five of those is reported to the regulators and law enforcement authorities. (*Note:* This is not unique to the United States.) While teaching a "Case Studies in Fraud" program in Europe, a high ranking official of Interpol, which serves more than 100 countries, told me that the U.S. figures I reported were "probably slightly better than those from the countries his organization served."

We all agree that "bank crime should never pay—but there's too much to handle. U.S. Attorneys, who prosecute it at the federal level, and the Federal Bureau of Investigation, which investigates it, don't have the resources to bring all guns to bear on every garden-variety embezzlement.... As a result, many cases involving smaller dollar amounts haven't been prosecuted—even when the bank involved has caught the cheat and obtained a confession."[171] As a result, although these thieves would be fired, "they had no criminal record and were free to move to another bank."[172] "One of the biggest complaints I've gotten over the years from bankers is, 'Hell, we send in hundreds of cases every year and nothing ever happens to them,'" says James R. Dundine, chief of the FDIC's Special Activities Section." As a result, a new approach known as "Fast Track" has come into being. It is now in "about half of the nation's 94 districts" in varying forms. The basic process is as follows:

1. "Careful work by the bank involved is essential. This includes a formal statement of the particulars of the case, a written or taped statement from the suspect, and copies of bank records.

2. "Each district offering the program has an officer in both the FBI and the U.S. Attorney's office in charge of handling Fast Track cases. Cases are reviewed by the U.S. Attorney's designated assistant U.S. attorney. If the bank clearly establishes that a crime has been committed, prosecution begins even if the loss is relatively small.

3. "This program puts bankers and local prosecutors into partnerships," says Ralph E. Sharpe, director of the Enforcement and Compliance Section at the Comptroller of the Currency.

"Normally, says Adamski of the FBI, the employee involved has confessed and is pleading guilty. The Fast Track system is generally set up so that such cases are packaged for bulk processing. On a designated court date, collected cases are processed through the court, almost assembly-line fashion. This may be through formal indictment or a less formal process in which an FBI agent swears to case information."[173]

The importance of all employees of the institution *knowing* that frauds, regardless of the amount involved, will result in prosecution and be made part of their personnel records can be a helpful fraud deterrent. Fast-Track, as summarized, should encourage institutions to diligently report all frauds identified and encourage prosecution so the crime is made part of the records of involved persons.

---

[171]"Put Fraud Cases on a Fast Track." *ABA Journal,* April 1989, p. 20.
[172]*Ibid.,* p. 20.
[173]*Ibid.,* p. 23.

Postscript to Chapter

In some recent professional literature, the term "forensic accounting" has been used, usually in relation to "investigative accounting." In reality, investigative accounting is one aspect of risk-oriented auditing. Where fraud auditing results from prior audit reviews or information from a source, known or unknown, the concept of forensic accounting can be something of a fishing trip; not knowing that anything is wrong but desiring to affirm that everything is all right or, during the reviews, to identify some irregularity (e.g., unrecorded assets or transactions or manipulated records, for better or worse). Forensic accounting has been used with success in personal matters (e.g., divorce and separation of joint assets) but it can, in fact, involve a total review of all transactions and related methodology. This kind of accounting can be extremely expensive and could, in the final analysis, find nothing. In business, I prefer the seven stages of fraud auditing over the concept of forensic accounting, because the scope of it increases on the basis of findings and concerns, and rarely, if ever, is a pure fishing trip.

Forensic is defined as "belonging to, used in, or suitable to courts of judicature or to public discussion and debate."[174] The definition goes on to say that it means "an argumentative exercise" or "the art or study of argumentative discourse."[175] For example, the intent of forensic medicine is to get to the truth. That should also be the objective of the forensic accountant as it is with the fraud auditor.

---

[174]*Webster's Ninth New Collegiate Dictionary, op. cit.,* p. 483.
[175]*Ibid.,* p. 483.

Part III
Audit Principles and Methods

9

Standards for the Professional Practice of Internal Auditing

"Internal auditors are employed by the enterprise whose activities they audit."[176] The Institute of Internal Auditors, Inc, which was formed in 1941 and formally adopted "operational auditing" as the preferred modus operandi of internal auditors, in 1959, has defined internal auditing as: "An independent appraisal function established within an organization to examine and evaluate its activities as a service to the organization. The objective of internal auditing is to assist members of the organizations in the effective discharge of their responsibilities. . . . The internal auditing department is an integral part of the organization and functions under the policies established by management and the board"[177] of directors. "The primary function of internal auditors is examining and evaluating the adequacy and effectiveness of their organization's system of internal control. In performing that function, internal auditors often conduct primarily operational audits that are broadly designed to accomplish financial and compliance audit objectives as well as the specific operational audit objectives of evaluating economy, efficiency, and program results . . . "[178]

"The independence of internal auditors is different from that of independent, external auditors. The independence of internal auditors comes from their organizational status—essentially, the level of management to whom they report—and their objectivity."[179]

To establish the function of internal auditors as a distinct profession, The Institute of Internal Auditors, Inc. during the 1970s established the certified internal auditor (CIA) which in a relatively short time has gained recognition that internal auditing is a distinct and separate profession from that of external auditors, certified public accountants or, in some states, professional accountants.

In the area of banking, the Bank Administration Institute has established the chartered bank auditor (CBA) and Cannon Financial established the certified trust auditor (CTA). While these indicate expertise in specific areas of banking, the CIA has gained worldwide recognition making internal auditing a distinct profession.

176Sullivan, et al., *op. cit.*, p. 25.
177*Ibid.*, p. 25.
178*Ibid.*, p. 25.
179*Ibid.*, p. 25.

As internal auditing has grown in stature, receiving recognition as a distinct profession, it has evolved into a higher level of auditing, in some organizations, which is known as management-oriented auditing, or sometimes called management auditing. The first term, more proper as Management Auditing, is a term developed and used by the American Institute of Management (AIM) in the 1940s through the 1960s as a form of managerial evaluation to indicate how effective management was at a specific plant or company, when related to "peer" organizations. Management auditing has actually received broader use than management-oriented auditing, which the writer strongly endorses. The following definition will put this higher level of auditing into perspective:

> "I see the internal auditor as an internal consultant, not as an internal adversary. Not a cop on the beat but a guest in the house. Not merely a searcher for errors, large or small, but a guide to improved operations. Not a second-guesser dedicated to putting people down but a counselor who lifts people up to do better and be better. Not only concerned with whether things are being done right but also . . . whether the right things are being done."[180]

The author of the preceding definition supplements it by indicating internal auditors are "members of a completely distinctive discipline; no longer junior siblings of other professions but professionals in their own right."[181]

Unfortunately, some years ago the auditors who were directly involved in electronic data processing pulled out of The Institute of Internal Auditors, Inc. and formed the EDP Auditors Association, Inc. Through their affiliate, the EDP Auditors Foundation, they started issuing the certified information systems auditor (CISA) title to qualified specialists in that field. Other professional organizations involved with systems and computers specifically have formed the Institute for Certification of Computer Professionals. They issue the following certifications:

- CCP for certified computer programmer.
- CDP for certified data processor.
- CSP for certified systems professional.

Because a large number of EDP auditors were originally computer specialists (CSP), programmers (CCP), or operators (CDP), the certifications indicate the experience and skill levels that make

---

[180]Lawrence B. Sawyer. *Elements of Management-Oriented Auditing*. (The Institute of Internal Auditors, 1983), p. 1.
[181]*Ibid.*, p. 1.

the holders worthy of becoming EDP auditors, where they could earn a CISA.

"An internal auditing function is a control procedure that, among other objectives, may ensure operational efficiency and monitor compliance with company policies and procedures. . . . The work of internal auditors provides evidence of accounting functions that are not being performed effectively, a warning system that they are not, and a deterrent to substandard performance of accounting functions subject to audit."[182] The preceding quotation refers to the perspective of internal auditing by the external auditors, as does the following quote. "Subject to appropriate review and evaluation by the independent auditor, effective internal auditing performed under the direction of appropriate management often allows the independent auditor to significantly reduce the audit scope in affected areas."[183]

Because the importance of internal auditing has been recognized by management, along with its professionalism, independence, and objectivity (PIO), a clear move has been made to improve the quality of personnel working in the function and use it as a training ground for administrative and operational management. For example, when I headed one of the three audit groups at the No. 15 bank in the United States, we worked in an operational auditing mode to meet the following self-imposed standards.

1. Seventy percent of our professional personnel came from the top 16 CPA firms.

2. About half of our professional personnel had (a) some form of certification (usually CPA, CIA, or CISA) and/or (b) a master's degree.

3. Ninety percent or more of our professional personnel had a minimum of one college degree. The other professional personnel were on the staff because of (a) their experience or (b) specific expertise in a high-risk area (e.g., wire/money transfers, foreign exchange).

4. All of the Standards for the Professional Practice of Internal Auditing were adopted, as summarized in Appendix A.

5. A budget was made to lose 12 to 18 percent of our professional staff to other areas of the bank each year.

---

[182]*Ibid.*, p. 2.
[183]*Ibid.*, p. 2.

6. A budget was set to lose 5 to 10 percent of the total professional staff to other organizations each year.

7. A "base" cadre of about 25 percent of the professional staff who would be career internal auditors was established, with their leaving only when a unique opportunity within the bank presented itself.

8. The operational auditing mandate from the board of directors and chairman was to develop our audit approaches and techniques by using the general audit risk component concepts, shown in Figure 14, which follows.

9. The "Seven Stages of Audit," as detailed in Chapter 7, was adopted.

10. Programs were built to give appropriate consideration to each of the "Twelve Building Blocks of Internal Controls/Checks," as illustrated in Chapter 7.

11. All of the *(a)* vertical auditing, *(b)* horizontal auditing, *(c)* situation/condition auditing, and *(d)* reactive auditing were adopted as well as the risk-oriented internal audit approaches discussed in Chapter 7.

12. General standards of the "Big 8" firm engaged by the bank were adopted. They pertained to *(a)* program format, *(b)* work paper format, *(c)* tick-marks, *(d)* continuing audit file (CAF), *(e)* cross-reference techniques, *(f)* familiarization format to enable scope determination, and *(g)* other methods and techniques that were suitable to our basic auditing methods. This enabled us to review their work papers and programs and vice versa; both feeling comfortable because most principles were similar.

Relative to the criteria established by The Institute of Internal Auditors, Inc. in their publication entitled *Standards for the Professional Practice of Internal Auditing,* as referred to in point 4 of the list preceding Figure 14, consider the following:

1. Independence

"Internal auditors are independent when they carry out their work freely and objectively. Independence permits internal auditors to render the impartial and unbiased judgments essential to the proper conduct of audits. It is achieved through organizational status and objectivity."[184]

---

[184] *Standards for the Professional Practice of Internal Auditing.* (The Institute of Internal Auditors, 1981), pp. 100-1.

Figure 14
Audit Risk Components

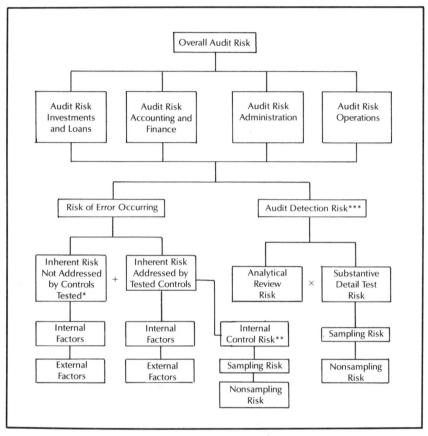

The following definitions are taken from SAS no. 55, issued by the AICPA and effective from January 1, 1990:

*INHERENT RISK: "Susceptibility of an assertion to a material misstatement assuming there are no related internal control structure policies or procedures."

**CONTROL RISK: "The risk that a material misstatement that could occur in an assertion will not be prevented or detected on a timely basis by the entity's internal control structure policies or procedures."

***DETECTION RISK: "The risk that the auditor will not detect a material misstatement that exists in an assertion."

The organizational position of the internal audit function must be such that *(a)* others in the organization recognize it is a management tool, and *(b)* it has lines of communication to the chairman, or another top officer, as well as the audit committee of the board of directors so excessive risks or critical conditions identified can be communicated effectively to them and they support internal auditing to get the risks under control. Banking is fortunate in that most institutions have a direct line to the chairman or president and a dotted line to the audit committee of the board. In most nondepository institutions, internal audit reports directly to the chief financial officer or controller but does have a dotted line to the audit committee, which obviously does not give them quite the freedom when their reporting line is to a more senior officer.

The mandate for the internal audit function should clearly indicate the authority and responsibility assigned and the purpose for the function as perceived by the audit committee of the board and the senior officer to whom they report directly.

2. Professional Proficiency

"Professional proficiency is the responsibility of the internal auditing department and each internal auditor. The department should assign to each audit those persons who collectively possess the necessary knowledge, skills, and disciplines to conduct the audit properly."[185]

Subfactors under the preceding primary heading include *(a)* staffing quality, *(b)* knowledge, skills, and disciplines, *(c)* quality of supervision, *(d)* full compliance with acceptable professional standards of conduct and the institution's code of ethics, *(e)* human relations and effectiveness of communications, *(f)* continuing education, and *(g)* professional care in the performing of internal audits.

3. Scope of Work

"The scope of the internal audit should encompass the examination and evaluation of the adequacy and effectiveness of the organization's system of internal control and the quality of performance in carrying out assigned responsibilities."[186]

Subfactors under the primary heading above include *(a)* reliability and integrity of information, *(b)* compliance with policies, plans, procedures, laws, and regulations, *(c)* safeguarding of assets, *(d)* evaluation on how economically and efficiently resources are being used, and *(e)* objectives and goals for operations or programs being reviewed and evaluated by the internal auditors to see whether they are being accomplished.

4. Performance of Audit Work

"Audit work should include planning the audit, examining and

---

[185]*Ibid.*, pp. 200-1.
[186]*Ibid.*, pp. 300-1.

evaluating the information, communicating results," and the follow-up.[187] Subfactors under the primary heading above include: *(a)* proper planning of the type and scope of the audit through familiarization, in most instances, or following up "leads" indicating that irregular conditions exist, *(b)* examining and evaluating information developed during the audit, and *(c)* effectively communicating results of the effects identified, causes resulting in the effects, and, where qualified, solutions; or, where not qualified, recommending persons with specified skills to effect solutions, which internal audit will evaluate to determine whether solutions have corrected the deficiencies and reduced the risks.

5. Management of the Internal Audit Function

"The director of internal auditing is responsible for properly managing the department so that *(a)* audit work fulfills the general purposes and responsibilities approved by management and accepted by the board, *(b)* resources of the internal auditing department are efficiently and effectively employed, and *(c)* audit work conforms to the Standards for the Professional Practice of Internal Auditing."[188]

Subfactors under the preceding primary heading include *(a)* purpose, authority, and responsibility for internal auditing being fully known, *(b)* sound planning for all audits, *(c)* the personnel of the function receiving written policies and procedures to guide the audit *(d)* a sound program establishing the quality and skills required within the internal audit function and, for other than the cadre, "general career planning" for persons performing well, *(e)* sound relations established between external auditors and regulatory examiners to minimize required reviews, wherever possible, by having test work done by the internal auditors, thereby reducing their work load, and *(f)* quality assurance reviews made of the function by qualified independent personnel from time to time to evaluate what is being done and what more should be done by the internal audit function.

6. Internal Audit and EDP Audit

"Internal audit has one of the most important roles in loss control. It is an independent review function, operating as a ser-

---

[187]*Ibid.*, pp. 400-1.
[188]*Ibid.*, pp. 500-1.

vice to management and a management control. EDP audit performs reviews and makes recommendations to strengthen the control process.

"To move the organization from a reactive mode of loss control to a preventive and deterrent mode, EDP audit must concentrate on systems development. This means it must assure responsibility for helping produce control standards and guidelines and for reviewing the development process and specific development efforts.

"A less tangible but equally important responsibility is to act in a constructive mode. In many organizations, the audit department performs adequate reviews but in an adversary mode. (Some EDP auditors believe that they are evaluated by the number of critical findings they produce.) Every effort should be made to build a positive, constructive working relationship between audit and EDP functions."[189]

The non-EDP auditor must prove to all levels of management that internal auditing is a constructive management tool and eliminate, as much as possible, the negative opinion that many internal audit functions have generated over the years. The auditor must eliminate such detrimental opinions that auditors are: "bean counters," "pencil pushers," "persons who bayonet the wounded after the battle is over," and, more commonly, "police dogs." They achieve the positive and constructive image by (a) how they perform, (b) their willingness to assist management, when prudent, and (c) their constructiveness relative to the best interests of the organization. In addition to accomplishing those results with management, they must convince the EDP auditors of the same things so they sell the virtues of the non-EDP auditors to EDP management. Too often, people forget how much of the EDP auditors' work deals with new programs or systems or revisions to existing programs or systems, leaving little time to check internal controls of operating systems.

---

[189]Eason and Webb. *Nine Steps to Effective EDP Loss Control.* (Bedford, Mass.: Digital Press), 1982, pp. 67-68.

10

Bank Administration Institute's Audit Principles

All the material in this chapter, which is quoted in its entirety, has been taken from *Internal Auditing in the Banking Industry,* Vol. 1, *Audit Principles and Methods,* published by Bank Administration Institute in 1986.

1. Statement of Principles
   "Internal auditing is that management function that independently evaluates the adequacy, effectiveness, and efficiency of the systems of control within an organization and the quality of ongoing operations.

   "The systems of control comprise the plan of organization and all methods and measures designed to:

   1. Provide reasonable assurance that assets are safeguarded, information (financial and other) is timely and reliable, and errors and irregularities are discovered and corrected promptly.

   2. Promote operational efficiency.

   3. Encourage compliance with managerial policies, laws, regulations, and sound fiduciary principles.

   "Ongoing operations are all activities involved in the conduct of the organization's business.

   "The internal auditor is accountable to the board of directors and executive management. This accountability precludes the auditor from organizational relationships that may conflict with his or her independence."

   (The last principle stated has been modified somewhat when internal auditing moves beyond normal operational auditing and performs some reviews in a management-oriented audit mode. Why? Because in a management-oriented audit mode, the internal audit function may have a member on the strategic planning committee, or in a similar "team" or "committee" member role for another management responsibility. In such case, the representative must honor the consensus of the "team" or "committee," even if in disagreement with what actions were agreed upon. However, as soon as some results relative to such actions are documented, the internal auditor can

(1) question variances, favorable or unfavorable, and (2) identify that the orginal data base was incomplete, inaccurate, or improperly used as a *cause* for part or all of the *effect,* which is the variance. Obviously, having an internal auditor on such a "team" or "committee" should improve the scope of data developed, its completeness, accuracy, and timeliness. But, membership on the "team" or "committee" could compromise the *independence* of the internal auditor. That is not true, where the auditor accepts the consensus, even if a minority of one is opposed, because of the ability to revert to the role of analyst and critic... based on performance against plan. When operating in a management-oriented audit mode, the auditor sometimes finds it difficult not to participate in some "team" or "committee" efforts, mostly in dealing with the forward planning for the institution. Such situations can, of course, be avoided if internal audit is functioning only in a financial audit or operational audit mode.)

2. Standards
   "Standards are essential to professional performance. They derive authoritative support from the organization's responsibility and commitment to provide for the internal audit function."

   Four categories of standards follow:
   (a) Organization Standards
   - (1) "The organization shall have an internal audit function responsible for evaluating the adequacy, effectiveness, and efficiency of its system of control and the quality of ongoing operations.
   - (2) "The organization shall maintain an environment within which the auditor has the freedom to act.
   - (3) "The organization shall maintain an environment within which the audit function can conform to the standards of normal auditing.
   - (4) "The organization shall require management to respond formally to adverse audit findings and... take appropriate corrective action.
   - (5) "The organization's system of control shall include measurement of audit effectiveness and efficiency."
   (b) Personal Standards
   - (1) "An internal auditor shall have adequate technical training and proficiency.
   - (2) "An internal auditor shall maintain a sufficiently independent state of mind to clearly demonstrate objectivity in matters affecting audit conclusions.

      (3) "An internal auditor shall respect the confidentiality of information acquired while performing the audit function.

      (4) "An internal auditor shall engage only in activities that do not conflict with the interests of the organization.

      (5) "An internal auditor shall adhere to conduct that enhances the professional stature of internal auditing.

      (6) "An internal auditor shall exercise due professional care in the performance of all duties and the fulfillment of all responsibilities."

(c) Performance Standards

      (1) "An internal auditor shall prepare a formal audit plan that covers all significant organizational activities over an appropriate cycle of time.

      (2) "The audit plan shall include an evaluation of controls within new systems and significant modifications to existing systems before they become operational.

      (3) "Audit procedures shall provide sufficient and competent evidential matter to support conclusions regarding the adequacy, effectiveness, and efficiency of the systems of control and the quality of ongoing operations.

      (4) "The organization of the audit function and related administrative pratice shall provide for the proper supervision of persons performing audits and for the proper review of work performed."

(d) Communication Standards

      (1) "The auditor shall prepare a format report on the scope and results of each audit performed.

      (2) "Each audit report shall contain an opinion on the adequacy, effectiveness, and efficiency of the systems of control and the quality of ongoing operations; the degree of compliance with previously evaluated systems of control; or an explanation of why an opinion cannot be expressed. When an adverse opinion is expressed, the report shall contain a statement about the exposures that may exist if corrective action is not taken.

      (3) "The auditor shall communicate audit findings in a timely manner to the managers responsible for corrective action.

      (4) "At least once each year the auditor shall make a summary report of audit activities to the board of directors and executive management. The report shall include an opinion on the overall condition of the organization's controls and operations."

3. Internal Auditing as a Discipline
"Internal auditing is developing a broader perspective by recognizing that all operations are properly subject to control and
within the scope of auditing. The internal auditor's concern for
control should extend beyond accounting matters. This
broader concept better serves the board of directors and executive management to whom the internal auditor is accountable.
Bank Administration Institute believes the systems of control
and ongoing operations, as defined here, provide a perferred
perspective for discussing internal auditing within the framework of the auditing discipline taken as a whole."

A number of disciplines are identified, with comments made
on each of them in the following text:

(a) Concepts of Control
"The systems of control exist to assure the achievement of
intended results, to promote operating efficiency, and to encourage compliance with policies and other established con-
straints. Although internal auditors have a definite interest
in verifying the results of business activity, their primary
concern must be the continuing effectiveness of the systems
of control that influence business results. The important
qualities that must be evaluated are adequacy, effectiveness,
and efficiency."

(b) Ongoing Operations
"Management must evaluate the quality of operations
based on information provided by the control systems. Adequate control systems produce sufficient information to re-
liably appraise operations. To confirm that the control systems are adequate and effective, the internal auditor should
independently evaluate the quality of ongoing operations,
since only ongoing operations have future significance. ...
Internal auditors should determine whether the quality of
ongoing operations is satisfactory or unsatisfactory." The
internal auditors should issue an opinion, based on their
reviews, and, if unsatisfactory conditions are identified,
they should be described in detail in their report. Where
possible, they also should identify a solution or recommend
hiring persons qualified to effect a solution, which the internal auditors would then evaluate. Remember that "circumstances may preclude the auditor from forming an opinion
on the quality of ongoing operations. This, by itself, is significant because the control systems should provide adequate information for the evaluation of ongoing operations."

(c) Accountability

"Accountability refers to the measures of effective audit performance. The organization standards of this statement define the conditions necessary to hold the auditor accountable for the other standards.... Only the board of directors can protect the auditor's need for independence; consequently, in over 85 percent of cases, the board [of directors] is the final judge of the auditor's performance.... The fact that the process of measurement may be done through an audit committee does not alter the auditor's ultimate accountability to the board.... The audit function serves many users, and the auditor has an obligation, if not accountability, to each of those users.... User satisfaction should be an important consideration in the board's evaluation of audit performance.... Independence is a matter of personal quality rather than of rules. The auditor's relationships, as indicated by the plan or organization and by the way in which the work is conducted, must always be such that a presumption of independence logically follows in the mind of the observer."

(d) Organization Standards

"The organization standards are prerequisites to the personal, performance, and communication standards. They simply state that an internal auditor cannot be accountable for adherence to the other standards without the necessary resources and support of the organization.... Many banks cannot afford the services of a competent and independent internal auditor. It should be clearly understood that those banks are not in compliance with these standards. Their directors and executive management, therefore, bear the burden of providing additional supervision to assure the adequacy, effectiveness, and efficiency of the systems of control and the quality of ongoing operations." Where there is an internal audit function, it should be understood that "the audit process is not complete until the auditor is satisfied that audit findings have received appropriate attention. By requiring management to respond formally to audit findings, the organization contributes to the effectiveness of the audit function.... The organization should measure the performance of its internal audit function in relation to the timeliness, efficiency, and quality of its work."

(e) Personal Standards

This relates "to the qualifications of auditors, the quality of audit practice, and the rules of professional conduct.... All persons engaged in the practice of internal auditing must have the technical training and proficiency necessary to conduct their audit duties in accordance with these standards. Technical training relates to education; proficiency relates to the skill and judgment acquired through experiences.... Proficiency is demonstrated by the proper exercise of professional judgment."

(f) Performance Standards

"The audit plan should be written and presented in a form that is suitable for critical review by audit committees, certified public accountants, regulatory examiners, and others who must evaluate the adequacy of audit coverage.... An audit plan is based on a catalog of examinations that include all significant activities of the organization classified by logical units for work scheduling.... The frequency of audit should be determined by factors affecting risk, management information, customer satisfaction, and the need to create an awareness of audit presence. Risk assessment involves audit judgment regarding how often and to what extent the systems of controls must be evaluated.... The audit plan, which usually represents work contemplated for the current year, should present the information necessary to schedule and assign the work."

(g) Communication Standards

"The auditor has a responsibility to report the results of all work performed.... Requiring auditors to express an opinion on the adequacy, effectiveness, and efficiency of the systems of control and the quality of ongoing operations enables the board of directors, management, and other interested parties to judge better their reliability. This service is a natural and logical part of the internal auditor's accountability.... Expressing an opinion imposes a serious obligation on the auditor; the requirement of due professional care extends to both the opinion and the commentary supporting it. Clear identification of the systems of control audit is the key to a meaningful opinion.... Auditors occasionally form adverse conclusions concerning the adequacy, effectiveness, or efficiency of the systems of control or the quality of ongoing operations. In these cases, they should qualify their opinion and identify exposures that may exist in the absence of corrective action. Risk measures the degree to which exposures are uncontrolled. The applicable equation is: Exposures minus control equals risk."

(h) Fraud and the Auditor's Responsibility

"Audit proficiency includes the ability to evaluate fraud exposures. Sufficient information is available concerning how fraud may be committed in banking (e.g., reports from the FBI and/or federal or state regulators).... The systems of control, not the internal audit function, provide the primary assurance against fraud. The internal auditor, however, must evaluate the systems' capability to achieve that end. When in doubt, the auditor should consider applying additional procedures to determine if fraud has actually occurred.... The internal auditor cannot be responsible for detecting irregular transactions for which there is no record (e.g., an unrecorded receipt of cash from a source for which there is no evidence of accountability); an isolated transaction that does not recur (e.g., a single fraudulent loan); or irregularities that are well concealed by collusion. ... In judging the preventive capacity of the control systems and the internal auditors' responsibility, the principle of relative risk should not be ignored—namely, cost must be balanced against intended benefit."

4. EDP Audit Principles

"The primary purpose of internal bank auditing is to determine that controls and operating procedures are functioning in a way to protect the banks from losses due to inefficiencies, inaccuracies, irregularities, and willful manipulations. The auditor's role is to help safeguard the bank's assets by carrying out tests and procedures that establish the validity and reliability of operating systems, procedures, controls, and the resulting records. The auditor is involved in all areas and activities of the bank. Electronic data processing continues to be pervasive in every application of audit, so today's auditors must be familiar with fundamental EDP control issues before they can effectively audit automated systems." Auditors have broad responsibilities relative to EDP, including:

(a) Proficiency

"The standard of proficiency states that audits of banking activities or functions that are affected directly or indirectly by electronic data processing are to be performed by a person with appropriate EDP technical knowledge and proficiency as an auditor.... Three levels of technical EDP knowledge are appropriate for the several operating environments that are encountered: (1) A basic knowledge of EDP concepts and the ways computers can be used is required of all internal bank auditors; (2) the internal auditors of banks that have their own computers will be trained

157

more thoroughly in EDP technology to become proficient at an intermediate level; and (3) in those banks that have major commitments to electronic data processing, one or more audit staff members should be fully qualified EDP professionals." Those levels of technical EDP knowledge are:

1. "Basic level. All internal bank auditors need a broad general knowledge of data processing.

2. "Intermediate level. In banks that have their own computers, some members of the audit staff must possess higher levels of knowledge. Banks with audit staff so limited in size that there is no real opportunity for EDP specialization will have at least one staff member trained as an intermediate level EDP auditor.

3. "Advanced level. Banks with extensive or highly sophisticated applications and with large investments in data processing systems should have at least one staff member trained as an advanced-level EDP specialist.... EDP audit specialists will have some programming skills, significant systems analysis skills, and general knowledge concerning the operating procedures of the EDP center. They will be able to design system tests and develop special-purpose computer audit programs independently of the data processing staff. Their level of competence will earn the respect of data processing personnel."

(b) Independence

"The auditor must maintain an independent attitude at all times and therefore must not be obligated or subordinate in any way to anyone in the activities or functions examined."

(c) Performance

"The auditor must discharge his or her responsibility with thoroughness, competency, and objectivity."

(d) Scheduling

"Audits requiring the use of automated records or procedures must be planned with due regard to the processing deadlines of the EDP department but without compromising essential control."

(e) Internal Control

"The auditor should evaluate the existing internal controls and use the results as the basis for determining the extent of other audit procedures and for recommending improved controls if necessary."

(f) Documentation
"The auditor should obtain adequate documentation to provide a reasonable basis for an opinion regarding the activity or function reviewed."

(g) Reporting
"The auditor should report his or her findings and recommendations in writing, and report any material variations in the usual scope of the audit."

5. Implications for Internal Audit Departments
"Following the principles of auditing and EDP auditing that auditors must be conversant with, today's audit department must be staffed by auditors who possess technical proficiency in the required areas. Also, audit programs must be reviewed to ensure that, taken as a whole, they can provide adequate assurance that the entire system of internal controls has been reviewed, and a continual education program and quality control review should ensure that those high standards are maintained."

As indicated at the beginning of this chapter, the quotations herein were all taken from the Bank Administration Institute's *Internal Auditing in the Banking Industry,* Volume 1. This three-volume work is useful as (1) a learning tool for new auditors in banking, or (2) as a reference for experienced auditors.

Chapter 3 of this text, "Electronic Data Processing Auditing," provides more details of what internal auditors "need to know" relative to auditing in an EDP environment. On the other hand, Chapter 8, entitled "Overview of Fraud Auditing," provides what fraud auditors "need to know" for auditing an EDP environment.

The Standards for the Professional Practice of Internal Auditors, as developed by The Institute for Internal Auditors Inc. (summarized in Appendix A) are basically the principles and standards for bank auditors.

11

Audit Disciplines

A definition, quoted earlier herein, taken from a 1973 issue of *The Internal Auditor,* is repeated here. It indicates how the audit disciplines of effective risk-oriented internal auditing, based on the framework of operational auditing, requires the auditor to (1) think like an owner, and have a reasonable understanding of all aspects of the business in the environment to be audited, and (2) know about the authority, responsibilities, tasks, duties, products, and services of the environment where the audit is to be performed, so that performance can be evaluated as to completeness of recording economic events, things are being done properly and promptly, and with adequate controls functioning as intended. The following definition is the framework around which all of the audit disciplines presented in this chapter are based:

"Operational auditing is using common sense, or logical audit techniques, with management perspective, and applying them to company objectives, operations, controls, communications, and information systems. The auditor is more concerned with the who, what, when, where, why, and how of running an efficient and profitable business than just the accounting and financial aspects of the business functions."

A. Seven Stages of an Audit

    (1) Familiarization:

        (a) Review organizational structure and job descriptions to become aware of the management mandate stipulated for (i) authority and responsibilities, (ii) tasks and duties, and (iii) other aspects of the "management mandate" relative to the environment to be audited.

        (b) Learn the principles and standards relative to the environment. This is usually accomplished by (i) reading the first four to six chapters of an accredited reference text on the environment to be audited (e.g., Purchasing: *Aljian's Handbook of Purchasing,* endorsed by the National Association of Purchasing Management; Foreign Exchange (FX): *"Foreign Exchange and the Corporate Treasurer,"* written by the head FX trader of a major banking organization). The order of preference for reference texts should be those endorsed by trade associations, such as the reference given for purchasing, with the second choice being a text written by a

professional practitioner, such as the reference given for foreign exchange. The third choice would be any text published by a reputable publishing house on the specific subject. Be aware of and knowledgeable about any internal policies and procedures, and also any regulatory requirements concerning the environment to be audited.

(c) Affirm all activities, functions, products, and services provided by (i) observation of personnel at work, and/ or (ii) discussion of those topics with supervisory and officer-level personnel.

(d) Evaluate competency of (i) officers, (ii) supervisors, and (iii) subordinate personnel, relative to the activities, functions, products, and services, as confirmed under item (c).

(e) Ascertain "risks," based on the efforts under items (a) through (d) earlier, and stratify them as to activity, total amounts involved, and level of controls dealing with each risk environment identified.

(f) Review information developed with management on the activity, function, facility, or entity to be audited to (i) be sure the information developed is complete and accurate, and (ii) ascertain what further reviews, if any, are necessary and should be performed promptly, before proceeding to the next audit stage.

(2) Planning

(a) Review previous audit reports and work papers if the environment has previously been audited. Focus on (i) any new products, services, activities, or functions that exist now but did not exist at the time of the most recent audit review; (ii) risk conditions that were identified at the time of the most recent audit review, which the "familiarization" phase identified now as being more effectively controlled or less effectively controlled and, if the latter, try to determine cause by familiarization efforts; or (iii) risks identified during the current familiarization effort that did not exist or were not found during the preceding audit review.

(b) Determine whether the audit recommendations of the most recent audit review were acted upon, as recommended in the audit report and/or as stated in re-

AUDIT DISCIPLINES

sponse to such a report by management.

(c) Based on all of the information developed from points (1)(a) through (2)(b) develop an audit plan deciding on (i) scope, (ii) compliance audit reviews to be performed in designated areas, (iii) substantive audit reviews to be performed in designated areas, and (iv) "special" audit reviews deemed appropriate in designated areas, because of risks, noncompliance with internal policies and procedures, or possible or identified violations of regulatory requirements (e.g., failure to properly report all cash transactions of $10,000 or more).

(3) Perform the examinations and reviews as stipulated in the audit scope requirements set out in the audit plan. Based on those findings, perform supplemental reviews, where the error rate, noncompliance with policies and procedures, noncompliance with regulatory requirements, or violations of required internal controls and checks raise concerns about the level of risks, so that reasonable audit conclusions can be reached from the work performed. (Note: This broadening of the original audit plan scope can continue through the seven stages of auditing, as described in Chapter 7.)

(4) Evaluate findings from the reviews performed under segment (3), and develop listings of primary, secondary, and tertiary findings. These should be reviewed with the audited management, except in the case of a fraud where its possible knowledge or participation warrants that the findings be reported at a higher level. This may vary by institution (e.g., direct to the chairman or direct to the chairman and audit committee of the board of directors). Obtain management agreement on the findings or, if there is disagreement, follow up to determine whether the findings are correct and the conclusions are appropriate, or disprove them and drop them, with regard to inclusion in the audit report. On agreed deficiencies, attempt to work out a timetable with the audited management as to corrective actions to be taken and when the undertakings will be completed. As appropriate, report such an agreement and management's commitment in the audit report on points of sufficient importance. For lesser findings, such follow-up can occur in Stage 6 or as a starting point when the next audit review is undertaken.

Where the auditors and management disagree, both positions should be stated in the audit report to (i) identify the disagreement, and (ii) put senior management on notice so they can support the audit or management position, or decide on a compromise solution that will be accepted by the auditors and management and thereby accomplish some efficiency, effectiveness, economy, or improved internal controls of the risk situation.

(5) Develop and present audit findings either orally, as an overview or on the most critical matters with a follow-up, written report or merely issue a written report. Because the scope covers accounting, administration, compliance, control, and operations, the findings may be bulky as compared to findings under traditional financial audit approaches. In such cases, it is recommended that findings and agreements with management be handled in a two-report format, except in fraud situations or "special" audit reviews requested by senior management, where a single report should be issued. Where a two-report format is adopted, it should be along the following lines:

(a) Primary Report: This should include the most serious or potentially serious and sensitive matters identified during the audit review. Agreement with auditee management as to corrective actions, and time frame to complete them, should be identified as well as where there is disagreement between the auditors and auditee management. This report should be directed to the chairman or other senior officer to whom the internal audit function reports, the senior officer to whom the auditee manager reports, the auditee manager, and, where requested, to the members of the audit committee of the board of directors, or other functions within the organization that should be aware of one or more findings in the report (e.g., law, risk management, human resources, or security units).

(b) Secondary Report: This covers matters that the auditors believe should be formalized in writing, for action by the auditee manager but are not significant enough to be included in the primary report. There will be instances involving a specific audit environment where some comments may go into the primary report while others are included in the secondary report. Where this is done, appropriate cross-reference should be in both reports which, together, identify the broad details of the audit. This report should be distributed to the senior officer to whom the auditee manager reports and the auditee manager. Those receiving the primary report would be made aware of such report and could request it if they desire.

Tertiary findings not considered important enough to include in the secondary report would be summarized in the audit work papers and could be followed up if an effort is being made in regard to more serious situations reported in either the primary or secondary reports. Or tertiary findings may not be checked out until the beginning of the next audit review of the environment.

(6) Follow-ups between audits are done when serious matters, usually in the primary report, but sometimes in both the primary and secondary reports, are of high risk, or noncompliance with policies, procedures, or regulations. This is done to assure that corrective actions have, in fact, been taken, as agreed to with the auditee management or, an increasing number of banks are requiring a reply to audit report findings within a stipulated time, usually 60 to 90 days, from issuance date of the reports, indicating what has been done and the time frame for completing other necessary actions to improve efficiency, effectiveness, economy, internal controls and checks, or control actions pertaining to identified risks. If there is any question that management of the audited area might be indicating the proper actions to be done in a reasonable time frame, but there is doubt that they are doing what they have committed to do, then a follow-up between audits is warranted at the discretion of the internal auditors. This is done to protect the institution and its management. It may be limited to specific audit report findings or, in more serious situations, could involve a complete functional audit of an area of great concern (e.g., foreign exchange section, futures trading, proper documentation on loans, or filing of liens on loans). There is great psychological value for the manager of the audited area and his superior to know that the auditors may decide to perform a special follow-up review, at their discretion. This encourages commitments to corrective actions be done within the time frame agreed by the audited area's management or its immediate superior.

(7) Summary: The preceding steps of each stage are not rigid. They can be repositioned when appropriate. To illustrate this, consider point (2)(a). This step of reviewing the work papers and reports of the preceding audit when in the planning stage can be changed, and that step moved up to the familiarization stage. Planning should not routinely be in the familiarization stage because the tendency there is to "test" information rather than do a thorough familiarization, as appropriate, to learn what is happening in the audit environment, and not assume that it is the same or virtually unchanged from the preceding audit. This is often rationalized on the basis of "saving time" but, in fact, the data of the familiarization stage, for the current audit, is reduced as to reliability, which could impair the final audit scope decided on in the planning stage. The key to the effectiveness of planning and the following stages is how well the work was done in the familiarization stage.

In the event of a fraud, possible fraud, mismanagement, or gross negligence situation, step (2)(a) can be moved into the familiarization stage to start the audit fieldwork. While that work is under way, the familiarization work, as described under step (1) should be performed, and once completed, the planning-stage work finalized as rapidly as possible. At that time, final-scope determinations would be developed and the fieldwork, already underway, modified according to the current plan.

Let me reemphasize that the familiarization stage is the most important of the six stages of an audit. The more sensitive the audit (e.g., possible fraud or noncompliance with regulatory requirements) the more important it becomes. It is interesting that the familiarization stage may be in progress while some fieldwork is underway on the audit review, but the final audit scope is built from findings of the familiarization stage or any "lead" that may have been cause to initiate sensitive reviews.

B. Audit Work Program

(1) A four-page work program will evolve during the planning of the audit, based on information accumulated from the familiarization stage and the work papers and reports of the previous audit, if one was done. This program follows

the step-by-step approach used. It also indicated how an EDP test package was used to reduce the clerical time needed to accumulate information or to test the data relative to the audit environment.

(2) Three pages of information relative to *(a)* Scope Memo-C/Ds, and *(b)* Computer Entry-C/Ds.

Think of the audit work programs as (1) guides to be followed when performing the audit reviews, keeping in mind that they must be flexible to adjust to review findings; and (2) a historical audit trail of what was done, which is supported by the work papers developed and the deficiencies, if any, reported relative to audit findings in the audit environment.

The *Internal Auditor's Handbook,* written by Paul E. Heeschen and Lawrence B. Sawyer and published by The Institute of Internal Auditors, Inc. in 1984 (on pages 128 and 129) presents its recommended criteria for working papers. My comments on each of the major headings follow:

Policy for Working Papers

All of the working papers of the last preceding audit should routinely be kept as a reference source for the next audit. If a fraud or other major problem occurred two audits previously, then both sets of working papers should be maintained to identify any negative turnaround since the last audit relative to the problem areas identified in the two preceding audits. A continuing audit file (CAF) or carry-forward audit file (CFA) should be kept and updated with each audit. Any material removed from the CAF or CFA file should be kept for reference purposes for two audits after its removal from such files.

General

The working papers should be uniform in a preparation format. Appropriate cross-reference, within the working papers, should comprise related materials. Common tick-marks should be established and used consistently. Special tick-marks created for a specific subject or audit action should be clearly described within the working papers, usually on the "lead schedule" for each audit phase.

Identification

Each working paper should clearly indicate the title of the audit project and a project number, with appropriate subheadings and section headings, as needed.

Form

Details relative to account analyses, reconciliation, and all other audit matters should be indicated clearly in the working papers.

Content

The lead schedule for each set of working papers should indicate the objective of reviews, degree of reliance strived for where sampling is used, sources of data, scope of work, and a summation of findings and conclusions with recommendations, as appropriate.

Deficiency Findings

The audit review findings and related recommendations should be stratified as primary, secondary, and tertiary. Also indicate any agreements with management of the audited environment on corrective actions and the time frame for implementation.

Indexing

Roman numerals should be used for each major section of the audit work. Each working paper developed for any section should start with that reference to be followed by a numeric reference. Where something must be inserted between two assigned numbers, use a tertiary alpha reference (e.g., "A," "B").

Disposition of Working Papers

Policy for working papers was discussed earlier. When working papers for previous audits are to be destroyed, (1) they should be microfilmed and (2) then destroyed under audit supervision. No more than one set of audit working papers need to be retained on microfilm. Some believe that this records control action is unnecessary. However, it is a safeguard to provide comparative analysis (e.g., current audit working papers, a prior set maintained for reference, and the microfilmed set of working papers). That may prove helpful particularly when a fraud is uncovered that has been going on undetected for several years. A comparative analysis could indicate, after-the-fact, how modifications of the audit program approach could have increased the probability of earlier discovery of the fraud.

Safeguarding Working Papers

The need for working papers of the most recent audit requires that they be in a fireproof cabinet or secure vault. An ordinary file cabinet with locks is inadequate and too easy to break into. Key pages of data might be removed unbeknown to anyone until specific

Work Program

XYZ National Bank
Deposits Cycle—Certificates of Deposit—Audit Date 12/31/89
Review Date 9/30/89 A.I.C.: RON MARTIN

ESTIMATED					PROGRAM BASED ON PRESUMED OR ANTICIPATED CONDITIONS*	WORK COMPLETED			
EXP LEVEL	PERSON	PHASE	SEC.	TIME	INCLUDE HERE OR IN SUPPLEMENTAL MEMORANDUM A BRIEF SUMMARY OF THE (A) NATURE OF THE ACCOUNTS, (B) CLIENT'S ACCOUNTING PROCEDURES AND INTERNAL CONTROL TECHNIQUES, AND (C) AUDIT OBJECTIVES TO BE ACCOMPLISHED.	...	W/P REF.	BY	TIME

As indicated in our audit approach, our work for the certificate of deposit subcycle will be substantive in nature and will address the accountability and accurate recognition of CDs in the books of the bank. Our approach will be primarily confirmation and recomputation.

[handwritten: noted RM]

AUDIT PROCEDURES—PRELIMINARY

1. Prepare a confirmation scope memo which will outline the reasons for selecting the number of confirmations selected, the means of selection of accounts, and the date which will be used for confirmation. *[handwritten: A-130 RN.]*

2. Since the certificate of deposit records are computerized and suitable for use by audit software, prepare inquiry and extract routines which will perform the following functions: *[handwritten: A-131 RN.]*

   a. Prepare a trial balance giving CD number, name, amount, date and due date, interest rate and accrued interest.

   b. A sequence report accounting for all CDs issued since previous yearend as being active, redeemed, or missing.

   c. Confirmation selection in printing and the related confirmation controls based upon the scope established in Step 1. *[handwritten: A-151 RM]*

3. For the date indicated in our scope memo in Step 1, obtain a backup copy of the certificate of deposit master file. Insure that the client has performed their weekly update for CDs through the current date. Maintain this file under our control and arrange for computer time to process our E/T routines. *[handwritten: A-131 RM]*

4. Utilizing our E/T routines prepared and the master file obtained above, obtain the E/T prepared trial balance, sequence report and the confirmations. *[handwritten: A-132 RM]*

5. Tie the trial balance prepared by E/T to the general ledger as of our preliminary date. Determine that reconciling items are the normal recurring items which result from timing differences in processing. Follow up on any large or unusually old reconciling items. Tie in accrued interest payable for the E/T trial balance to the general ledger.

*IF PROGRAM IS CHANGED AS A RESULT OF CONDITIONS FOUND IN THE FIELD, DESCRIBE THE CHANGES IN AN ATTACHED MEMORANDUM (INDICATE LOCATION) AND STATE THE GENERAL REASONS FOR SUCH CHANGES.

***Cycle schedule cross-reference   E/T: EDP Test Package

W/P REF.: Workpaper reference

Work Program

XYZ National Bank
Deposits Cycle—Certificates of Deposit—Audit Date 12/31/89
Review Date 9/30/89 A.I.C.: RON MARTIN

PROGRAM BASED ON PRESUMED OR ANTICIPATED CONDITIONS*						WORK COMPLETED			
ESTIMATED					INCLUDE HERE OR IN SUPPLEMENTAL MEMORANDUM A BRIEF SUMMARY OF THE (A) NATURE OF THE ACCOUNTS, (B) CLIENT'S ACCOUNTING PROCEDURES AND INTERNAL CONTROL TECHNIQUES, AND (C) AUDIT OBJECTIVES TO BE ACCOMPLISHED.				
EXP LEVEL	PERSON	PHASE	SEC.	TIME		***	W/P REF.	BY	TIME
					6. Obtain the sequence report and test the activity shown as follows:		A-133	RM	
					a. Follow up and determine disposition of CD numbers shown as missing. These should represent CDs which have been voided and maintained by assistant branch managers or the assistant cashier in the main office.				
					b. Select 20 C/Ds indicated as redeemed and examine documentation of poceeds paid to depositor.				
					c. Relate the first CD number issued this year to the last CD number issued based on our audit work papers for 1984. Visually examine the CDs under the assistant cashier and assistant branch manager's control on the date of our examination and relate to the last CD number per the sequence report.				
					7. Select 20 C/Ds and using information for issue date, maturity date and interest rate and amount, recompute CD accrued interest payable by use of our timesharing terminals.		A-134	RM	
					8. Obtain the confirmations prepared by E/T and review them before mailing and control them during the review. After having this review performed, mail the confirmations.		A-135	RM	
					9. Send second request on all nonreplies after two weeks using this same control process.		A-135	RM	
					10. Sort all replies into the following groups: no exceptions; exception reconciled; exception not reconciled; unable to confirm; returned from post office.		A-136 to A-137	RM	
					11. Make copies of exceptions and give them to a staff auditor for reconciliation (Xerox copies are the primary control over return of these replies).		A-137	RM	
					12. Examine documentation of reconciliation and if letters are appropriate control the mailing of these letters. These letters should request the depositor to respond to us that they are in agreement with the reconciliation.		A-137	RM	

*IF PROGRAM IS CHANGED AS A RESULT OF CONDITIONS FOUND IN THE FIELD, DESCRIBE THE CHANGES IN AN ATTACHED MEMORANDUM (INDICATE LOCATION) AND STATE THE GENERAL REASONS FOR SUCH CHANGES.

***Cycle schedule cross-reference   E/T: EDP Test Package

W/P REF.: Workpaper reference

Work Program

XYZ National Bank
Deposits Cycle—Certificates of Deposit—Audit Date 12/31/89
Review Date 9/30/89 A.I.C.: RON MARTIN

ESTIMATED					PROGRAM BASED ON PRESUMED OR ANTICIPATED CONDITIONS*	WORK COMPLETED		
EXP LEVEL	PERSON	PHASE	SEC.	TIME	INCLUDE HERE OR IN SUPPLEMENTAL MEMORANDUM A BRIEF SUMMARY OF THE (A) NATURE OF THE ACCOUNTS, (B) CLIENT'S ACCOUNTING PROCEDURES AND INTERNAL CONTROL TECHNIQUES, AND (C) AUDIT OBJECTIVES TO BE ACCOMPLISHED. •••	W/P REF.	BY	TIME
					13. Post office returns should be listed for control purposes and given to the staff auditor for research:	A-139	AM	
					a. Obtain new addresses and indicate the date remailed on our control listing.			
					b. For those CDs which a better name of address could not be obtained, examine CD copy and compare signature to signature card for other accounts maintained at the bank.			
					14. Perform the procedure above for confirmations that have been returned by the depositor indicating he is unable to confirm.	A-138	AM	
					15. Summarize the results of confirmation procedures and statistically evaluate the errors noted. Conclude as to the propriety and completeness of the certificate of deposit file as of our confirmation date.	A-135	AM	
					AUDIT PROCEDURES—FINAL			
					1. Using specified software, prepare a sequence report listing CD disposition since preliminary date. Follow up on those CDs indicated as missing.	A-140	Ron	
					2. Using average balances and recorded expense for interest, prepare an analysis of yields comparing this year to the prior years and explain significant variations. Relate yield for interest expense to the stated rates and determine reasonableness.	A-141	AM	
					3. Reconcile the CD trial balance for outstanding principal and accrued interest to the general ledger. Determine propriety of reconciling items and prepare AJE if appropriate.	A-142	Ron.	
					4. Review the lead schedule and comment on fluctuations between years of all accounts that show unusual activity.	A-1	Ron.	

*IF PROGRAM IS CHANGED AS A RESULT OF CONDITIONS FOUND IN THE FIELD, DESCRIBE THE CHANGES IN AN ATTACHED MEMORANDUM (INDICATE LOCATION) AND STATE THE GENERAL REASONS FOR SUCH CHANGES.

***Cycle schedule cross-reference   E/T: EDP Test Package

W/P REF.: Workpaper reference

Work Program

XYZ National Bank
Deposits Cycle—Certificates of Deposit—Audit Date 12/31/89
Review Date 9/30/89 A.I.C.: RON MARTIN

PROGRAM BASED ON PRESUMED OR ANTICIPATED CONDITIONS*						WORK COMPLETED			
ESTIMATED					INCLUDE HERE OR IN SUPPLEMENTAL MEMORANDUM A BRIEF SUMMARY OF THE (A) NATURE OF THE ACCOUNTS, (B) CLIENT'S ACCOUNTING PROCEDURES AND INTERNAL CONTROL TECHNIQUES, AND (C) AUDIT OBJECTIVES TO BE ACCOMPLISHED.				
EXP LEVEL	PERSON	PHASE	SEC.	TIME		***	W/P REF.	BY	TIME
					5. Prepare blueback recommendations generated through our review of procedures and audit steps above.		D-106	ML WT	
					6. Senior review.				
					7. Clear senior review points.		N/A	per	
					Note: This audit work program concentrates on substantive auditing review efforts. The program should be supplemented, if deemed appropriate, by appropriate compliance audit review requirements. As a general statement, audit reviews combining both substantive and compliance reviews are (1) cost effective, and (2) analytically more effective, relative to any specific audit environment.				

*IF PROGRAM IS CHANGED AS A RESULT OF CONDITIONS FOUND IN THE FIELD, DESCRIBE THE CHANGES IN AN ATTACHED MEMORANDUM (INDICATE LOCATION) AND STATE THE GENERAL REASONS FOR SUCH CHANGES.

***Cycle schedule cross-reference   E/T: EDP Test Package

W/P REF.: Workpaper reference

XYZ National Bank
Confirm Scope Memo
Certificates of Deposit
Dec. 31, 1989

This memo summarizes the confirmation plan for XYZ National Bank's certificates of deposit. We have determined, based on our review of client procedures followed in the certificates of deposit area, that our approach will be to test the CD balance as of 9/30/89 substantively.

To perform this test, we will use attribute sampling to develop an estimate of error occurrence rates in the population. Our population will be the certificate of deposit masterfile certificates. There are about 4,000 certificates.

An error will be defined as a bank processing error that has not been detected or corrected before our follow-up. Our sampling method will be unrestricted random using the E/T random sampling routine. A random selection method is necessary to have a valid basis for statistical evaluation.

Sample Size Considerations

This test is the primary one we are using to determine the validity of the certificate of deposit balance. As such, our degree of reliance on the test will be great. Therefore, we will develop a sample size sufficient to evaluate the results at a 85 percent confidence level. We expect few, if any, errors to occur; however, to "cushion" our sample size, we will estimate a 0.5 percent error rate. Further, we want a high degree of precision in our evaluation and will use a 1 percent one-sided precision interval.

Confidence level	95% (one-sided)
Precision interval	1% (one-sided)
Error rate expected	0.5%

Estimated sample size <u>299</u>

Sample Testing

We will use all positive confirmations to test the sample selected above. For confirmations returned with possible exceptions, we will perform sufficient procedures to determine whether an error occurred as we defined it. We will address past office returns by attempting to obtain a better address and, if unsuccessful, we will examine the signed copy of the certificiate.

XYZ National Bank
Computer Entry—Certificates of Deposit
Dec. 31, 1989

I.A. prepared E/T routines that generated the following reports:

—CD trial balance including CD number, name, amount, date and due date, interest rate, and accrued interest.

—Sequence report including all CDs issued since 12/31/88 and noted them as being currently active, redeemed or missing.

—Confirmations selected according to the confirmation scope outlined on A-130 and the related control listings.

On 9/30/89 I.A.s entered the computer room on a surprise basis to prepare to run the above E/T routines. Van Flick, EDP officer, accompanied us during the entry.

We determined through discussions with the computer operator that they were running the weekly update of the CD activity. Once the process was completed we obtained a backup copy of the certificate of deposit master file and obtained computer time over the weekend to process our routines.

On Saturday we ran the E/T routines against the copy of the master file which was maintained under our control. See the following schedules for the reports generated and the work performed on them:

CD trial balance —A-132
Sequence report —A-133
Confirmations —A-135 to 139

information is needed from the working papers.

The *Internal Auditor's Handbook,* on page 130 recommends a formal control record be kept on the destruction of working papers, saying (1) when, (2) where, (3) by whom, (4) observed by which IA personnel, and (5) disposition (e.g., of shredded materials or ashes or mixed in with other destroyed materials).

C. Continuing Audit File (CAF)

The CAF also may be known as the carry-forward audit file (CFA) or permanent file (PF). While the contents of such file may vary from company to company, some general criteria are stated in the *Handbook for Auditors,* edited by James A. Cashin, and pubished by McGraw-Hill Book Co. in 1971. On pages 14 and 20-21, the handbook indicates that such a file should include "those working papers that have current importance year after year. The information included has been accumulated in current and past audits and will be required in future audits. . . . It briefly summarizes recurring items that must be reviewed, thus avoiding the necessity of rereading lengthy. . . documents year after year." The book goes on to state the "deleted items are either destroyed or put into a dead file." Some of the contents may be:

(1) Activity, function, product, service, entity, or affiliate ID, and location.

(2) Table of contents.

(3) Sources of information included.

(4) Copies of articles of incorporation and bylaws, where applicable.

(5) Management of board meeting abstracts.

(6) Organization and authority structure.

(7) Specific information on accounting, administrative, organizational, control, operational, data processing, and security matters.

(8) Data on significant contracts or leases.

(9) IA assessment of permanent accounts and schedules of carry-forwards.

(10) Other pertinent information; discretionary.

D. Summary

Without question, the familiarization stage of the audit will result in either coming up with effective planning or the audit will be developed along (1) financial perspective primarily, and (2) audit theory secondarily. The audit will not be planned on the basis of a *real* understanding of the audit environment and, specifically, the risks that exist. Without knowing the risks, or having a broad understanding of the audit environment, how is it possible to develop an effective audit plan? If the plan is deficient, its scope and approach probably will not produce the fieldwork needed to determine deficiencies, potential problems, or the recommendations to deal with either.

Remember that the audit programs developed for reviews are alive in that they can be enhanced, revised, or shifted from a standard audit to a fraud audit approach at any time, based on information arising from the fieldwork.

As for reports, either one or two level reports are acceptable. However, if the review gets beyond accounting and finance into administration, management, controls, systems, compliance with policies, procedures, and regulations, and security, the findings inevitably will be broadened. My recommendation is the two-level report, so senior management will get all of the "need-to-know" information, and the manager of the audited area and that person's superior will get the "need-to-act" information that supplements the "need-to-know" information.

12

The Increased Professionalism Required by Risk-Oriented Internal Auditing as Against All Other Internal Audit Formats

The *Standards for the Professional Practice of Internal Auditing,* published by The Institute of Internal Auditors, Inc., 1981, under heading 250, on page 200-2, states, regarding knowledge, skills, and disciplines, that:

"Internal auditors should possess the knowledge, skills, and disciplines essential to the performance of internal audits.

.01 "Each internal auditor should possess certain knowledge and skills as follows:

.1 "Proficiency in applying internal auditing standards, procedures, and techniques is required in performing internal audits. Proficiency means the ability to apply knowledge to situations likely to be encountered and to deal with them without extensive recourse to technical research and assistance.

.2 "Proficiency in accounting principles and techniques is required of auditors who work extensively with financial records and reports.

.3 "An understanding of management principles is required to recognize and evaluate the materiality and significance of deviations from good business practice. An understanding means the ability to apply broad knowledge to situations likely to be encountered, to recognize significant deviations, and to be able to carry out the research necessary to arrive at reasonable solutions.

.4 "An appreciation is required of the fundamentals of such subjects as accounting, economics, commercial law, taxation, finance, quantitative methods, and computerized information systems. An appreciation means the ability to recognize the existence of problems or potential problems and to determine the further research to be undertaken or the assistance to be obtained."

177

The book goes on to state under 260 Human Relations and Communications that "internal auditors should be skilled in dealing with people and in communicating effectively."

All of these skills, as well as others, are summarized effectively by Lawrence B. Sawyer in his *Ten Commandments of Auditing*, as discussed earlier in the text. Of the preceding text from IIA, let us focus on paragraph .01-.3, dealing with "an understanding of management principles." Earlier, I indicated that the auditor, in a risk-oriented auditing environment, must be thinking like an owner evaluating a specific manager. To do so, the owner must understand that phase of the business. He begins by recognizing that, in many phases of the business the manager must have a number of skills (e.g., training, education, and experience) that he may not have. Even so, he can still check on and evaluate the performance of any manager, except in assuming expertise and educational skills that manager may possess. How? Simply by:

1. Knowing the business and the specific authority and responsibilities given to the manager as well as the total staffing of the activity, function, product, service, entity, or facility.

2. Knowing the general goals and objectives of the environment involving the manager and a broad perspective of the general modus operandi plus all the established policies, procedures, practices, standards, and controls and laws or regulations affecting the business.

The third element to understand is the theory and principles pertaining to the environment. As indicated earlier, the best reference book available on the general business environment should be found, and the fundamentals can usually be learned by reading the first four to six chapters of the book. This enables an owner or his representative, the internal auditor, to (1) understand much of the who, what, when, where, why, and how of the environment and (2) know the theory and principles, and general terminology relative to the environment. Let me prove it with the following two real examples:

Example 1: Controllership

This would be the actual section, group, or division of medium and larger banks or the equivalent phase of the bank's administration and operations under the direction of the bank's cashier in smaller institutions.

The reference book selected is *Controllership: The Work of the Man-*

agerial Accountant—3rd edition, written by James D. Willson and John B. Campbell, published in 1981 by Ronald Press Co., a subsidiary of John Wiley & Sons. Now, let's consider what in the book should be read and understood by the risk-oriented internal auditor:

Chapter 1: Accounting and its Relation to Management

Subheadings:

(a) The Business Objective.

(b) The Management Task.

(c) An Enlightened Philosophy of Management.

(d) Complexities of Management Greatly Increased.

(e) Managerial Skill Essential.

(f) Accounting as an Aid to Management.

(g) Business and National Economic Goals.

(h) The Management Process:

- Planning
- Organizing (including proper staffing)
- Directing and
- Measuring

(i) Measuring Business Management.

(j) Accounting Information for Business Decisions.

Chapter 2: The Controllership Function

Subheadings:

(a) Evolution in Duties of Financial Executives.

(b) An Essential to the Function.

(c) Various Titles Applied to Position.

(d) Controllership Principles Applicable to All Types and Sizes of Concerns.

(e) Basic Controllership Functions:

- Planning
- Control
- Reporting
- Accounting and

179

- Other Primary Responsibilities (e.g., Taxes, Relationships with External and Internal Auditors, Insurance Coverage; Maintain Systems and Procedures; Records Retention Programs; Investor and Financial Public Relations Programs; and other Assigned Functions)

(f) The Planning Function.

(g) The Control Function.

(h) The Reporting Function.

(i) The Accounting Function.

(j) A More Detailed List of Functions.

(k) Organizational Status.

(l) Source of Controller's Authority.

(m) Specific Responsibilities.

(n) Characteristics of the Controllership Task.

(o) Qualifications of the Controller.

Chapter 3: Organization Structure for Effective Controllership

Subheadings:

(a) Organizing for Control.

(b) Typical Organizational Problems for the Controller.

(c) Typical Organizational Structure for Controller's Department.

(d) A Centralized vs. Decentralized Accounting Organization.

(e) Delegation of Responsibility and Authority.

(f) The Controller's Authority over Accounting and Statistical Activities.

Chapter 4: Accounting Principles and Practices

Subheadings:

(a) Generally Accepted Accounting Principles.

(b) Development of Accounting Principles.

(c) Financial Accounting Standards Board (FASB).

(d) Changing Accounting Principles and Practices.

(e) Conceptual Framework.

(f) Statements of Financial Accounting Concepts.

(g) Other Accounting Organizations.

Chapter 5: Role of the Computer in Business and in Financial Analysis

Subheadings:

(a) A New Environment.

(b) A Planning and Control Overview.

(c) Role of the Controller.

(d) Computer Applications.

(e) Corporate Models.

(f) Financial Planning Models.

(g) Components of Financial Models.

(h) Sensitivity Analysis.

(i) Distributed Systems.

(j) Security, Confidentiality, and the Computer.

(k) The Computer and the Management Reporting System.

The reference book has a total of 39 chapters but from the five chapters for which the subheadings are detailed, the internal auditor will understand the theory and principle relative to the controllership environment.

The three factors indicated for controllership can be viewed as follows:

1. Knowing the Business and the Specific Authority and Responsibilities of Controller

2. Knowing the General Goals and Objective of the Controller Environment

3. Understanding the Theory and Principles Relative to Controller Environment

Example 2: Cash Management

This would be the range of services offered to client or potential client organizations on cash management. Internally, this involves the loan or contact officer promoting use of the bank's cash management services; the cash management consultant, who assesses the client or potential client treasury function and recommends which cash management services should help them by *(a)* increasing availability of funds, *(b)* clearing deposits so that available funds are maximized, and *(c)* supplemental services such as lockbox and other collection systems or money movement systems, either for getting payments from customers or making payments to customers, usually the other party being in another country, although possibly used domestically but not with quite the same *time* advantages; and the operations people who man the various cash management services. It could be viewed as:

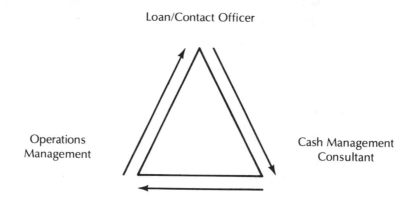

Loan/Contact Officer

Operations Management

Cash Management Consultant

The reference book selected is *Cash Management,* by John M. Kelly and published in 1986 by Franklin Watts. Here's what should be read and understood by the risk-oriented internal auditor:

Chapter 1: Laying the Groundwork for Cash Management
Subheadings:
(a) Introduction.
(b) Cash Management at Work.
Chapter 2: The Goals and Importance of Cash Management
Subheadings:

(a) Introduction.

(b) The Cost of Cash.

(c) The Banking Environment.

(d) What is Cash Management?

(e) The Goals of Cash Management:

- Liquidity.

- Earnings.

(f) Using Cash as a Resource.

(g) Integration with Operations.

(h) Customizing Cash Management.

Chapter 3: Preparing a Cash Forecast:

Subheadings:

(a) Introduction.

(b) The Elements of Cash Forecasting.

(c) Formulating the Forecast.

(d) The Long-Term Cash Forecast.

(e) The Adjusted Net Income Technique.

- Estimate net income for the period.

- Adjust for noncash items.

- Add other sources of funds.

- Estimate the total outflow of funds.

- Calculate the increase or decrease in working capital.

- Analyze the components of working capital.

(f) Intermediate-Term Cash Forecasting.

(g) Cash Thinking.

(h) Goals of Intermediate Forecasts.

(i) The Cash Receipts/Disbursements Technique.

(j) Short-Term Cash Forecasting.

(k) Developing the Short-Term Forecast.

(l) Computerized Forecasting Models.

Chapter 4: Analyzing the Concept of Float

Subheadings:

(a) Introduction.

(b) A Banking System in Action.

(c) Assessing the Implications of Float.

(d) Calculating Marginal Interest.

(e) Float in International Cash Management.

(f) The Cash Cycle.

Chapter 5: Utilizing Proven Collection Techniques

Subheadings:

(a) Introduction.

(b) Analyzing Collections.

(c) Lockbox Banking.

(d) Economies of a Lockbox.

(e) Drawbacks to Lockboxes.

(f) Lockbox Evaluation.

(g) Using Preauthorized Checks.

(h) Special Handling.

(i) Accounts Receivable Processing.

(j) Other Collection Improvement Techniques.

Chapter 6: Cash Concentration Techniques

Subheadings:

(a) Introduction.

(b) Advantages of Cash Concentration.

(c) Concentration Strategies.

(d) Depository Transfer Check.

(e) Wire Transfer.

(f) Economy and Timing.

(g) The Company as Banker.

The reference book has 16 chapters, but from the 6 chapters listed, the internal auditor will understand the theory and principle of cash management environment.

In summary, the skills required of the risk-oriented internal auditor are:

1. The traditional education, training, and knowledge expected of an experienced internal auditor who can do *(a)* operational, *(b)* management-oriented, and *(c)* special audits up to and including fraud reviews.

2. The capability to think like an owner who is reviewing or having a review done by qualified personnel with the managerial competency and fulfillment of those responsibilities assigned to the manager and performed by him and his subordinates.

3. The curiosity to identify *risks* and to put them into perspective as to their probability (e.g., frequency and amount per incident). To do so in any audit environment, the auditor must first have a reasonable knowledge of risk, which is indicated by the two examples provided, or personal experience of functioning in such an environment or using a specialist or consultant.

All of the skills combined are needed by risk-oriented internal auditors to function properly.

It is important for the risk-oriented internal auditors to recognize the limit of their capabilities in any audit environment even if they have followed the steps under points 1 through 3. In addition to the use of specialists/consultants in specific audit environment where high-risks are assumed, based on a "tip" and/or audit review findings, all skills must be used. That would include any or all of the specific skills of the CHARLES team, to supplement and assist the auditors where possible. The risk-oriented internal auditor also should have the freedom to bring in valued, outside skills needed in a specific audit environment (e.g., real estate: independent appraisers; credit: use of qualified personnel of the bank's credit committee; abuse of rank/authority/responsibility: chairman or his designate, except where that officer may be involved in the audit matters or the bank's audit committee, or a designated member, whose authority enables the risk-oriented internal auditor to review and evaluate the actions of all bank officials). Obviously, the risk-oriented internal auditor must be prudent when exercising the primary level of support. Consider the use of support personnel as follows:

- Tertiary: Use of any or all of the staff support functions of the CHARLES team or other internal personnel (e.g., credit specialists—loan review or officials from the bank's credit committee).

185

- Secondary: Use of outside support personnel (e.g., experts in specific areas—engineers; real estate appraisers; investigative agencies; Dun & Bradstreet or similar services to perform background checks on employees at any level, usually with focus on such special concerns as drug or alcohol use, personal conduct inappropriate for bank personnel such as pornography, and particularly child pornography, and gambling debts incurred by persons being investigated).

- Primary: Use of power of chairman and/or members of audit committee of board of directors. This is the option of last resort.

Risk-oriented internal auditors should be competent in the following *critical* interpersonal skills areas:

1. Effective interviewing.

2. Effective listening.

3. Effective interrogation.

Let us briefly define those terms:

EFFECTIVE. "Producing a decided, decisive, or desired effect."[190]

INTERVIEW. "A meeting at which information is obtained."[191]

LISTENING. "To hear something with thoughtful attention."[192]

INTERROGATE. "To question formally and systematically. . . . To give or send out a signal . . . for triggering an appropriate response."[193]

Most auditors of the staff accountant or semisenior level are mechanics when it comes to effective interviewing or effective listening. Give them a list of questions to ask or have them prepare a list, which you, as their superior, revise to cover the primary points and some supplemental points that you want answered in the audit to be undertaken or in progress. The auditors will come back with answers but they forget that accurate and complete answers are desired, *not just answers*. One should not assume the interviewee is totally honest, or totally unaware of any deficiencies in the area you are asking him about. Experienced officers or supervisors in the environment have been through audit interviews before and know pretty much what answers the interviewer *wants to hear*. As a result, they respond in a way that will satisfy the interviewer and enable them to get back to

---

[190]Webster's *Ninth New Collegiate Dictionary, op. cit.,* p. 397.

[191]*Ibid.,* p. 633.

[192]*Ibid.,* p. 697.

[193]*Ibid.,* p. 633.

work as quickly as possible. The auditor forgets what I jokingly refer to as (1) the Jack Webb syndrome of TV's "Dragnet" fame; and (2) the Missouri syndrome. Restated, first it is "get the facts," which means the auditor has to probe and ask "what if" or "could this happen" type of questions, supplementing the original questions so that, in the end, the auditor feels that (i) interviewees know what they are talking about and (ii) the answers, considered together, leave the auditor reasonably confident that he understands what is going on, relative to the audited area. Second, it is "show me," which means the auditor requires the interviewee to take him to where things are being done, or show him how information is processed or entered into a computer system, how records are controlled through the environment and how systems are controlled. Too often, the inexperienced auditor merely takes what the interviewee tells him, with no effort made to assure that he "got the facts" or confirmed what he heard by seeing for himself. The auditor may be more interested in completing the interview in an allotted time, getting *an answer* for every question but not making sure the responses are complete and correct.

Unfortunately, slipshod questioning leaves the auditor vulnerable to (1) the supervisor or manager who wants to mislead the auditor with partial, incomplete, or totally incorrect answers, and (2) the supervisor or manager who believes they have given an honest response but have not in one or more of their responses because practices have arisen of which they are unaware.

The more experienced auditor is usually better at (1) getting the facts as Jack Webb did and (2) seeing what is going on as in Missouri the "show me" state. Both must be done to assure that the auditor is working with sound information in conducting fieldwork and assessing the adequacy of systems and procedures (e.g., the 3-Es, efficiency, effectiveness, and economy, and 3-Cs, character, capacity, and capital). Unfortunately, even the more experienced auditor seems to be overly conscious of time while at an interview. As a result, many interviews do not give the auditor what they might on questionable or improper practices. The auditor hears what he expects to hear and does not listen well to comments of the interviewee. Further, when the interviewee makes a statement that does not truly focus on the question but indicates strange or questionable practices interrelated to the audited area, the auditor doesn't catch it and, naturally, does not ask follow-up questions to develop more information on a potentially odd or questionable practice.

It is vital for the auditor to come to the interview with a list of questions, but that is only the "alpha" part of the interview. In addition to answers to the "alpha" questions, the auditor should be listen-

187

ing carefully to the answers of the interviewee that might (1) result in further questioning when unexpected information arises or (2) take the interview down a totally unplanned avenue based on unusual information given by the interviewee. The extensions of the originally planned scope of the interview, as in points (1) and (2), quite often develop into more meaningful information than responses coming from the original list of questions. However, only effective *listening* will pick up on the interviewee's statements, bringing the supplemental questions, as under points (1) and (2). This interview approach is called "flexible." The "rigid" approach is merely getting answers, whether correct or not, to the list of questions the auditor came with, nothing more or nothing less. The flexible approach only will be successful when the auditor (1) is a good listener and picks up on leads for further questioining; or (2) has a secondary list of questions designed to supplement the primary list, from which the auditor will "cherry pick" those related to comments of the interviewee. A good interviewer is prepared to use these supplemental questions, when appropriate, based on responses to the primary questions. Most of the secondary questions are concerned with risks or possible risks, relative to the audit environment. Getting-the-facts and show-me factors are equally important in the secondary questioning as in the primary.

Because the auditor is prepared to (1) follow up with secondary questions, as appropriate, or (2) follow up on points raised by the interviewee's responses, time for the interview must be such that either point (1) and/or point (2) matters are given appropriate time. If none is used during the interview, it should be completed in less than the scheduled time.

Since experienced supervisors and officers know auditors are always fighting the clock, some will quite cleverly use as much time as possible discussing anything but the questions that the interviewer plans to ask (e.g., family, home, favorite sports, change in approach being followed by internal auditor—risk-oriented as against "financial" auditing). While casual banter is a means of breaking the ice and relaxing the interviewee, it should be limited. The interviewee should not be permitted to control the interview. Nonetheless, some high-level executives might attempt to do so. However, the auditor *must* control the interview!

Let us summarize the criteria for an effective interview:

1. Adequate time should be allotted to cover all of the primary questions, as well as secondary questions and/or leads from statements of the interviewee. They should be followed up appropriately.

2. The objectives of the interview should be stated at the beginning. Spend a few minutes breaking the ice with general conversation before getting to the interview. Once into the interview, distractions or efforts to revert to casual conversation must be avoided. Insist that "we will have to stay at this until I have developed the information needed."

3. At his discretion, the interviewer should choose when he wants more facts or when he wants to see something. He should not let the interviewee show him records or anything else that may keep the auditor from following up what he desires to pursue. Let interviewees show whatever they want but don't let that influence your decision in selecting what additional information you want or decide to see in a specific function or activity in the audited environment.

4. Go to the interview with both a primary and secondary list of questions. The latter should be used when appropriate (e.g., the answer to the primary questions did not provide details wanted or probably did not approach the subject from the truly desired direction).

5. Be a good listener and pick up on leads provided by the answers that make you want to learn more about something the interviewee said or implied, not covered in either your primary or secondary questions.

6. Be sure your approach to the interview is flexible so *(a)* you can take matters further than originally planned when appropriate, or *(b)* you can reduce the scope, because answers to one question may have, in fact, answered two or more questions.

7. Conduct the questioning in a relaxed and friendly manner. On occasion, you will encounter a difficult interviewee but you must persist until you are satisfied that all questions are answered and confident the responses are accurate. The interviewee knows your authority, responsibility, and mandate so you only have to exert or state your intent to the difficult interviewee.

8. Review at the end of the interview the sensitive points you want the interviewee to confirm. (*Note:* Some auditors advocate asking the interviewee to permit a taped interview. This may be useful in the adversarial environment of an interrogation, but it may work against you because the interviewee becomes overly careful in answering questions. In such instances, this carefulness in responding also will assuredly result in less "side" leads

or statements that you would want to follow up on because the answers will be shorter and mored carefully worded).

The interview approach described involves primary and secondary questions prepared in advance. The interviewer should include "bait" questions that are deliberate efforts to get the interviewee to change a previous answer. Along with bait questions, quick secondary questions should be ready when the interviewee takes the bait. Somewhat similar to the bait question is the follow up on leads exposed unintentionally by the interviewee. Leads also warrant quick follow-up questions. This type of interviewing is known as the "behavioral analysis" approach.

Information has been developed in interviews, and audit fieldwork, where incorrect statements were found relating to the audit environment. In this event, psychological testing generally has replaced polygraph testing. And we will discuss that as the next level of personal information development. I have always had more confidence in psychological testing than in the polygraph. Why? Because on occasion, I have seen the polygraph used improperly as a substitute for sound fraud auditing techniques. For example, a major bank, incurring a low, seven-figure loss, had a general auditor, who had been demoted to that post from comptroller, where he headed the comptroller's loan review and internal audit functions when the organization was restructured into three separate departments. He had no public accounting or internal audit experience. Operational deficiencies reported in the fraud environment had not been pursued by the general auditor to correct the situation, as recommended by one of his group heads and subordinates. That action at a low cost would have made the fraud that was perpetrated virtually impossible. After the fraud occurred, instead of initiating sound, fraud-audit procedures in reviewing the situation, he relied on the polygraph to find the fraud perpetrators or persons who knew what had happened. Fifty clerks, supervisors, and officers were ordered to take polygraph tests. When those were unsuccessful, he ordered another 50 and, finally, a third group of 50 underwent polygraph tests. No one was identified as a perpetrator of the fraud. The "fishing expedition" resulted in bad will toward auditing and some key employees resigned.

Some of the 150 persons who were tested were required to take a second, and, in some instances, even a third polygraph. Again, these tests did not prove anything. The audit tests conducted while this was going on were limited and provided little insight on who stole the money. The operational risks had been identified in several earlier audit reports, but the general auditor did not use his clout to make the recommended corrective actions.

The psychological tests, given in a far less adversarial mode than a polygraph test, always have reduced negative side effects of abuse and misuse of polygraph tests. Also, if five or six selected persons had been identified by logical and sound fraud-audit techniques as the possible fraud perpetrators or turned up leads as to whom they were, then, based on the conclusions of the psychologist, who evaluated the tests, the number of persons who should have been interrogated could have been reduced by at least one-half. However, test results in some instances could indicate that the auditors have not identified anyone who should be interrogated. In such cases, the audit should be expanded. At some later point in the reviews, if others are identified who have perpetrated or have knowledge of perpetrators, they should undergo the psychological testing. Psychological testing should never be a "fishing expedition." A valid audit reason must be given for selecting people in a fraud situation for psychological testing.

Where audit and psychological test findings clearly identify persons suspected of fraud or knowing about a fraud, interrogation is quite proper.

In interrogation, the approach is confrontational and accusatory. Unlike interviewing, *you* do most of the talking in an interrogation. Good interrogation is a sort of psychological *tour de force*. It calls for extremely subtle ploys.

In an interview, you normally conduct it on their turf, preferably in a conference room to minimize interruptions, which inevitably occur in their offices. If you must, you can hold it in their office. In an interrogation, you *do not* hold it on their turf! Use your own office, a conference room, or another neutral site. During an interrogation, you always address people by their first name (e.g., Bill, Jane), never by last name or rank. This is to keep the suspect ever so subtly from taking control.

Place yourself face-to-face with the suspect, only a few feet apart. If possible, nothing (no desk or table or other object) should be between you. Seat yourself between the suspect and the exit. Obviously, that is most effective in a room with only one door. The objective is to make the suspect feel hemmed in, and that the only way out is a confession.

So the suspect has to concentrate on you, try to pick a room with no windows, no phone (or disconnect the phone) and where no one will enter the room accidently to break the mood. In some instances, I have positioned an associate outside the door to prevent interruptions, but with the assistant not taking that position until after the suspect and I have entered the room. If a third person (e.g., a union representative, the individual's attorney, or an attorney working with you) must be present, ask that they do not speak and are seated slightly behind the suspect so they won't cause any visual distraction. If the suspect attempts to break the tension by getting up, pacing, or interrupting you, demand that he or she be seated and not interrupt.

Begin your interrogation with a direct accusation of guilt (e.g., "Our investigation indicates you deliberately turned your back, thus failing to fulfill your control duties, thereby enabling the fraud to occur" or "Our investigation indicates you took the money"). You must be trained in and always conscious of the suspect's body language and verbal responses (e.g., swift and angry; persistent; rationalizations).

Swift and angry responses or rationalizations could be signs you have the right person, and you should pursue the interrogation strongly. Persistent and controlled responses could indicate you have the wrong person. Then you must decide whether to pursue the matter or shift gears and attack from a different angle (e.g., from indicating he or she is the perpetrator *to* indicating he or she knows who the perpetrator is).

Psychologists say the strong opening accusation will result normally in weak or evasive answers (e.g., "Who me?" "How could I have done that?"). Such guilt-oriented responses are *green lights* to go ahead with your train of questioning. Then you seek reasons for making it easier for a confession (e.g., "The theft was no big deal, everybody does it"; "You must have needed the money for family problems; someone must have been seriously ill"). The fact that a number of themes or approaches can be tried on a suspect does not mean they should be. The objective is to find a theme to which the suspect's responses make you feel you are heading in the right direction; then develop that theme. If you have the guilty party, you ultimately may receive disconsolate, crestfallen admissions to what you are asking. Often, that is the beginning of a confession. You may be only a question or moment away from the point where you ask a witness to come in, such as a bank attorney or the auditor guarding the room. Then you ask the suspect to sign a statement or confession. Be sure to sharpen your questions on a specific topic when the response or body language signals you to do so.

Things you *imply* to the suspects may help persuade them to go along with you. The key word is *imply*. You must *not* state the ideas as facts. If that is done it could negate the confession obtained from suspects when legal actions are initiated. For example, you can *imply* you have been in positions similar to theirs (e.g., "I can relate to what you're going through"). That may convince them of your sympathy. Most importantly, you may *imply* that their confession *may* help them, though that usually is not the case.

Here is a summary of the preceding discussion.

1. Interviews (Psychological and Behavior Symptom Analysis)

    (a) Each question should address specifically the primary issue.

    (b) Ask questions in a casual not challenging manner.

    (c) Observe casually behavioral reaction (nonverbal).

    (d) Meet the person initially with *(a)* greeting, *(b)* clerical information, and *(c)*, where sufficiently sensitive, indicate Miranda warning; although, in my opinion, this is more appropriate in interrogation.

    (e) Make a history of objectives of interview.

    (f) Determine motive of interview.

    (g) Indicate situation and persons under suspicion.

    (h) Make suspect think about situation, indicating possible punishment. (Again, my experience places this tactic in the interrogation and not the interview mode.)

    (i) Indicate possible psychological testing, if audit findings do not confirm statements made by interviewee. (Personally, I tend to withhold this comment till the end and ask whether the interviewee wishes to change or enhance any of the answers.)

    (j) Be sure "bait" questions are included in lists of primary and secondary questions. Follow up where answers are inconsistent.

2. Interrogations

    (a) Direct positive confrontation.

    (b) Develop theme.

    (c) Observe body language constantly and note tone of verbal responses.

    (d) Handle denials by pursuing them as far as appropriate.

    (e) Overcome objections by reacting to them and indicating the implications are different than the words said.

    (f) Maintain suspect's attention.

    (g) Press forward when suspect gets passive; this could be sign of guilt.

    (h) Be prepared with alternate questions (e.g., Plan "B," when Plan "A" fails).

(*i*) Strive for verbal confession and attempt to have it put into writing.

Two of the "Seven Attributes of an Internal Auditor" are *curiosity* and a *constructive approach*. To communicate audit findings effectively, the internal auditor must use all of the tools available. They include *traditional* tools as well as *imaginative* tools. Let us consider some in each category:

1. Traditional Audit Tools

   (*a*) Using the flow chart: "Flow charting [sic] is a technique that uses graphic symbols and brief phrases to describe a series of steps in a given operation. It may represent document flow or the flow of logic required to complete a task. Flow charting is useful to the auditor in systems analysis, and it is essential in documenting any systems analysis and design or programming activities."[194]

   (*b*) Cycle Auditing: "The concept of dividing banking activity into cycles."[195] The most usual division being the following cycles:
   - Treasury.
   - Payroll Expenditure.
   - Trust.
   - Deposit.
   - Loan.
   - Nonpayroll Expenditure.
   - Financial Reporting.
   - Investment.

   The concept focuses on economic events that are factual happenings. Each cycle follows the format below:
   - Authorization.
   - Transaction processing.
   - Classification.
   - Substantiation.
   - Evaluation.
   - Physical safeguards.

   The intent is to assure integrity of information and its completeness as well as the internal controls and checks in processing each economic event.

---

[194]Jeffrey S. Seglin. *Bank Administration Manual.* (Rolling Meadows, Ill.: Bank Administration Institute, 1988), p. 184.
[195]*A Guide for Studying and Evaluating Internal Accounting Controls—Banking.* (Chicago: Arthur Andersen, 1980), p. 7.

(c) Professional Requirements for Evaluating and Reporting on Internal Accounting Control (SAS No. 1, Section 320.01): "Under the profession's standards, auditors first review a company's system of internal accounting control and make an evaluation of it. Based on the evaluation, they determine whether to perform functional (compliance) tests of internal accounting controls, or to proceed directly to the validation (substantive) testing of account balances. If the evaluation of internal accounting controls indicates that a control procedure has been established, the auditor has the option of functionally testing the control to gain reasonable assurance that the procedure is in effect, is operating as prescribed, and can be expected to continue to do so throughout the period under examination, and thus can appropriately reduce the validation testing of related account balances. If, on the other hand, the evaluation uncovers a control weakness, the auditor cannot rely on the control and has to select validation tests of the appropriate nature, extent, and timing to compensate for the control weakness, and apply them to the related account balances."[196] Revised and updated AICPA criteria on "Internal Control" are set forth in Appendix B of this book.

(d) Psychological Testing: Described earlier in this chapter.

(e) Interviewing: Described earlier in this chapter.

(f) Interrogation: Described earlier in this chapter.

2. Imaginative Audit Tools

(a) Cameras: Security would be responsible for administration relative to cameras used for security related purposes (e.g., at ATM locations; at lockbox rooms, so activities of employees can be monitored). The auditor, however, can use cameras to (1) make photos of facilities where the housekeeping or entry controls are not adequate, and (2) make photos of such other situations, where appropriate (e.g., ATM facilities where lights or cameras are not working; improper security at branches when armored trucks are making deliveries or pickups; or at records retention facilities). (*Note:* Video equipment use falls in this category.)

(b) Audio: Such as taping conversations where either controls

---

[196]Seidler and Carmichael, *Accountants' Handbook*, 6th ed. V. 1 (New York: Ronald Press, 1981), p. 10-3.

are explained or ongoing activities in a specific environment. Also can be used for interviews or interrogations, where deemed appropriate. Be sure to get legal advice as to (1) any restrictions placed on taping, or (2) what verbal permission must be obtained on the tape before recording an interview or interrogation. The auditor should never assume that any conversation can be taped without notice and/or authority, as appropriate.

(c) Testing

(1) In a noncomputer environment, process a number of either (i) selected valid transactions and/or (ii) created transactions to determine whether appropriate systems are operational and that all specified internal controls are in place and functioning to hold risks to the levels acceptable to management. The opening balance on any accounts affected, plus the impact of processing the transactions, should agree with a predetermined result. The entries under item (ii) would then be reversed to remove any impact on the general or subsidiary records.

(2) In a computer environment, the same approach as under items (i) and (ii) in paragraph (1) above should be processed following the same proof and balance approach indicated. Again, the internal controls must be validated as being in place and functioning as intended.

(d) Transaction Walk-Throughs

Follow a transaction from inception of the subject *economic event* through to its final destination on the general or subsidiary records and determine that adequate internal controls and checks are in place and functioning as intended to hold risks to the levels acceptable to management.

(e) Psychological Testing

Use this tool on new hires to determine competency and honesty. This testing also can be used on officerrs and staff to affirm competency and honesty when appropriate.

Summary

The risk-oriented internal auditor must be constantly trying to determine what can go wrong, who could be involved in wrongdoing, how could something go wrong, when could something go wrong, who would perpetrate the wrongdoing, where would the wrongdoing occur. The auditor must have put into place adequate controls and checks to insure that the internal procedures and processes will operate so that the risks and threats in doing business are held at the level accepted by management. Imagination is important. It is not satisfactory to let wrongful acts be detrimental to the institution. Actions must be taken to prevent wrongdoing. If the actions are unsuccessful, safeguards must be in place to provide an early warning of any irregularity. Finally, the seven stages of fraud auditing should be followed to uncover all aspects of wrongdoing. All of the preventive and early warning methodology must be cost efficient, except in the most extraordinary situations, when some specific control(s) may be only marginally inefficient but, with the overall control environment cost efficient. Finally, the auditor's imagination, heightened by curiosity, must be stirred continually in normal reviews so they can be expanded when conditions warrant.

13

The Internal Auditor as Consultant

In *Elements of Management-Oriented Auditing,* by Lawrence B. Sawyer, and published by The Institute of Internal Auditors Inc., he writes:

> "I see the internal auditor as an internal consultant, not as an internal adversary. Not a cop on the beat but a guest in the house. Not merely a searcher for errors, large or small, but a guide to improved operations . . . . "

What exactly is internal audit consulting? Management has a responsibility of controlling business risks, which can be separated into *(a)* operating risks and *(b)* financial information risks.

Operating risk refers to optimizing efficiency, effectiveness, and economy of producing and delivering a product or service. The objective is to generate the greatest return on investment (ROI) possible for the institution.

Financial information risk concerns that related to internal and external financial information and accurate reports that can be relied on for business decisions (e.g., internal: strategic planning, budgeting, performance evaluation; credit decisions, credit exposure, decisions to extend or reject requests for credit, or decisions relative to financing of acquisitions either for the institution or clients).

Internal audit consulting can be separated into the following four services (1) consultation, (2) quality assurance reviews, (3) manpower, and (4) contract/replacement. Their descriptions follow.

1. Consultation Services

   This consists of such things as:

   (a) Start-up of an internal audit function.

   (b) Conversion of a financial internal audit function into a risk-oriented operational internal audit function.

   (c) Identification of major business risk areas for (i) internal audit review and/or (ii) management action.

   (d) Specification of management missions (e.g., strategic planning or budgeting and evaluation of economic feasibility for current or planned products, services, or facilities).

   (e) Review and assessment of existing policies and procedures and recommended changes to improve them.

    (f) Review and evaluation of policy and procedure to draft instructions before issuance and implementation.

    (g) Formalization of communication procedures and report writing formats for the internal audit function.

2. Quality Assurance Reviews

This consists of such things as:

    (a) Internal audit reviewing the organization, administrative, and operational procedures and practices, and training and evaluating whether management is satisfied with the performance of a given division, group, department, facility, or entity.

    (b) Assisting personnel doing a review, such as under point 2*(a)* of the internal audit function. Such reviews should evaluate the functions in terms of The Institute of Internal Auditor's *Standards for the Professional Practice of Internal Auditing*. Section 560.04 states:

> "External review of the internal auditing department should be performed to appraise the quality of the department's operations. These reviews should be performed by qualified persons who are independent of the organization and who do not have either a real or an apparent conflict of interest. Such reviews should be conducted at least once every three years. On completion of the review, a formal, written report should be issued. The report should express an opinion as to the department's compliance with the *Standards for the Professional Practice of Internal Auditing* and, as appropriate, should include recommendations for improvement."

3. Manpower Services

Such services consist of providing personnel:

    (a) From internal audit on a short-term basis to help deal with serious audits in other areas.

    (b) From other areas to help internal audit by providing expertise to complete specific tasks the function does not have time to conduct.

4. Contract Audit Services

This consists of public accountants taking over the responsibilities of the internal audit department on a contract basis or performing a specific function (e.g., EDP auditing) on a project basis. When undertaking such duties, the external auditor must be aware of the quality control policies recommended by The Institute of Internal Auditors Inc.

This *will be* a high-focus area for some of the larger public accounting firms as they strive to increase the profitability of audit functions to that more comparable with their tax and consulting functions. However, the one question to be resolved is:

Can a public accounting firm provide the independent personnel to direct and perform internal audit responsibilities for an audit client?

The same question exists regarding public accountants auditing a computer system or program developed by the consulting area of their firm. Some experts argue that the question of independence has not been resolved. There is, however, no question that a specific public accounting firm can direct and perform internal audit responsibilities for a nonaudit client.

Sawyer in his IIA publication *Elements of Management-Oriented Auditing,* contends that internal auditors are "not accounting-oriented tickers and checkers under the domination of external auditors, the professional accountants, but [are] members of a completely distinctive discipline. [They are] no longer junior siblings of other professions but professionals in their own right."

Because the audit function of public accounting has, as some people contend, become almost a commodity in that firms seek a certification that can be relied on by investors, creditors, or depositors and the marketplace, public accountants are striving to improve profitability in that area. The internal auditor, however, must be aware of the potential threat to their position or the discipline of "internal auditing as a profession" because public accountants are making intrusions on internal auditing. In some instances, particularly with EDP auditors, public accountants will take personnel from the internal audit function where they contract to provide internal audit services.

On the other hand, the internal audit function of a parent organization can contract to *(a)* provide on-site local audit personnel to affiliates and subsidiaries and *(b)* perform routine internal audit reviews on a broad risk-oriented operational auditing format for affiliates and subsidiaries, either as a parent company directive or on a contract basis.

For those who have no fear of public accountants displacing the full-time employees of internal audit, let me say that they will compete on the basis of:

1. Experience.

2. Reputation.

3. Knowledge of the business and industry.

4. Cost.

No one should be surprised with points 1 through 3. However point 4 may be somewhat surprising. Recognize that staffing may be made up of a mix of full-time personnel, exclusively devoted to internal audit contracted services, and they will be supplemented from time-to-time by personnel who normally perform public accounting reviews but *not* at the specific firm where they would be assigned as internal auditors. That could be a conflict of interest.

Recognize also that any income generated from public accounting personnel when working under contract as internal auditors can be classified as "contribution margin" or "marginal income." The *Handbook of Cost Accounting*, edited by Sidney Davidson and Roman Weil, and published in 1978 by McGraw-Hill Book Co. is defined as "the excess of sales price over variable expense." Hours not chargeable to specific public accounting audit assignments or for required training could be considered as "variable expense" that has to be applied against revenues generated from time charged to clients, with training time also offset against such revenues. When viewed from this perspective, public accountants clearly are able to meet or beat the direct cost of full-time internal audit personnel. They also have back-up personnel available in times of vacation or illness to replace someone assigned to a contract internal auditor and can call on people with specific skills (e.g., consultants, EDP experts) when needed.

Summary

The internal auditor acting in the capacity of *internal consultant* can be of service in any way that the skills, experience, and competency of the personnel in the function will permit them to be of assistance to management. This assistance can include *(a)* profit-improvement programs, *(b)* efficiency evaluation (e.g., operations analysis procedures, *(c)* merger and acquisition deals, *(d)* economic feasibility (e.g., whether to get into specific products and services or whether existing products, services, or facilities can pay their own way, and *(e)* any other projects assigned to them by the board of directors and/or senior management.

14

Techniques and Approaches

Computers

1. Transaction Processing:

    (a) "A series of processing steps that result in a specific function or activity being completed. With respect to real-time systems, the term 'transaction' generally refers to a number of interactions between a terminal operator and the computer. The result of these interactions is usually the addition, deletion, or change of a single record or group of records in a file or data base. However, a transaction may be set up for displaying information, without changing it in some way" such as "a single interaction with a computer system. For example, sending a message between a computer and a remote terminal . . . . As a general term, any series of procedures that accomplishes a task . . ."[197]

2. Transaction File:

    (a) "A file that contains the results of a series of data processing transactions that have occurred over a period of time. A transaction file normally is used to update periodically a master file. A typical transaction in a transaction file is a record of each payment by a company's customers during a given month. Synonymous with Update File. The term 'transaction file' is often used as a synonym for the term 'detail file.' "[198]

3. Control (Processing):

    (a) "Within a computer system, instructions that control activities or a sequence of events. Control may imply manual intervention to 'override' computer-controlled activities."[199]

    (b) "Generally, a manual check over computer processing. For example, a user might manually determine a total count

---

[197]Robert A. Edmunds. *The Prentice-Hall Standard Glossary of Computer Terminology.* (Englewood Cliffs, N.J.: Prentice-Hall, 1984), p. 455.
[198]*Ibid.,* p. 455.
[199]*Ibid.,* p. 97.

of a number of records to be processed by the computer to check that all records were processed."[200]

4. Control File:

"A computerized file designed specifically for 'controlling' functions as opposed to a file designed to hold data for processing. A control file is used to hold information about processing that was done on data after a computer's processing run has been completed."[201]

5. Control System: "Synonymous with closed-loop system."[202]

6. Closed-Loop System: "A computer system with a feedback type of control. The output of the system is used to modify the input."[203]

7. Control Objective: "The objective of every control should be to prevent an undesired event from occurring, and/or contain the impact of an undesired event to a predefined level of tolerability."[204]

8. Control Function: "A control function defines how the control meets its objective."[205] Optimally, a control should:

    (a) "Deter intentional attempts to compromise the control.

    (b) "Detect an intentional or unintentional act or event that the control seeks to prevent.

    (c) "Prevent the undesired action or event from occurring.

    (d) "Notify an appropriate function that the undesired event or action has been attempted or has occurred.

    (e) "Provide an audit trail."[206]

9. Application Controls: These "are the manual and computer processing procedures that either prevent or limit the impact of an undesired event from occurring. They also verify the performance of a function as intended by management within an application program or system. An alternative term of an application control is a basic control."[207]

---

[200]*Ibid.*, p. 97.

[201]*Ibid.*, p. 98.

[202]*Ibid.*, p. 100.

[203]*Ibid.*, p. 74.

[204]Rolf T. Moulton, *Strategies and Techniques for Preventing Data Loss or Theft.* (Prentice-Hall, 1986), p. 15.

[205]*Ibid.*, p. 16.

[206]*Ibid.*, p. 16.

[207]*Ibid.*, p. 17.

10. System Controls: They "are those manual and computer processing procedures that protect the application controls from being compromised. The term integrity control may be used synonymously with system control. System controls are the joint responsibility of the EDP department and the application system manager."[208]

11. Compensating Controls: They "are those procedures (manual or computerized) that offset the need to have a control at the particular point during the processing cycle. In . . . payroll examples . . . , the clerk may have also checked for the completeness of information on each time card that was submitted. This task could have been performed at a later time, after the data was [put into] the computer, by the application program. The absence of the manual control would have then been compensated for by the presence of a computer program procedure control."[209]

12. Network: "A widely used term that applies to any type of computer system or communications system that involves the use of more than one component. The term 'network' can apply to the group of components themselves, such as computers, controllers, terminals, and printers, together with the communications channel, which links them all together."[210]

13. Systems Security (Computer System): "Those procedures necessary to protect a computer system, including its related software, from damage, destruction, malfunction, or unauthorized access. System security includes such techniques as: *(a)* the provision of backup, recovery, and restoration facilities; *(b)* provision of alternative resources in the event of a disaster; and *(c)* protection of data through such techniques as password protection and encryption. The matter of privacy is a related concern."[211]

14. Privacy (Data Security): "The concept that information should not be made accessible to unauthorized people. The issue of privacy is more important because of the general trend toward maintaining information on individual citizens

---

[208]*Ibid.*, p. 17.
[209]*Ibid.*, p. 19.
[210]Edmunds, *op. cit.*, p. 294.
[211]*Ibid.*, p. 434.

within large computer systems and the relative ease with which that information can be made available."[212]

15. Data Privacy: "Synonymous with privacy."[213]

16. Test Plan: "A formal, written document that contains the procedures for testing a program or computer system."[214]

17. Test Data: "Data that is created purely for the purpose of testing a program or a computer system. Test data is often 'extracted' from real data, usually selected from a larger file or data base. Test data will often be set up to contain deliberate errors or in such a way that the expected results of the test will be known in advance."[215]

18. Auditing Through the Computer: "The sophistication of computers eventually reached the point where auditors could no longer audit around the system. They were forced to treat the computer as the target of the audit and audit 'through it.' Auditing through the computer requires that the auditor submit data to the computer for processing. The results are then analyzed for the processing reliability and accuracy of the computer program. Technology and other developments that require this approach include:

- On-line data entry. In some systems, customer orders are received by phone and entered directly into the system with cathode-ray tube input devices. No source documents are created. The auditor cannot trace from source documents to output. The auditor is forced to enter the system to determine the reliability and accuracy of controls and processing.

- Elimination or reduction of printouts. With on-line direct inquiry and reports prepared only on an exception basis, printouts may not be available to trace transactions. The auditor is again forced to enter the system to determine the accuracy of processing and contents of files.

- Real-time file updating. With real-time file updating, transactions are posted as soon as they occur. A printout supplied to the auditor showing the content of such files

---

[212]*Ibid.*, p. 340.
[213]*Ibid.*, p. 118.
[214]*Ibid.*, p. 446.
[215]Watne and Turney. *Auditing EDP Systems.* (Englewood Cliffs, N.J.: Prentice-Hall, 1984), p. 14.

may not be accurate even for an instant. This is because by the time the printer is halfway through the file listing balances, those at the beginning may already have changed. The auditor is again forced to enter the system to perform the audit.

"In addition to technological and other developments that forced the auditor to use the computer system in the performance of the audit, some auditors decided to audit through the system for the following reasons:

- An inability to locate the source documents or printouts because of the filing system used.

- An apprehension that the amounts shown on the computer printouts might not agree with the balances actually contained in the computer files."[216]

Considerations in Testing Internal Controls

The risk-oriented internal auditor must test constantly the internal controls of a computer environment. The tests do the following:

1. Assess adequacy, in theory, of the system of internal control.

2. Assess compliance in implementation of the system of internal control as under point 1 above.

3. Determine:

   (a) Whether situations of noncompliance under point 2 and requirements under point 1, have worked at cross-purposes on the desired control level and as a result have increased risks in computer environment.

   (b) What action(s) are required to bring risks in the computer environment down to acceptable levels, through strict compliance with requirements as now stipulated and/or by enhancing or modifying current controls.

4. Enable management to give auditing unlimited scope in determining what reviews are appropriate to test the computer systems and environments.

The review scope, as under point 4 must deal effectively with each of the following:

---

[216]Javier Kuong. *Computer Auditing, Security, and Internal Control Manual.* (Englewood Cliffs, N.J.: Prentice-Hall, 1987), p. 9.

- Risks: "You must identify the risks . . . to effectively test internal controls in a computerized environment. . . . Controls should not be considered a cost of doing business but, rather, a cost-effective means of reducing risks to an acceptable level. . . . Few systems designers identify risks prior to building systems of internal control. Most systems of internal control are built using the intuition and judgment of users and systems personnel. Risks are neither identified nor measured. In this environment, it is easy to miss or misapply controls."[217]

- Approaches: "You must determine the type of test needed to evaluate controls relating to a specific risk. The specific risk will lead you to pinpoint the area that should be subject to the testing of controls."[218]

- Methods: "The methods or means for testing internal control are provided by the tools and techniques available to you to conduct the test. . . . You should be familiar with the tools and techniques available for testing internal control . . . "[219]

- Level: "You must determine what major components and elements of the computerized environment need to be tested to measure the adequacy of controls. . . . The level of testing can be determined only after the risk has been isolated to specific points in the computerized environment. This isolation of risk is performed by using testing methods."[220]

With the preceding as a foundation, here are other risks to be considered when reviewing systems of internal controls:

- Product risk: "The system does not do what the user wants it to do. This can result from forcing a system to perform functions it was not designed to do."[221]

- Technology risk: "Problems in mastering the technology result in system problems."[222]

- Use risk: "The user does not understand the information and limitations in reports and/or makes faulty decisions based on that information. Violations of the boundaries of applicability of the system can lead to this."[223]

---

[217]*Ibid.*, p. 9.
[218]*Ibid.*, p. 9
[219]*Ibid.*, p. 9.
[220]*Ibid.*, p. 9.
[221]*Ibid.*, p. 12.
[222]*Ibid.*, p. 12.
[223]*Ibid.*, p. 12.

- Security risk: "Valuable information of the organization is stolen or [has] compromised privacy or confidentiality."[224]

A number of methods are used for testing internal control in the computer environment, but those used mostly are:

- Checklist: Developing a series of questions and getting appropriate answers thereto; enhancing the list when appropriate to cover points not considered in developing the initial listing.

- Static: Work from policies, procedures, practices, standards, and regulations to determine theoretically whether adequate internal controls are provided for, then confirm implementation and ascertain whether they are achieving the risk control expected of them.

- Test data: These can be created entirely for testing or supplemented by deliberate incorrect entries to determine what occurs when data is processed.

- Live data: These are alive and are run through normal processing. Their impact is to compared figures that are expected after processing is completed (e.g., opening balance plus or minus accounting impact of entries resulting in a closing balance).

- Parallel: Processing the live data twice, once under normal conditions and then through a parallel computer or another computer with matching results. In many parallel situations, both runs are simultaneous on different equipment with differences printed out promptly as an exception report.

Testing can be viewed from different perspectives, as follows:

- Stress: This test is designed to push the application systems to their limits.

- Functional: This test affirms that the system does, in fact, perform specific functions as designed.

- Regression: This determines whether changes to application systems have not adversely affected controls or existing functions before a modification.

- Environmental: This test focuses on the interrelationship between hardware and software as well as chains of applications.

- Performance: Systems when designed are intended to perform certain tasks "efficiently, effectively, or economically." Perfor-

---

[224]*Ibid.*, p. 12.

mance tests see whether application systems accomplish the 3 Es (efficiency, economy, and effectiveness) in a properly controlled environment.

- Portability: This test is to ensure that a system is working effectively at several selected locations of the network or distributed processing system.

Bringing the preceding elements together, the auditor has six levels of testing to consider. They are:

- Module: Testing one part of a program.
- Program: Testing the entire program.
- Computer System: Testing all programs interconnected in a series.
- Application System: Testing the computer system and the manual interfaces.
- Intersystem: Testing to validate links between two or more computer systems or application systems.
- Operating environment: Testing the functions of all the operating systems necessary for proper functioning of computer systems.

Everything up to this point, as to definitions, approaches, or techniques are conventional. The risk-oriented auditor must go *one step further* into the "twilight zone," if you like, to assess and test, as necessary, the weaknesses in each program and system.

The concept of reactive auditing is no longer acceptable, because the risks are too high. When best estimates indicate that only 2 to 15 percent of computer frauds are discovered; that only 1 of 5 discovered computer frauds are reported to the law enforcement and/or regulatory authorities; that the average discovered computer fraud is about $525,000 and growing at an alarming rate; and that more than 90 percent of such fraud is perpetrated by officers and staff, it is time for risk-oriented internal auditors to be highly proactive. They must anticipate what can go wrong; not just see what is controlled adequately. Auditors determine this by evaluating and eliminating areas that are controlled adequately and concentrating on areas of concern. Here is where the proactive, imaginative, and inquisitive auditor performs reviews and tests to determine what the real risks are and what can be done to control them at acceptable levels, relying on adequate controls and checks and effective monitoring, particularly of the high risk situations.

It is inadequate to merely confirm that a program or system does what the user has requested. Why? Because other capabilities in a program or system may enable someone trying to manipulate or destroy records or steal from the institution to do so successfully with little chance for discovery. Let me illustrate. Between World War I and World War II, the French Maginot Line and German Siegfried Line were built across from each other along the common border of France and Germany. Unquestionably, the Maginot Line was stronger and would be more difficult to penetrate. It was enhanced continuously, increasing the assurance that Germany could not penetrate the French defenses. What did the Germans do when they decided to attack the French? They simply went through Luxembourg, Holland, and Belgium and bypassed the Maginot Line and its guns that could only swing 120 degrees.

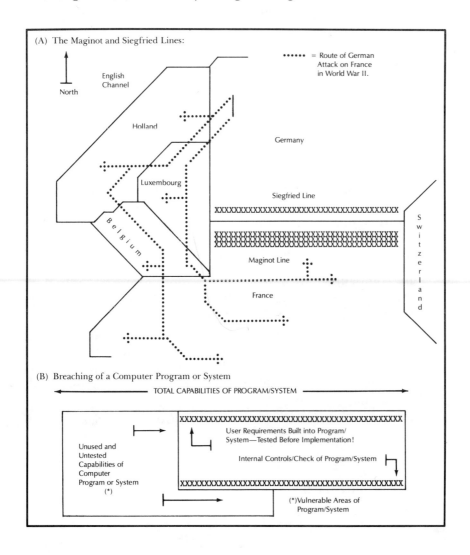

(A) The Maginot and Siegfried Lines:

North

English Channel

•••••• = Route of German Attack on France in World War II.

Holland

Germany

Luxembourg

Siegfried Line

Belgium

Switzerland

Maginot Line

France

(B) Breaching of a Computer Program or System

TOTAL CAPABILITIES OF PROGRAM/SYSTEM

Unused and Untested Capabilities of Computer Program or System (*)

User Requirements Built into Program/System—Tested Before Implementation!

Internal Controls/Check of Program/System

(*)Vulnerable Areas of Program/System

Look at the situation and then its comparability on how easy it is to bypass the internal controls and aspects of a program/system tested, *unless* the *total environment* is considered:

The risks and actions to defend against them are obvious, in both situations.

Think of the Siegfried Line as the "user requirements" of a program/system. Think of the Maginot Line as the "implementation of controls" relative to the "user" related *risks*. Left *unused* and *untested* is the program/system environment that is geographically identified as Holland, Luxembourg, and Belgium. Being untested, the results were risks not considered. They bypassed and breached the controls established for the "user" of the program/system environment. The same fundamental conditions existed in illustration B where only the user requirements were tested and controls were established, leaving untested what resulted in risks that could bypass and breach the controls of the user aspects of the program/system.

The principles are that:

1. The entire potential use of a program/system must be tested and controls established even though only a part of it is used to fulfill user requirements.

2. Never assume that established controls cannot be bypassed or breached.

3. Test not only to determine whether *(a)* user requirements are fulfilled, *(b)* adequate controls are in place relative to user requirements, and *(c)* other risks exist in the program/system that should be controlled, even though the user does not need them.

Some companies have individuals or groups whose task is to find ways to bypass or breach the controls built into any selected program/system. Why? So that the total environment of a selected program/system is under controls that prevent bypassing or breaching that could result in manipulation of records, distortion of stored or current transaction information, and/or theft of the institution's assets. Merely testing user requirements of a program/system is no longer adequate.

The fundamentals in a test of internal controls can be classified as:

1. Determining what to test.

2. Ascertaining how to perform the appropriate tests.

3. Performing the necessary tests.

4. Evaluating and reporting the findings and conclusions, and making recommendations on necessary changes.

The following 12 steps are required to make the preceding test of internal controls:

1. Perform a Risk Analysis

   (a) Identify the threats (*Note:* A threat is the potential for an adverse event to occur, assuming a given set of circumstances/conditions) that could result in a loss. Threats are always present in any program, system, or operating environment. Then the probability of specific threats occurring must be determined.

   (b) Do a risk analysis, which establishes the (1) probability of risk occurrence, and (2) the severity of the risks based on a number of situations that could occur to enable the assessor to concentrate on the highest or primary risk situations.

2. Establish Testing Objectives
   Information developed under segment 1 should provide a perspective of what to test pertaining to identified threats and risks.

3. Establish Acceptable Levels of Risk
   Determine, in advance, what levels of risk will be acceptable relative to each threat or risk identified under segment 1 so review findings can be evaluated against this standard, and find out what, actions if any, are (a) needed to reduce specific risks, and (b) warranted to expand initial review scope to get a better perspective before drawing the conclusion under point 3(a).

4. Ascertain the Type of Testing to be Performed
   Tie in the testing to be performed with the objectives, under segment 2. The various testing techniques used in the aggregate must accomplish the original objectives or, where appropriate, enhance the objectives.

5. Determine Level of Testing to be Performed
   Break down the system into primary, secondary, and tertiary levels of possible threats or risks. The time provided for the testing should be allocated so appropriate efforts are performed on each level of threat or risk.

213

6. Select Method of Testing
Effective testing usually involves tackling the threat or risk from two different approaches, creating a "grid" as shown below:

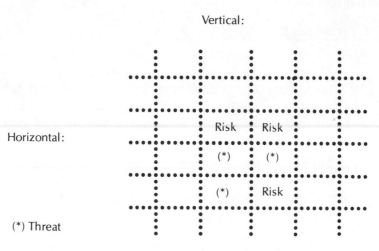

Vertical:

Horizontal:

Risk   Risk

(*)   (*)

(*)   Risk

(*) Threat

Generally, a single testing approach does not provide the perspective on a threat or risk as does vertical and horizontal bracketing. Keep in mind that the objective of testing is to understand fully the threats and risks, and thereby decide on appropriate solutions.

7. Prepare for Final Testing:
Bring together objectives in the testing, type of testing, level of testing, and method of testing. Then determine how to gather or create data necessary to perform the tests, including development of questionnaires, checklists, procedures or programs, and necessary documentation.

8. Test the Integrity of Environment
Be sure the environment where the testing is to be done is the same as the operating environment when procedures, programs, or systems are tested. Then you can be confident that what you are testing is comparable to the real operating environment.

9. Perform Tests
Do the test procedures. They can be limited to a checklist or questionnaire, flow charts on the program or systems, preparation of test matrices, development of test data, and processing the test data, or some combination of two or more of these testing approaches.

10. Evaluate Test Results:
Compare test findings under point 9 with the acceptable risk

and threat levels under point 3. Differences should be explained and/or further tests done to make sure they are representative of the transactions processed by the program or system.

11. Summarize and Disseminate Test Results
    Achieve the title objectives and supplement with recommendations that are appropriate.

12. Follow Up
    Make sure recommendations have been acted on prudently and promptly to bring the risks and threats down to acceptable levels.

The allocation of your time budget for a special program/system review follows:

(a) Steps 1 through 8 should take 25 to 35 percent of the budget.

(b) Step 9 from 30 to 40 percent.

(c) Steps 10 through 14 from 25 to 35 percent.

(d) Total of items (a) through (c) should be adjusted to equal 100 percent.

Remember, based on review findings additional time may be allocated to (b), increasing the total time for the internal control review. Also, keep in mind that the indicated reviews are to assess controls against both internal and external threats and risks.

Disaster Planning Evaluation

For purposes of this text, contingency planning and disaster planning are synonymous. The importance of disaster planning can not be overemphasized. The risk-oriented internal auditor *must* do periodic reviews to make sure such plans are in place and have been tested to assure they will, when needed, function as intended. The basic elements of such a plan are:

- "Proper backup vaulting procedures. Computer programs should schedule back-up copies of your data and programs on a schedule that has been defined" by internal EDP/MIS management and approved by the EDP auditors. "The physical back-up copies should be moved to the off-site storage facility on a schedule that reflects your recovery requirements."[225]

---

[225]Moulton, *op. cit.*, pp. 86-87.

- "Adequate separation of the off-site data and program storage facility. Look for a storage facility [away] from the computer room. A location several miles away from the computer room would be better than one in a nearby building."[226]

- "The computer room, tape library, and off-site storage vault. [They] should have fire and intrusion detection and response equipment. Video equipment wired to a security location would be a plus."[227]

- "Regular audits of library contents. [They would be] performed by the operating department. A weekly physical match of what is supposed to be in the off-site storage facility to what is actually there should be performed by the computer operations staff."[228]

- "Systems should be designed so that they can be operationally recovered and disaster recovered. Operational recovery is effected when program or data problems occur during processing at the usual data center."[229]

The basic elements of sound disaster planning are:

1. Defining and Establishing Goals Through:
   - "A statement of importance as to the need for business resumption following disruption or loss of the computer facility. The ultimate objective of every plan is to restore service promptly and efficiently. . . . By indicating the value of computer services, it is . . . easier to shape strategies that are cost effective."[230]
   - "A statement of priorities as to the relative importance of the functions or applications performed."[231]
   - "A statement of organizational responsibility. This is important to establish authority and responsibility for implementing the plan and to foster cooperation across all organizational elements."[232]
   - "A statement of urgency and timing. Management should establish at the outset firm target dates for the implementation

---

[226]*Ibid.*, pp. 86-87.
[227]*Ibid.*, pp. 86-87.
[228]*Ibid.*, pp. 86-87.
[229]*Ibid.*, p. 121.
[230]Hutt, Bosworth, and Hoyt. *Computer Security Handbook* (Englewood Cliffs, N.J.: Prentice-Hall, 1988), p. 84.
[231]*Ibid.*, p. 84.
[232]*Ibid.*, p. 84.

of the plan and also indicate the need for maintaining operational effectiveness through regular updating and testing."[233]

2. Emergency Response Procedures
   When an emergency actually arises, the institution must react to it with dispatch and efficiency. That is why emergency response procedures should be established in advance. They are the first line of defense so proper actions, after quick analysis of the situation, can be undertaken.

3. Hardware Backup
   Some consider hardware backup synonymous with sound disaster planning. Actually, it is only one element in developing a logical and efficient disaster plan. When dealing with this subject both on-site and off-site protection strategies must be considered. One approach is:
   - "Nondisasters. Disruptions in service stemming from a system malfunction or other failure. Requires action to recover to operational status...to resume service. May necessitate restoration of hardware, software, or data files."[234]
   - "Disasters. Disruptions causing the entire facility to be inoperative for a lengthy period of time, usually more than one day. Requires action to recover operational status, usually the use of an alternative processing facility. Restoration of software and data files from off-site copies may be required. It is necessary that the alternate facility be available until the original data processing facility is restored."[235]
   - "Catastrophes. Major disruptions entailing the destruction of data processing facility. Short-term and long-term fallback is required. An alternate processing facility is needed to satisfy immediate operational needs, as in the case of a disaster. In addition, a new, permanent facility must be identified and equipped to provide for continuation of data processing service on a regular basis."[236]

4. Software and Information Backup
   "There are several approaches to back up information and software. All entail copying files onto machine-readable media."[237]
   Tiered backup can be accomplished by:
   - On-site local backup, used in a fire-resistant environment.

---

[233]*Ibid.*, p. 84.
[234]*Ibid.*, p. 87.
[235]*Ibid.*, p. 87.
[236]*Ibid.*, p. 87.
[237]*Ibid.*, p. 88.

- Off-site local backup, also in a fire-resistant environment, usually within one mile of the primary site.
- Off-site remote backup, also in a fire-resistant environment but located a minimum of five miles from the primary site.
- Archival storage, which is an underground, fire-resistant, and possibly an earthquake-resistant storage facility, usually a minimum of 50 miles from the primary site. Example, First Chicago has an underground records retention center at Harvard, Ill., more than 50 miles from its downtown headquarters.

5. Procedures and Documentation
   "Procedures and documentation are an important extension of hardware and software and are equally vital to ensure the continuity of business activities. . . . Systems and program documentation also require attention and must be protected through the use of off-site backup."[238]

6. Backup for Related Activities
   The overall plan also should provide for:
   - Vendor or third party to resupply hardware.
   - On-the-shelf hardware.
   - Mutual aid agreements with other organizations.
   - In-house dual sites.
   - Third party hot sites *(Note:* A hot site is for emergency operations for a short-time use only).
   - Third party cold sites and warm sites *(Note:* A cold site does not provide immediate back-up needs. It is to provide for longer-term back-up requirements, after hardware is physically installed. The warm site is a basic computer facility equipped with some peripheral equipment and, possibly, a small CPU. With additional hardware, it can be made ready for operations on a partial basis rather quickly and for the long haul more quickly than a cold site).
   - Mobile back-up sites are relatively new but two hardware vendors offer computer-ready trailers that can be set up in a user's parking lot or other site after a disaster. Other trailers serve as an office and library.

7. Emergency Procedure Training
   "Personnel should be trained on key emergency procedures and on the use of ad hoc equipment. One of the most common aspects of emergency training is to hold fire drills as well as

---

[238]*Ibid.,* p. 90.

indoctrination sessions on how to handle such things as telephone and bomb threats."[239]

8. Defenses Against Program/Systems Viruses
   A new area to be included in disaster planning concerns viruses and related data alterers and destroyers (e.g., Trojan horses or trap doors limiting access to programs. Software packages are available that can (a) test programs periodically and (b) identify and destroy viruses and related factors, thereby protecting the integrity of a program and stored data.

The risk-oriented internal auditor must review disaster planning both from a passive and proactive basis. A passive review observes all aspects of the plan including training of personnel, location of back-up facilities, and use of software. In a proactive review, the risk-oriented internal auditor should have the authority to simulate a disaster so the conduct of management and staff can be observed, and vendors who would provide equipment in a real disaster should be involved. Deficiencies identified in either a passive or proactive review should be identified, and appropriate corrections should be made in the disaster plan.

Computer Security

"Computer security may be defined as the protection of computing assets from loss or damage. As a natural extension, the avoidance of loss or damage to other assets through abuse or misuse of computer facilities is also within the scope of this topic."[240]

The basic cause of the problem is perceived simply: "The use of computers has grown to the point where [they have] become almost indispensable to the continuing operations of many organizations....Larger organizations, particularly, are dependent upon data processing because this resource has been used to extend, and often substitute for, scarce and expensive human resources in performing a variety of essential functions. In many instances, loss of the data processing resource, even for short-time intervals, may result in serious consequences to the user organization. On-line, real-time systems are particularly sensitive to disruptions."[241]

Relative to computer security, the risks are generally categorized as:

* Physical hazards.

---

[239]Kuong, *op. cit.*, p. 219.
[240]Hult, Bosworth and Hoyt, *op. cit.*, p. 3.
[241]*Ibid.*, p. 3.

- Software malfunction.
- Misuse of data. (*)
- Equipment malfunction. (*)
- Human error.
- Loss of data. (*)

(*) Could be accidental, or deliberate but made to appear accidental.

Many institutions have established the position of computer security manager. His job "is to provide leadership, and it must be provided in an organized and creative manner. Management is dynamic, not static, and the manager must deal with change—change in the organizational environment, change in people and change in the management methods. The laws of inertia apply, particularly in that people will resist change. The challenge to the manager is to manage change.

"Even a successful security program will usually result in higher costs as well as in changes in the organizational structure and in the working environment. To compound the problems, the benefits of a security program are not highly visible. Security is essentially preventive and often regarded as capital expenses and overhead of questionable value.

"The tools of the manager include planning, organizing, integrating, and controlling. These are not independent activities that can be completely separated; rather they represent a matrix. Taken as an interrelated process, they achieve balance and direction."[242]

The risk-oriented internal auditor should work closely with the computer security manager. However, the risk-oriented internal auditor must recognize the danger of making the computer security manager a "Caesar's wife," which could result in treating that official as part of the audit function. The computer security manager is *not* part of the internal audit function but an officer of the EDP/MIS environment. The very nature of the position normally provides the officer with total access to (1) the EDP systems planning and development area, (2) the EDP operations area, (3) the EDP library and records retention areas, and (4) all testing results that ensure controls are in place. His scope of authority creates a vulnerability if someone in that position misuses data and the freedom of access to all EDP/MIS activities, records, and equipment. Therefore, while his position is an important control function, the computer security

---

[242]*Ibid.*, pp. 11-12.

manager, by the very high risk he could represent, must be audited closely and his activities monitored by the risk-oriented internal auditors.

Consider the following facts in knowing that the risk-oriented internal auditor finds no one of position or rank above being audited:

1. *Computerworld* Focus on Integration
   (June 5, 1989):

   Whom do you consider to be a threat against your network?

   - Internal employees, 81.6 percent.
   - Outside hackers, 17.3 percent.
   - Someone else, 1.1 percent

2. New York Times News Service article published in the *Chicago Tribune* (June, 1989):

   - "You cannot make a computer system 100 percent safe except by turning off the computer."
   - "It's a jungle out there for computer security officials.... Threats come from all over, and it takes an alert, well-trained staff to deal with them."
   - A partner of a "Big 8" accounting firm's consulting arm states that "danger comes from supposedly trustworthy employees more often than from the outside."
   - "Companies tend to go outside to hire experts" in computer security. They don't have time to train people. They want specific systems knowledge."

   My comment to the last point is that it is better to use someone who has the technical competence and experience with the bank and its general EDP/MIS activities than going outside. That is a band-aid approach because it will take the outsider, no matter how competent, time to learn all of the critical EDP/MIS aspects of the organization. Meanwhile, during catch-up time, the institution has a computer security officer who is not functioning fully at that position.

3. *Chicago Tribune* article (May 7, 1989):

   It is important psychologically to make personnel, in sensitive positions, aware that not only their work, through regular and EDP auditors, regulators, and external auditors, is being checked, but they also are being evaluated.

   Therefore, I encourage periodic psychological testing of selected personnel. This makes others in the sensitive environment aware that they too could be tested. The *Tribune* article states, "The vast majority of people don't object. Reid Psychological's statistics showed 92 percent of test-takers accepted the test while only 3 percent resented it, and the rest had no opinion."

4. *Bankers Monthly* (April, 1989):

An article in this publication, titled "Are Employees Robbing Your Bank?" makes the following two important statements:

(a) "Nearly 90 percent of all computer fraud at banks is committed by insiders."

(b) "For some reason, CEOs of small banks think that big banks are more prone to employee abuse while their big bank counterparts view small banks and S&Ls as easy targets because they lack the more sophisticated security systems. The truth is that every bank is vulnerable; every institution's security chain has its own weakest link. Set out to find it and strengthen your defenses before an employee exploits you."

5. *Computer Disaster Recovery—A Structured Appraoch to Corporate Survival:*

This bulletin, published in 1987 by Price Waterhouse, states that:

(a) "According to reliable statistics 90 percent of businesses who suffered a computer disaster and who had not developed a contingency plan, ceased trading within 18 months. Will your company survive?"

(b) "Experts in the industry have calculated that one computer room in 1000 will suffer a computer disaster." This is an annual rate. The disasters will "result from the following causes:

- Fire explosion, 50 percent
- Water damage, 15 percent
- Employee action, 6 percent
- Lightning/power surge, 15 percent
- Building defects, 10 percent
- Others, 4 percent"

6. *Journal of The Institute for Financial Crime Prevention* (Fall, 1988):

A survey by The Institute for Financial Crime Prevention,

publisher of the Journal, showed that 111 banks out of 241 contacted about white collar crime, had a "medium loss experience [of]…$38,000. Fifty-five institutions reported losses less than the median, and 56 reported losses of more than $38,000. The largest loss reported by a single institution was $2,235,014 and the smallest loss was…ten dollars."

Seventeen of the reporting banks had losses of $250,001 to $1 million. Another eleven banks had losses of $1,000,001 to $2,235,014.

The six sources just cited are provided as food for thought. The threats and risks are major ones now. They will increase as we rely more on computers and other automation. If your bank does not have a computer security manager, we strongly recommend that:

1. Such an individual be designated from current personnel or hired from the outside.

2. If your bank is reluctant to hire an extra full-time employee, assign a senior officer to those duties and let him draw on the skills of the consulting arm of a public accounting firm, or other consulting organization, to do the reviews necessary to provide approximately the same level of comfort and confidence in computer operations that a full-time computer security manager would be expected to achieve.

3. Have the audit committee of the board of directors assume the responsibilities similar to those of a full-time computer security manager, and let it engage outside consultants, as under point 2, to conduct the appropriate reviews to give the comfort and confidence in computer operations that a full-time computer security manager would be expected to achieve.

Action is required now, if not already set in place, to control effectively the threats and risks that are inherent in computer operations. It is too late after a catastrophe occurs to say, "I wish we had done…" The risk-oriented internal auditor must encourage management to add a computer security manager or implement one of the options from points 1 to 3 to hold threats and risks to acceptable levels.

Virus Proofing Computers
Introduction

The following headlines and supplementing comments came from newspapers and magazines published in November, 1988:

"Virus Infects Huge Computer Network"[243]

"One of the fastest moving, most widespread computer viruses yet devised forced a number of major U.S. universities and some corporations overseas to shut down their computer systems ... " The "virus moved via a mail program on an academic research network called Internet, which is used primarily by government-funded university researchers to communicate with each other via computers connected by telephone lines.... The virus caused much inconvenience as it slowed the computer systems—sometimes to a halt.... But the virus' rapid movement over worldwide networks shows the vulnerability of major computer systems to such attacks.... This isn't the last we're going to see of this kind of thing.... This virus is a symptom of our poor security systems. If it had been malicious, it would have destroyed many, many systems."

"Virus Shows Computers' Vulnerability"[244]

"Computer viruses hold the potential for great devastation to modern technological society as we know it." The head of a computer security firm stated, "This could just be a warning for the big one ... " Another expert was quoted as saying, "Within an hour, hundreds of thousands of computer files could have been wiped out.... Going a step beyond such a scenario, government officials are suddenly worrying about what terrorists or hostile foreign governments could do by planting such viruses in computers used for national defense systems. Or the IRS. Or hospital records. Or financial transfer systems.... There also is the fear that the widespread publicity given the current virus will spur copycats."

"Could a Virus Infect Military Computers?"[245]

"A computer virus introduced by a university student swept through interconnected networks last week, bringing hundreds of computers at defense-research centers and universities to a halt." Military experts indicated Pentagon computer systems could be affected by a virus but "that the chances are remote." They base this on the fact that "access to sensitive Pentagon computer systems is extremely limited.... Elaborate audit trails record what each user does. Transmitted data are encrypted in hard-to-break codes. Special 'vaccine' programs detect unauthorized changes to computer software. The most crucial systems are not connected by networks to others, so damage could be contained if they were hit by a virus. A

---

[243]*Chicago Tribune,* 4 November 1988.
[244]*Ibid.,* 11 November 1988.
[245]*InformationWeek,* 7 November 1988.

former top Pentagon information-security chief concedes, "No one has ever built a system that can't be broken. . . . The Defense Department has been on the lookout for additional safeguards for more than a year."

"Virus Bombards DOD Nets—Data Survives, But Software Treatments Are Unsuccessful"[246]

"Virus busters at several universities and government laboratories around the country were struggling to debug a virus that hit Internet and Arpanet, two Department of Defense networks, late last week. . . . While the virus has not destroyed data, researchers say it's 'very worrisome' because the virus appears to be extremely persistent, perpetuating itself on Unix-based Sun workstations with DEC VAXes even after treatment with software fixes."

Aftermath

"Companies aren't expected to beef up computer security, despite a virus that infected 6,000 university and military computers, experts say. . . . It will scare some companies into looking into what they should do for security," the editor of *Computers & Security* magazine is quoted as saying. He continues, "But most will cry about it, say that they are in danger, and that the sky is falling, and in two weeks, they'll be back to business as usual. . . . Businesses are safer from viruses because they're more protective with the data in their computers." A spokesperson for a major U.S. airline is quoted as saying, "Still, no one's immune from a virus. . . . [A]irlines have long feared someone getting access to their computers, so they've taken precautions. . . . Many other companies say they're constantly trying to keep out computer vandals. But security consultants say they should be doing more." The security experts concluded: "It's sort of the shuttle syndrome. Nobody does anything until something happens."[247]

Perspective on Viruses

"A computer virus is a rogue program planted by a high-tech saboteur. It can spread to other computer systems and make them do things they're not supposed to do—such as send harmless messages or destroy information."[248]

"A computer virus, a renegade program that sabotages computer

---

[246]*Ibid.*, 14 November 1988.
[247]*USA Today,* 18 November 1988.
[248]*Ibid.*

systems, can cause them to slow down, damage, or alter data or plant instructions for future electronic vandalism. They are called viruses because, like their [human] biological counterparts, they give instructions to reproduce themselves. Such bugs are planted by knowledgeable vandals who design them to spread rapidly over electronic networks or through shared software before they are detected."[249]

The virus is created by a knowledgeable vandal who makes relatively simple moves:

1. Programs virus.

2. Places virus on disk.

3. "Command[s]: copy self to all other computers. Virus replicates by changing a program.

4. Shares disk and infects computer systems.

5. Virus does what it has been told to do (e.g., alters or erases data, etc.)

"A virus is a delivery system that can carry any warhead the programmer wants it to," according to a university computer science professor.[250]

Another perspective of a "typical virus life cycle":[251]

1. Vandal's system
   "Virus code is placed in popular public domain software. Software is unloaded to a bulletin board using phone lines."

2. Bulletin board host
   "Infected program is then downloaded to the user's system and stored on a hard or floppy disk."

3. User's System
   "When the program is run, the virus copies itself to an operating system file on the active disk drive. Copies of the virus are then spread from each user's system to other disks' operating systems files when DIR or other DOS commands are executed."

4. Dissemination
   "The virus spreads quickly from the original bulletin board file to other micros through the infected disks. When a predetermined state occurs, the virus attacks the system files on the hard disk, leaving the programs and data files inaccessible."

---

[249]*Chicago Tribune*, 4 November 1988.
[250]*Miami Herald*, 16 November 1988.
[251]*Journal of Accounting*, December, 1988.

Viruses have many forms and inflict their damage in various ways. They have enough in common to create a representative description of how they can spread and the degree of havoc they can inflict. Following is an example:

"When a micro is turned on with the contaminated operating system file on its active disk drive, the virus is loaded into its memory. Then, whenever a common DOS command like DIR, COPY or TYPE is used, the virus becomes active. It copies itself onto other disk files and waits until it is triggered. For example, when the current date hits the date programmed by the culprit, the virus might activate and destroy critical system files.... The result is a hard or floppy disk with inaccessible files. The programs and data on that disk can't be read or copied onto another disk without some arduous work to repair the systems. The damage would not stop there because the virus would have spread itself to other disks and computers."[252]

In addition to the classic virus, as described at the beginning of this article, and to illustrate how broad the risks are in this area, consider some other virus situations:

1. A virus infected shrink-wrapped copy of a graphics software package intended for retail sales.

2. A virus planted in a data file was able to infiltrate an internal communications network. This was a nonmalicious virus. It displayed a holiday greeting and made clones of itself to do that same thing.

3. A major university, however, encountered a vicious virus that attacked the institution's computer system with a virus that spread itself to all available copies of one of the operating system files. Once that had been accomplished, it destroyed the disks' system files, which resulted in widespread data loss. That rendered the disk useless until it was reformatted.

4. A major systems' consulting firm had its computers infiltrated by a virus called SCORES. It attacked valuable proprietary trade-secret programs.

Some risk areas of concern regarding virus transmission:[253]

1. Viruses can sneak into PCs on borrowed disks and programs:

   (a) Received over the telephone.

---

[252]*Ibid.*
[253]*U.S. News & World Report,* 21 November 1988.

227

(b) Received from electronic bulletin boards.

(c) Received from mainframes.

2. A PC linked to other computers should be turned off when idle because infected programs can only be sent to your computer if it is turned on.

Protective Measures

1. Guidelines
   A panel of spokesmen from 3COM, BANYAN, DATAPOINT, MICROSOFT, NOVELL, and others representing more than 60 computer vendors endorsed a *set of guidelines for computer virus prevention.* They point out that the best way to control the virus problem is to focus on *total system reliability,* with the full support from senior management to achieve that. Among the guidelines agreed on were these:
   - "Back-up copies of all original software should be made as soon as the software package is opened. Copies should be stored off-site."
   - "Once purchased, all software should be reviewed carefully by a systems manager, before it is installed on a distributed system."
   - "New software should be quarantined on an isolated computer."
   - "System administrators should restrict access of system programs and data on a 'need-to-use' basis."
   - "All programs on a system should be checked regularly for size changes. Any size deviations could be evidence of tampering or virus infiltration."
   - "Many 'shareware' and 'freeware' programs are useful applications."
   - "System managers should develop plans for quick removal from service of all copies of a suspect program, and immediate backup of all related data. These plans should be made known to all users, and tested and reviewed periodically."[254]

2. Another Set of Guidelines
   - "Don't use strange software without careful examination."
   - "Don't share software."
   - "Test your programs periodically to see if they've changed."

---

[254]*Information Week,* 21 November 1988.

- "Isolate an infected computer until its data storage can be electronically wiped clean and reloaded with untainted software."[255]

3. Security Strategies

(a) LeeWah Datacom Security Corp., of Hayward, California, has come up with a technique for "personal computers to screen attempts to obtain data by telephone by automatically calling back to confirm the identity of the caller before releasing any data."[256] They have installed nearly 2,000 systems to protect computers. Their clients include Apple Computer Inc., Chase Manhattan Bank, and American Express Co.

(b) An official of a "Big 8" CPA firm has stated that "now is the time for companies to plan for the worst, just in case." He says that "the scope and nature of the problem (viruses) is one that isn't likely to be solved in the short- to medium-term by vaccines or antidotes."[257] He recommends:

(1) Examine your systems, especially personal computers, research computers, and other end-user systems that operate outside conventional data processing department "to make sure that only authorized programs can be used and that only authorized people can use the machines either directly or remotely. This means creating very stringent password systems that [are] changed frequently."[258]

(2) "Companies should devise a plan for reacting to and recovering from such a catastrophe (viruses)."[259]

(3) It should be routine to make "systematic, day-by-day backups of data, not just periodic backups." Why? "Because most viruses are designed to go off like time bombs.... You simply replace lost data with the latest copy..."[260]

(c) A computer security specialist at a major U.S. governmental laboratory is so concerned about the virus risk that he

---

[255]*Miami Herald,* 16 November 1988.
[256]*The Wall Street Journal,* 20 November 1988.
[257]*Ibid.*
[258]*Ibid.*
[259]*Ibid.*
[260]*Ibid.*

said, "This whole situation is worrisome, because it points out the fragility of the whole system."[261] He does not believe vaccines are the ultimate solution. He says, "The 'vaccine' is really another computer program—a filter which checks for software attempting to perform suspicious operations. Using this safeguard represents additional overhead costs, processing time, and protocol procedures. In the end, the user is still susceptible to being outflanked or undermined by some other programmer in the future."[262] While he has no final solution, he warns against excessive reliance on vaccines to control the virus risk.

(d) Testing Software

All programs whether (1) developed internally, (2) purchased from retail dealers, or (3) those available as public domain programs should be tested. The tests should be conducted on micros with any disks used during the tests isolated so as not to be used on any other system or copied to disks used by other PCs. This prevents a virus from spreading. Suspicious text found in these programs is often a clear giveaway that something is wrong. Software should be used in this isolated environment a minimum of 15 to 20 times, and longer if there is some concern about the program. This should be long enough to detect virus activity. It also is wise to change the date so the next 365 days are exposed to the system while the program is being tested. Repetitive commands that change the date and then execute a DOS command such as DIR or TYPE will make this task easier. The objective is to trigger any virus lurking in the system files if its execution is based on a particular date. Any virus present should attack during such testing.

When a virus is found, remove all disks from the PC and turn the machine off. Label the infected disks and keep them separate from disks which can be used. The *Journal of Accountancy* issue of December, 1988, indicates that "infected disks can be sent to Dr. Harold Highland, Editor, *Computers & Security, Virus Research,* 562 Croydon Rd., Elmont, New York 11003-2814."[263] He is conducting research on viruses.

---

[261]*Information Week,* 12 December 1988.
[262]*Ibid.*
[263]*Journal of Accountancy,* December 1988.

(e) Some Available Backup Software:

(1) COREFAST, developed by Core International Inc., 7171 North Federal Hwy., Boca Raton, FL 33421. Telephone 305-997-6044.

(2) PC-FULLBACK, developed by Westlake Data, P.O. Box 1711, Austin, TX 78767. Telephone 512-328-1041.

(f) Some Available Virus Software:

(1) FLUSHOT PLUS, developed by Software Concepts, 594 Third Ave., New York, NY 10016. Telephone 212-889-6431.

(2) MACE VACCINE, developed by Paul Mace Software, 400 Williamson Way, Ashland, OR 97520. Telephone 800-523-0258.

Note: There are a number of other backup software and virus software packages available. The information under segment 3*(e)* and 3*(f)* is merely to show the availability of such software.

Summary

As stated earlier, "a computer virus is a program that 'infects' other programs by modifying them to include a copy of itself. With this 'infection' capability, a virus can spread from program to program, user to user, computer to computer, and network to network . . . corrupting programs and data." In the six months from the last third of 1987 "roughly 100,000 computer systems sustained some form of damage from computer viruses."[264]

"There are three fundamental differences between computer viruses and other known attack techniques: generality, persistence, and extent."[265]

- "Generality: Because a virus can carry other program codes along with it, the nature of the damage it can do is only limited by the creativity of the attacker."[266]

- "Persistence: Because viruses can reinfect programs that have been 'cleaned up,' they can survive many generations of program changes and upgrades. Even the most thoroughly verified

---

[264]*Datamation Magazine* supplement: *Computer Security: Issues and Trends,* November 1988, developed by the Computer Security Institute.
[265]*Ibid.*
[266]*Ibid.*

program might become infected in its executable form, and typical change control mechanisms do not stop or detect this."[267]

- "Extent: Because a virus can spread far and wide, a single programmer with a PC could cause computer problems worldwide. Many known viruses have spread to thousands of computer systems, crossing both national and [other] geographical boundaries."[268]

"There are products on the market designed to provide limited protection against computer viruses. Unfortunately, most offer little more than a false sense of security. Recent theoretical studies, however, have stimulated a new generation of products which are expected to offer . . . better protection and convenience than their predecessors. These 'integrity shells' will likely be improved over time to provide extensive services such as integrated backups and restores, integrated networking capabilities, and high-integrity information exchange between mainframes and microcomputers."[269]

While steps have been taken to protect systems and identify risks relative to viruses and other computer threats, much more needs to be done before security is a reality.

---

[267]*Ibid.*
[268]*Ibid.*
[269]*Ibid.*

15
Audit Methodology

Statistical Sampling

"The process of obtaining information about a whole collection of things by examining a portion of that collection is called sampling."[270] "The foregoing collection of things is variously called a population, universe, or field. These are synonymous terms. Population has been chosen for exclusive use here . . . "[271] "Statistical sampling is the whole of the process by which the size of a statistical sample is determined, items are selected and examined, and results are evaluated."[272] It is a most useful audit tool when properly used. "It requires determination of the sample size based on an acceptable level of risk and an unbiased selection of items included in the sample. It permits projection of the sample results to the entire population."[273] Greater accuracy is achieved by the auditor "when larger populations are involved because it reduces the"[274] number of items in the population to be checked. Restated, it enables drawing broader conclusions from reduced testing than random, block, or selected item audit reviews. "When samples are selected using statistical probability, a heavy burden is lifted from the shoulders of the auditor. He or she no longer has to establish an arbitrary sample size. Nor will the auditor be faced with the impossible task of defending an arbitrary determination of size to superiors, associates, and perhaps even a court of law."[275] The auditor *(a)* identifies the population size, and *(b)* determines the confidence level (i.e., 80, 90, 95) desired and the reliability factor acceptable (i.e., ± 1, 2, 3, 5, or other percentage variance). "Statistical measurement requires a truly random selection, i.e., each item in the population must have an equal or otherwise determinable probability for selection. The most important advantage of statistical sampling is that it permits the auditor to generalize, i.e., to infer from observations of the sample that the characteristics are probably present in the entire population—and to do so with the confidence of scientific support."[276]

"Statistical assurance is a specific measure of the reliance that the auditor can place upon the inferences drawn from the characteristics

---

[270]Seglin, *op. cit.,* p. 378.
[271]*Ibid.,* p. 379.
[272]*Ibid.,* p. 379.
[273]*Ibid.,* p. 379.
[274]*Ibid.,* p. 379.
[275]*Ibid.,* p. 379.
[276]*Ibid.,* p. 379.

of a sample. This measure is based upon the laws and theories of probability that require that sample elements be randomly selected from the entire population. Assurance is stated in terms of precision and reliability."[277]

"Random, in statistical parlance, is a precise term. Random selection is selection governed solely by the laws of chance."[278]

"Sampling error is the amount that the sample projection might deviate from the value that could be obtained from a census of the population. The objective of statistical sampling is to control this difference so that it is kept within acceptable limits."[279]

"Control over the sampling error is established by means of statistical measurements leading to a statement of statistical inference referred to as the assurance, reliability, or probability statement. We refer to the statement of statistical assurance as a probability statement."[280]

"The probability statement is the keystone that distinguishes statistical sampling from all other forms of sampling. The statement contains two important assertions: reliability and precision."[281]

"Reliability is the proability that the statistic (value of the characteristic observed in the sample) is within a stated range of the parameter (value of the same characteristic) in the population. Reliability also is called the confidence level and the assurance level."[282] It is generally stated as a percentage.

"Precision is the extent to which the population parameter may differ from the sample statistic and still be acceptable to the auditor. Precision also is referred to as confidence interval or reliability."[283]

SAS No. 39, Audit Sampling (AU Section 350.01) "Provides a formal definition of audit sampling: 'Audit sampling is the application of an audit procedure to less than 100 percent of the items within an account balance or class of transactions for the purpose of evaluating some characteristic of the balance or class.' "[284]

"Audit sampling is used by auditors in both compliance and substantive testing. It is especially useful when the auditor's selection of items to be tested is drawn from a large population, and the auditor has no specific knowledge about the characteristics of the items being tested, such as whether an account may be overstated or under-

[277]*Ibid.*, p. 380.
[278]*Ibid.*, p. 380.
[279]*Ibid.*, p. 380.
[280]*Ibid.*, p. 380.
[281]*Ibid.*, p. 380.
[282]*Ibid.*, p. 380.
[283]*Ibid.*, p. 380.
[284]Sullivan, et al., *op. cit.*, p. 417.

stated as a result of various types of errors."[285] Sampling is not used in a variety of audit areas. As an example: "For the purpose of confirming the understanding of the system of internal controls over a particular type of transaction, the auditor traces one or two transactions through the"[286] operating, administrative, or accounting system.

Two types of *risk* that must be considered are:

1. Nonsampling Risk

   This "encompasses all risks that are not specifically the result of sampling, including the risk that the auditor will form incorrect conclusions, because of failing to employ appropriate and effective audit procedures, applying audit procedures improperly or to inappropriate or incomplete populations, or drawing incorrect conclusions from evidence examined."[287]

2. Sampling Risk

   This "is the risk that, when an audit test is restricted to a sample, the conclusion reached from the test will differ from the conclusion that would have been reached if the same test had been applied to all items in the population rather than to just a sample."[288]

   (a) Relative to compliance tests of internal accounting controls:

   (1) Overreliance on Tests: "Is the risk that the auditor will conclude, based on a sample, that the compliance rate justifies the planned level of reliance on a control when examination of every item in the population would reveal that the true compliance rate does not justify such reliance."[289]

   (2) Underreliance on Tests: "Is the risk that the audit will conclude, based on a sample, that the compliance rate does not justify the planned level of reliance on a control when examination of every item in the population would reveal that the true compliance rate justifies such reliance."[290]

---

[285]*Ibid.,* p. 417.
[286]*Ibid.,* p. 418.
[287]*Ibid.,* p. 422.
[288]*Ibid.,* p. 422.
[289]*Ibid.,* p. 423.
[290]*Ibid.,* p. 423.

(b) Reliance to substantive tests of account balances:

    (1) Incorrect Acceptance: "Is the risk that the auditor will conclude, based on a sample, that the recorded account balance is not materially misstated when examination of every item in the population would reveal that it is materially misstated."[291]

    (2) Incorrect Rejection: "Is the risk that the auditor will conclude, based on a sample, that the recorded account balance is materially misstated when examination of every item in the population would reveal that it is not materially misstated."[292]

*Beta risk in statistical literature. A beta test is one performed under controlled conditions.

**Alpha risk in statistical literature. An alpha test uses actual data and transactions.

Audit objectives for statistical sampling

1. "To understand the characteristics of the population . . . "[293]

2. "To estimate, with a specified degree of reliability, the characteristics of a population (error rates, etc.) and to determine 'how many'."[294]

3. "To estimate, with a specified degree of reliability, the value of a population of one of its characteristics (e.g. dollar value of inventories, dollar value of improper travel vouchers, etc.) and to determine 'how much.'"[295]

In most instances, a population is viewed totally. To increase the dollar percentage of total transactions in a population, it can be segmented by stratification and different testing rates used for each segment. For example:

| 1. Transactions or balances over "X" dollars each: | Up to 50 percent of balances in 20 percent of transactions or balances. | 90 percentage confidence level, with ± 2 percent reliability factor. |

---

[291]*Ibid.*, p. 423.
[292]*Ibid.*, p. 423.
[293]Heeschen and Sawyer, *Internal Auditor's Handbook.* 1984, p. 143.
[294]*Ibid.*, p. 143.
[295]*Ibid.*, p. 143.

2. Transactions or balances under "X" dollars but above "Z" dollars each:	Up to 30 percent of balances in 35 percent of transactions or balances.	80 percent confidence level, with ± 3 percent reliability factor.
3. Transactions or balances of "Z" dollars or less:	Up to 20 percent of balances in 45 percent of transactions or balances.	70 percent confidence level, with ± 4 percent reliability factor.

Once the criteria for segmenting a population are made, each segment on its own becomes a population for evaluation, although statistically the results are not considered by many as being as meaningful as not segmenting any population. My actual experience, in more than two decades of using statistical sampling, has not indicated segmentation materially affects the conclusion. This has been proved by taking a population and conducting tests, with different audit personnel (1) on the total population, and (2) on the population segmented into three lesser populations which, in the aggregate, make up the whole population under item (1), using the criteria for the *middle* segmented population, i.e., 80 percent confidence level, with a ± 3 percent reliability factor, for the total unsegmented population tests.

If in a given population the auditor were concerned about an official breaking down a fraudulent transaction into smaller amounts for recordation, assuming it would be less likely to be detected by audit examination (e.g., $10,000 transaction broken into five segments of $2,000 each) then the auditor could reverse the level of testing shown and perform a higher level of sampling on transactions or balances of "Z" dollars or less. This is entirely a judgment call.

Confirmations

(Auditing) Confirmation

This is the "substantiation of the existence and sometimes the condition and value of a claim against another or of an asset in the possession or control of another, or the existence and amount of a liability. A confirmation usually takes the form of a written request and acknowledgment, but it also may be obtained [verbally] or through observation, as by the inspection of a passbook containing entries for deposits, or of records reflecting a certain transaction. . . . Either of two types of confirmation is commonly employed: a positive confirmation requesting a reply in any event, or a negative confirmation requesting a reply only in the event of a discrepancy."[296]

Selection of confirmation format

"It is important to impress on debtors the necessity for communicating directly with the auditor when discrepancies exist. If the auditor has reason to believe that the negative form of confirmation request will not receive consideration, sending out that form of confirmation request does not constitute compliance with generally accepted auditing standards. In that respect, SAS No. 1 (AU Section 331.05) states, in part:

"The negative form is useful particularly when internal control surrounding accounts receivable" or loans receivable "is considered to be effective, when a large number of small balances are involved," such as credit card balances, "and when the auditor has no reason to believe the persons receiving the requests are unlikely to give them consideration. If the negative rather than the positive form of confirmation is used, the number of requests sent, or the extent of the other auditing procedures applied to the receivable balance, should normally be greater in order for the independent auditor to obtain the same degree of satisfaction with respect to the accounts receivable balance."[297]

Negative Confirmations

These can be in the following forms:

1. A special confirmation letter which details the account and balance as of an indicated date.

2. A rubber stamp or sticker affixed to a statement showing balance of a specified account on a particular date, usually with activities for a day, week, or month detailed.

"The value of negative confirmation requests has been the subject of much discussion" in audit and management circles. "Although the incident of debtors who simply ignore and discard requests is unknown and unmeasurable, the results can nonetheless be relied on to an appropriate degree for two reasons."[298]

They are:

- "Since the objective of confirmation is to provide reasonable assurance of the validity and accuracy of the aggregate" of the

---

[296]Kohler, *op. cit.*, pp. 100-101.
[297]Sullivan, et al., *op. cit.*, pp. 531-533.
[298]*Ibid.*, pp. 531-533.

accounts being confirmed, "a discrepancy is significant only if it is evidence of a condition that affects a great many accounts." If that is true then negative confirmations are not appropriate.

- "Confirmation of accounts or loans receivable or accounts payable or depositor balances is only one procedure that provides evidential matter. Audit evidence is cumulative, and one procedure tends to corroborate another. Therefore, some audit detection risk can be tolerated in a single procedure because that procedure does not serve as the sole basis for a conclusion."[299]

Positive Confirmations

"A positive confirmation is a request that a debtor reply directly to the auditor stating whether the account balance is correct. Positive confirmations may be used for all accounts or for selected accounts, such as those with large balances, those representing unusual or isolated transactions, or others for which an auditor needs greater specific assurance of validity and accuracy. The positive form of confirmation is called for if there are indications that a substantial number of accounts may be in dispute or inaccurate or if the individual receivable balances are usually large or arise from "transactions involving a few major customers. "The request may be conveyed by a letter or directly on the statement by means of a rubber stamp or sticker. To facilitate replies, a postage-paid envelope addressed to the auditor should be enclosed. Because the form of the request specifically asks for a reply, an auditor may not assume that failure to reply indicated that" the account holder or firm "agrees with the stated balance. Second requests should be sent, and sometimes third requests by registered mail."[300]

"It is impracticable for an auditor to determine the genuineness or authenticity of signatures on replies to confirmation requests. Accordingly, if the account being confirmed is material or the auditor has determined that inherent risk is high, the auditor should ask the client to request an officer of the "firm in whose name the account is recorded "to sign the confirmation reply. The auditor may then wish to communicate with that officer by telephone or other means to corroborate the validity of the confirmation."[301]

"Auditors often employ various techniques to improve the response rate, such as 'personalizing' the request by using postage stamps rather than a postage meter."[302]

---

[299]*Ibid.,* pp. 531-533.
[300]*Ibid.,* pp. 534-535.
[301]*Ibid.,* pp. 534-535.
[302]*Ibid.,* pp. 534-535.

Whether positive or negative confirmations are to be used, the computer can be helpful in (1) statistical selection of balances to be confirmed and (2) maintaining a record of responses, whether in agreement or indicating a difference to the records on which the confirmations were mailed. Whether positive or negative confirmations are used, *all* exceptions must be followed up and explained, whether clerical error or deliberate balance manipulation is involved.

Selection of Accounts

This can be done on the basis of:

1. Customer service complaints on previous balance problems.

2. Statistical sampling techniques to achieve a desired confidence level with a suitable reliability factor. As noted earlier, the accounts can be treated as a single population or stratified into two or more segments, each treated as a population.

3. Block, random selection, or other auditor selected basis can be used.

4. Accounts on which a difference was identified at the time of the last most recent audit.

5. Any combination of items 1 through 4.

Analytical Auditing

"Analytical auditing is the use of flow chart techniques to develop audit programs, survey internal control, and structure recommended revisions of system flows. By using flow chart techniques, the auditor can look upon the subject of the audit as a system. The auditor can make a critical analysis of the system's functioning, audit the inputs and the processing, and, ultimately, arrive at conclusions concerning the outputs. Surveys of internal control usually are accomplished by using internal control questionnaires. Answers to the questions are obtained by inquiry, observation, or testing. . . . The preparation of tailor-made questionnaires is facilitated by using flow charts of the systems of paper flow," or data flows, in a partial or fully paperless system. The procedural steps for an analytical audit include:

1. "Making a general review of the system or department. During this review the auditor should obtain copies of forms, study applicable operations manuals, and draw a rough flow chart of the system.

2. "Developing a detailed flow chart of the system or department

to show the flow of work, operation steps, actions required, and certain positions or persons involved in key" areas of responsibility and authority.

3. "Making a detailed analysis of the flow chart to determine the strengths and weaknesses in the system of internal control. A step-by-step detailed analysis of the procedure is necessary ...

4. "Investigating potential weaknesses in the internal control system. This step could require additional use of test checks, observations, samplings, or other audit techniques to determine the extent of the weakness.

5. "Making recommendations for procedural changes to improve the internal control.

"Because analytical auditing requires considerable attention to detail and may require a substantial amount of time (at least on the initial review), it is probably not an appropriate technique to use in functions with low volumes or in which control weaknesses are apparent on the surface."[303]

Anticipatory Auditing

This concept is built on the foundation of *key indicators*. This is using a integrated audit approach, dealing with (1) risks, (2) threats, (3) internal control deficiencies, (4) questions as to personnel competency, and (5) irregular practices or conditions. Key indicators are supplemented by the *call program*. The two key terms, as indicated, are described below:

1. Key Indicators: These "contain information—extracted from reports, data, or statistics—of either a financial, operational, or managerial nature. Tracking these indicators over time serves to highlight potential problems, unfavorable trends, and abnormal fluctuations."[304]

2. Call Program: "This is used to facilitate the exchange of knowledge and ideas between the audit department and line personnel. The program consists of regularly scheduled meetings with line managers, with the objective of enhancing the auditing department's awareness of banking trends, new products and systems, and other relevant changes with each area of the bank."[305]

---

[303]Seglin, *op. cit.*, pp. 22-23.
[304]*Ibid.*, pp. 29-30.
[305]*Ibid.*, pp. 29-30.

The concept of anticipatory auditing is not to replace the traditional approaches of auditing but to complement them. "One result of the audit department's continuous monitoring of critical risks is that the scope and frequency of scheduled work paper audits often can be reduced."[306]

Internal Control Questionnaires

"An internal control questionnaire is designed to ask a series of questions about the controls in each audit area as a means of indicating to the auditor aspects of the system that may be inadequate. In most instances it is designed to require a yes or a no response, with 'no' responses indicating potential internal control deficiencies. . . . The primary advantage of the questionnaire approach is the relative completeness of coverage of each audit area that a good instrument affords. Furthermore, a questionnaire can usually be prepared reasonably quickly at the beginning of the audit engagement. The primary disadvantage is that individual parts of the client's system are examined without providing an overall view of the entire cycle. In addition, a standard questionnaire is often inapplicable to some audit clients, especially the smaller ones. In using questionnaires, it is important to determine whether the controls believed by management to exist are actually being followed. Questioning the personnel actually performing each procedure, observation, and verification by examining documents and records are convenient methods of obtaining information for completing the questionnaire."[307]

The auditor must be satisfied that the answers received are correct. This can be achieved by using either:

1. The Jack Webb (from Dragnet) syndrome: "I just want to get the facts!"

2. I'm from Missouri syndrome: "Show me!"

The audit must recognize that the person giving the answers (1) may think they are giving correct answers but procedures may have been changed without their knowledge or (2) may be deliberately attempting to (a) misdirect, or (b) misstate the true conditions because of deficiencies that management would like to hide.

Using the Flow Chart

"A flow chart of internal control is a symbolic, diagrammatic representation of the client's documents and their sequential flow in the

---

[306]*Ibid.*, pp. 29-30.
[307]Arens and Lobbecke, *Auditing—an Integrated Approach.* (Englewood Cliffs, N.J.: Prentice-Hall, 1976), pp. 174

organization. An adequate flow chart shows the origin of each document and record in the system, the subsequent processing, and the final disposition of any document or record included in the chart. In addition, it is possible for the flow chart to show the separation of duties, authorization, approvals, and internal verifications that take place within the system. . . . [The flow chart] is advantageous primarily because it can provide a concise overview of the 'specific' system, which is useful to the auditor as an analytical tool in his evaluation. A well-prepared flow chart aids in identifying inadequacies by facilitating a clear understanding of how the system operates." Generally, "it is simply easier to follow a diagram than to read a description. It is also usually easier to update a flow chart than a narrative description. . . . The three basic elements of a flow chart are symbols, flow lines, and areas of responsibility."[308]

There are two fundamental approaches in using a flow chart. They are:

1. Conventional: Where a procedure is detailed step-by-step, using the three basic elements of a flow chart, as stated above.

2. Cycle Concept: Where a flow chart of a procedure is reduced to primary elements of processing, internal control, or internal check.

The second approach, as above, can reduce the detail work of the conventional approach substantially—at least 50 percent but usually 75 percent or thereabouts.

---

[308]*Ibid.*, pp. 170 and 172.

16

Risk Assessment Matrix Procedures (RAMP)

Introduction

One of the most difficult things for the auditor to determine is the proper scope for a planned audit examination. The RAMP concept is to build on (1) the foundation of the familiarization phase of the audit review; (2) data developed during previous audits of the subject environment, if any; and (3) any information developed, from any source concerning potential problems.

Familiarization is by far the most important single phase of an audit. This is really the key aspect of the three stated above in learning about and understanding what the authority and responsibilities are of the environment to be audited, the competence of the people in performing their duties, and the level of compliance with policies, procedures, practices, and standards.

Time is the auditor's constant enemy. The auditor wants to do an adequate audit but does not have the luxury of doing extra work because other assignments are always waiting. However, when reducing time on an assignment, the auditor always must be careful so critical review aspects are not overlooked and the audit work can draw conclusions on the how well or how poorly a specific function, activity, product, service, entity, or facility is performing against acceptable standards.

To achieve the foregoing, the auditor must develop sources of basic knowledge on the audit to be performed. Examples of internal and external sources follow:

What Auditors Should Know

The sources of basic knowledge (for the auditor) should be:

Internal

Familiarization of area/function to be audited:
1. Organization
   A. Mandate from management/authority and responsibility.
   B. Activities and work tasks.
   C. Structure.
   D. Competency of management (including supervisors).
   E. Turnover rate.

2. Equipment and facilities used/forward plans for same.

3. Universe of activities: In units, dollars, or other measure basis.

4. Budget/strategic plan and performance against budget for last three years.

5. Interviews with both management and line personnel.

6. Historical or current problems.

7. Observation of office and line operating environment.

8. Evaluation of internal controls.

9. Regulatory environment/requirements.

10. Policies, procedures, standards for area/function.

External

1. Contact with appropriate industry and/or trade organization.

2. Normal industry/function/activity standards.

3. Definition of functions/activities.

4. Interdepartmental relations.

5. Objectives.

6. Contribution to cost and/or profit effectiveness.

7. Traditional organizational structure.
   A. Centralized or decentralized.
   B. Pyramid or matrix.

8. Industry/function/activity "competitive" information (independently or related to item 1 above).

9. Reference materials on industry/functions/activities.

History of the Basic Matrix Approach

In 1978, Arthur Andersen & Co. in its courses "Operational Auditing—I and II" came up with the first use of this basic matrix concept. It was given the acronym FIRM, meaning functional internal risk matrix. That matrix consisted of the first four columns of the RAMP concept.

In 1985, in an issue of *The Internal Auditor,* a college professor modified the first three columns of Andersen's FIRM concept and renamed it. In my opinion, it was a "polishing" job of an existing concept but not a new concept.

In 1984, an associate in the Chicago office of Arthur Andersen and myself talked about how to broaden the value of the matrix. We experimented and found a way to take it all the way from (1) understanding the operational objectives for the audit function to (2) developing a final audit program for that audit function. In a rough format, we used this with two clients, a firm in the pharmaceutical business and another in food processing. Even though successful, the concept was never formalized or incorporated into either of the courses at Arthur Andersen. I formalized the concept after starting my own firm.

Matrix Concept

This matrix approach is designed for any type of audit (e.g., function/activity/area/facility). The matrix, however, should be developed for each function and all of the matrixes developed used to together to prepare the full deck of audit programs for the overall audit, or a separate audit program can be established for each function but assuring that organizationally no work phase/activity is overlooked in the overall audit.

Column by Column Explanation of Matrix Concept

Column 1, Operational Objectives
The definition of objective: "Something that one's efforts are intended to attain or accomplish, i.e., purpose, goal, target.

For example, an objective for the purchasing function might be as simple as to assure that the function will obtain the proper items, i.e., equipment, material, supplies, and/or services in the proper quantity, at the right quality, at the correct price, and from a reliable and acceptable source.

On any function, objectives will be one or more, but usually seven or less.

Column 2, Management Techniques
The definition of technique: The matter, methods, or ability to fulfill the technical requirements of a job/function; technical skill; the ability to apply procedures or methods to produce a desired result.

The techniques for each objective will be one or more, but usually seven or less, as in Column 1 of the matrix described above.

Column 3, Risks, If Techniques Are Not Used
The definition of risks: The exposure to the chance of injury or

loss; a hazard or dangerous change. A person or thing with reference to the hazard involved. Synonym: Venture, peril, jeopardy, imperil, endanger, jeopardize.

With each risk technique exists one or more risks, usually seven or less, as described in Column 2 of the matrix.

In this instance, the more risks increase in probability the less effective the managerial controls, processes, and overall internal systems, including internal controls/checks. The risks are reduced as management more effectively monitors and, if you wish, manages the function with effective implementation of techniques to achieve its objectives.

Column 4, Operational Auditing Objectives

These are the audit techniques that are planned for use in the performance of the audit of the function. The techniques are set up to integrate with the data in the three preceding columns and for each objective in Column 1 of the matrix. This can be used in financial auditing as well.

Column 5, Internal, External Sources of Basic Knowledge of the Function

1. The data profile of information developed internally during familiarization phase of the audit.

2. The data profile of the function as developed using external sources.

(*Note:* Refer to overhead 3 on this subject, which details Internal 10 and External 9 data sources).

Column 5, in effect, is to establish (a) standards, (b) practices, (c) universe of activities, (d) understanding the function, (e) historical data, and (f) normal practices for function as set forth in internal policies and procedures and external information from industry/trade sources and normal performance standards for the function.

Column 6, Preliminary Draft of Audit Program

1. First, start with the internal/external knowledge of the function, which is set forth in Column 5 of the matrix. This is the foundation of what should exist.

2. Next, rate the data in Column 4, the operational auditing principles, with the risks, as set out in Column 3. This action focuses on the risks and the appropriate audit scope and criteria, which should be used in the performance of the audit to give you "reasonable comfort and knowledge" on the risks and related aspects of control.

3. Last, relate the operations' objectives of Column 1 and the management techniques to achieve those objectives in Column 2.

Be sure they are considered in preparing the preliminary draft of the audit program. Be able to assure upper management whether the management being audited is striving to achieve the same objectives and using appropriate management techniques toward that goal.

4. All the management techniques incorporated in the preliminary draft of the audit program must be compared with the contents of Column 2. If similar, proceed to Column 7. If a management technique is found in Column 2 or Column 6, but not both, then the matrix must be revised to have it in both or out of both, based on your evaluation of its importance.

Column 7, Audit Approaches to Be Followed

While Column 6 concentrates on areas/activities/work phases/controls to be reviewed, Column 7 focuses on methods of performing audit reviews. For each program, a step identifies the methods to be used:

1. Substantive auditing.

2. Compliance auditing.

3. Use of confirmations and type (positive or negative).

4. Interviews.

5. Observations.

6. Test counts.

7. Sampling and approach.
   —Statistical (confidence/reliability).
   —Random.
   —Block.
   —Attribute.
   —Stratified.
   —Other?

8. Cycle audit techniques (e.g., Arthur Andersen, TFA, Peat Marwick, Seadoc).

9. Follow-up (previous findings or current known problems/ potential problems).

10. Using flow chart (where 9 did not use one).

11. Policy, procedure, standards, law, or regulatory environment compliance (supplementing general review under 2).

12. Evaluation of organization (including competency, training, turnover).

249

13. Other reviews of nature and scope deemed appropriate.

Column 8, Final Audit Program

Final program means the one with which you began the review. All audit programs must be flexible so you can adjust the approach and increase or decrease the scope, based on findings.

Column 8 then becomes Column 6, modified by a technical agreement with Column 2 and the identification of audit approaches to be followed for each program step, combining the review principles of Column 4 with the specific approaches of Column 7.

Conclusion

The RAMP concept has proved to be one of the most effective approaches to assure that sound auditing concepts and scope are incorporated into the actual review program used to start a review of any function. Its use also gives a degree of consistency that often did not exist in the past when different people prepared programs for different functions, because they worked using their own bias and prejudices. Thus, the result was inconsistency in approach and scope relating to historical, known, or potential problems.

Perspective of RAMP

Matrix Phase

RAMP Column

1. Identifies the management mandate, including organizational structure, authority, and responsibilities. Specifies the techniques that management should be implementing to assure the objectives, as assigned, are achieved. Last, it identifies the risks, if one or more of the specified techniques to achieve objectives are not used effectively.

1. Operational objectives.
2. Management techniques.
3. Risks, if techniques under 2 are not used effectively.

2. Sets forth the theoretical operational steps/approaches that should be used for each operational objective and management technique set forth in Column 1 and Column 2 (Column 4). It then supplements that data with

4. Operational auditing objectives.
5. Internal/external sources of basic knowledge of the function.

250

internal/external sources of basic knowledge of the function to be audited (Column 5). This is the data base on which you evaluate *(a)* what the function should be doing, *(b)* what it is doing, and *(c)* where its policies, practices, standards, procedures, systems, controls, and organization are either (1) in basic compliance with normal practice or (2) not in basic compliance with normal practice.

3. Develop the preliminary draft of the audit program, be sure that the management techniques in Column 2 and Column 6 are synchronized. Adjustment should be made to either or both columns until the management techniques are synchronized.

    Then identify the various audit approaches you plan to use in doing the audit, auditing step by step through the program.

    On the basis of the work done above, and a comparison of same to assure that all of the risks in Column 3 of RAMP have been considered in proper perspective, make final revisions. Complete the audit program.

6. Preliminary draft of audit program.
7. Audit approaches to be followed.
8. Final audit program.

Note: The matrix can be set up as eight consecutive columns, on a 14-column work pad or as two sections of four consecutive columns each, which is the format I recommend.

Column 1	Column 2
Operational Objective	Management Techniques to Achieve Objective
Column 3	**Column 4**
Risks, If Techniques Not Effectively Implemented	Operational Auditing Techniques
Column 5	**Column 6**
Internal/External Data Sources	Preliminary Draft of Audit Program
Column 7	**Column 8**
Special Audit Impacting Conditions	Final Audit Program

Summary

Use of the RAMP format will greatly assist in determining the proper scope for an audit review, whether it is for a standard review or for a fraud-audit review. It takes data that is known and developed and identifies areas of highest risk and threat so that appropriate focus will be made from that knowledge.

The time spent on developing the RAMP will be more than returned by establishing proper audit scope for any audit review to be done, one that can be defended as reasonable and adequate while asserting that unneeded review efforts are not a part of the final scope as a safety measure for audit management.

17

Questionnaire to Evaluate the Internal Audit Planning Process

The following questionnaire is a guide for evaluating the soundness of the techniques and approaches used to plan the scope of (1) any specific audit review, or (2) the overall reviews of the internal audit organization. It is not intended to evaluate all functions and responsibilities of internal auditing, only the planning process. As with any questionnaire, it is *alive*. This means it is not in concrete. Questions may be dropped, added, or broadened.

	Yes	No	Remarks
1. Does the internal audit organization have established documented standards for planning an internal audit project?	_____	_____	_____
2. Is there a formal process for the planning phase of an internal audit project?	_____	_____	_____
3. Is the planning phase of the internal audit project documented in the work papers?	_____	_____	_____
4. Is there a checklist or other control to determine whether all steps of preliminary planning are executed by the audit staff?	_____	_____	_____
5. Does the internal audit organization have a system to keep time, for recording all hours allocated or charged to audit projects?	_____	_____	_____
6. Does the internal audit organization have a budgeting system to project or budget audit hours?	_____	_____	_____
7. Are previous year actual and budgeted hours used to plan for current year audit requirements?	_____	_____	_____
8. Are audit assignments matched with appropriate available personnel whose qualifications and experience ensure that audit objectives will be attained?	_____	_____	_____
9. Are staff assignments scheduled to maintain an even workload throughout the audit and permit timely release of people not required for the entire audit?	_____	_____	_____
10. Is the audit supervisor's time scheduled to allow him or her the opportunity to perform in-field review before the release of assigned personnel?	_____	_____	_____

	Yes	No	Remarks
11. Does each staff participant in the audit have complete knowledge of the role he or she must play to meet planned objectives?	_____	_____	_____
12. Do staff members set their own goals within the guidelines of the audit objectives to accomplish assigned responsibilities?	_____	_____	_____
13. Does the internal auditor maintain permanent files for various areas of examination?	_____	_____	_____
14. Does the internal auditor obtain background information about activities to be audited?	_____	_____	_____
15. Does the auditor perform a preliminary review to become as familiar as possible with the operations and management of the area to be audited to prepare a satisfactory and adequate audit program?	_____	_____	_____
16. If the question 15 answer is yes, does the internal auditor review the following types of information during the preliminary review?			
Prior audit work papers.	_____	_____	_____
Prior audit reports and replies.	_____	_____	_____
Permanent files.	_____	_____	_____
Post audit reviews.	_____	_____	_____
Auditor's comments from previous audits.	_____	_____	_____
Audit programs.	_____	_____	_____
Audit reports of other company divisions.	_____	_____	_____
Management reports.	_____	_____	_____
Historical financial information.	_____	_____	_____
Organization charts.	_____	_____	_____
Chart of Accounts.	_____	_____	_____
Flow charts and descriptions of operations.	_____	_____	_____
Summary of audit time.	_____	_____	_____
Bylaws.	_____	_____	_____
Examination by regulatory agents.	_____	_____	_____
Examination/comments by outside auditors.	_____	_____	_____
Minutes of board/committee meetings.	_____	_____	_____
17. Does the internal auditor organize his work and perform in-office type work between the time he receives his assignment and starts his preliminary survey?	_____	_____	_____
18. If the answer to 17 is yes, does the auditor's preliminary work include the following:			
Prepare a reminder list.	_____	_____	_____

	Yes	No	Remarks
Block out various work papers.	_____	_____	_____
Prepare table of contents.	_____	_____	_____
Prepare areas for cost reduction.	_____	_____	_____
Prepare a summary of prior deficiencies.	_____	_____	_____
Prepare data processing requirements.	_____	_____	_____
19. Does the internal auditor perform an on-site preliminary survey to become familiar with the activities and controls to be audited and identify areas for audit emphasis?	_____	_____	_____
20. Does the internal auditor conduct preliminary meetings with members of management before the audit?	_____	_____	_____
21. Does the internal auditor use questionnaires to obtain information from the audit subject during the preliminary survey?	_____	_____	_____
22. Does the internal auditor use a flow chart as a tool for reviewing the area under audit?	_____	_____	_____
23. Does the internal auditor use the results of the preliminary survey to evaluate risks, set the scope of his audit, and establish audit objectives?	_____	_____	_____
24. Following the preliminary work, but prior to the fieldwork, does the internal auditor review the results of his preliminary survey with audit management?	_____	_____	_____
25. Does audit management have the opportunity to set the scope of the audit?	_____	_____	_____
26. Does audit management challenge the preliminary work and proposed audit scope?	_____	_____	_____
27. Do all staff members assigned to the audit have an opportunity to meet with audit management before the fieldwork starts?	_____	_____	_____
28. Does the internal audit organization prepare a comprehensive audit plan?	_____	_____	_____
29. If the answer to 28 is yes, does the comprehensive audit plan include:			
Organization activities to be audited.	_____	_____	_____
Scheduled date to begin audit activities.	_____	_____	_____
Scheduled date to begin the audit.	_____	_____	_____
Estimated hours to complete the audit project.	_____	_____	_____
Frequency of audits in areas of organization.	_____	_____	_____
Staffing requirements.	_____	_____	_____
30. Does the internal auditor allow time in his audit plan for special projects (board, management requests)?	_____	_____	_____

	Yes	No	Remarks
31. Does the internal auditor know in advance how, when, and to whom audit results should be communicated?	_____	_____	_____
32. Does the internal auditor communicate with all who need to know about the audit, both inside and outside the organization?	_____	_____	_____
33. Does the internal auditor have written audit programs?	_____	_____	_____
34. Does the internal auditor accumulate audit programs in an audit manual for all areas audited by the internal audit division?	_____	_____	_____
35. Are audit programs updated for changes resulting from the preliminary phase of the internal audit project?	_____	_____	_____
36. Does the internal audit organization have a formal staff training program for new staff members?	_____	_____	_____
37. Is the formal staff training program supplemented with preplanned on-the-job training?	_____	_____	_____
38. Does the in-house staff training program include instruction on how to plan the internal audit project?	_____	_____	_____
39. Does the internal audit organization have plans to establish or enhance the planning process for internal audits?	_____	_____	_____
40. As it relates to the planning of an internal audit project, does the internal audit organization meet the standards for the professional practice of internal auditing?	_____	_____	_____

Part IV
Special Reviews

18

Special Reviews

Introduction

The scope of risk-oriented internal auditing is only as limited as the auditor's imagination and management's mandate. Let us consider some of the more standard "special reviews" done by risk-oriented internal auditing.

Management Audits

This is defined as "an independent examination of objective evidence, performed by trained personnel, to determine whether integrated management systems, which are required to fulfill the contractual and legal obligations of the company to its customer and the community, are being effectively implemented, and the true and fair presentation of the results of such examination."[309]

Who can use management audits effectively? "All companies and enterprises regardless of size can benefit by examining their management systems. This applies no less to local government, civil service, commerce, and the service industries than to manufacturing industry."[310]

With regards to the traditional operational audit, the management-oriented or management audit is considered the second or higher level of that concept. At level one, the concept focuses on dealing with activities, functions, products, services, entities, or facilities, concentrating on (1) organizational authority and responsibility, (2) accounting, administration, and operational procedures, standards, and practices, and (3) level of internal control and check to deal with the risks and threats therein. At level two, the auditor gets involved with such key factors as *(a)* capital adequacy, *(b)* budgeting and strategic planning, *(c)* asset/liability management, *(d)* risk asset mix, *(e)* liquidity, *(f)* competency of management, at all levels, *(g)* adequacy of policies, procedures, standards, and code of ethics, and *(h)* profitability. Senior audit management actively functions as a member of the management team, in all of the indicated areas, to assure (i) adequate data bases are developed and used in the

---

[309]Allan J. Sayle. *Management Audits—The Assessment of Quality Management Systems.* (McGraw-Hill, 1981), p. 4.
[310]*Ibid.*, p. 4.

decision-making process, (ii) risks and threats are understood, regarding any aspect of the current or planned business environment, and (iii) actions are taken promptly by management relative to performance, income, balance as to financial matters, and risks and threats. Some would say that auditing in this role serves as the conscience of senior management to assure that areas involved are always kept in proper perspective with up-to-date information.

In summary, management audits involve any aspect of management planning, implementation, or performance measurement. Management is defined as "as [an] integrating process by which authorized individuals create, maintain, and operate an organization in the selection and accomplishment of its aims. This basic concept has the advantage of denoting a process being carried out continuously over time. It includes the idea of a goal-oriented organization as the fundamental arena of managerial action as well as the concept of persons specifically charged with managerial responsibility." Specific aspects are (1) "management is getting things done through other people. This definition stresses teamwork, delegation, and results," (2) "management is partly an art and partly a science. This definition recognizes the presence of intuitive, subjective skills in the management processing and the growing importance of verified knowledge as a guide to managerial decision and action," and (3) "management is the performance of the critical functions essential to the success of an organization. This definition essentially holds that management is what managers do in performing roles as managers."[311] Risk-oriented auditors focus on assuring that whatever they do, they do with an adequate knowledge and consider all of the risks and threats inherent in the environment so the final decision is viewed with knowledge of them and whether resulting decision(s) will possibly increase them. When viewed at the higher end of possible risks and threats, managers may seek another course of action. If they have made decisions without adequate knowledge, the risk-oriented auditor would identify the risks and threats and alternative ways of reaching desired goals, by holding risks and threats at or below levels acceptable to management.

Remember, in management auditing the auditor has two distinct roles to fulfill. They are (1) assisting in developing facts and assuring they are complete, current, and reliable for making decisions and (2) evaluating performance against plan (e.g., budget) or levels of risks and threats that exist concerning the impact made by the decisions. The auditor always has the responsibility of point (2). Where in-

---

[311]Lester R. Bittel and Jackson E. Ramsey, eds. *Handbook for Professional Managers.* (McGraw-Hill, 1985), p. 487.

volved with point (1), the auditor must accept the management team decision (e.g., strategic plan) and concentrate on point (2) solely because the decision is a consensus and may be against the auditor's recommendations. Therefore, where involved with point (1) the auditor must insist strongly that adequate information be available on which to make the final decisions. Where not involved in point (1), as a management team participant, the auditor may evaluate the data on which the decisions were made and criticize their completeness, accuracy, and timeliness, and also on how the decision was made or implemented.

Reviews of Managerial Mismanagement, Negligence, or Gross Negligence

The risk-oriented auditor who has the skills and competency to perform management and management-oriented audits can investigate properly situations of possible managerial mismanagement, negligence, or gross negligence. Let us define those terms before reviewing how each such audit should be approached:

1. MISMANAGEMENT. "To manage or administer badly or dishonestly."[312]

2. MISFEASANCE. "Illegal or improper exercise of a legal responsibility; failure to properly perform a lawful act, or ... performing ... an action without proper notice of those involved. cf. nonfeasance."[313]
   (*Note:* Misfeasance should be considered a form of mismanagement.)

3. ORDINARY NEGLIGENCE. "The omission of that care which a man of common prudence usually takes on his own concerns ... based on fact that one ought to have known results of his acts."[314]

4. GROSS NEGLIGENCE. "Rests on assumption that one knew results of his acts but was recklessly or wantonly indifferent to results."[315]

Before reviewing specific approaches to the special review, consider Figure 15.

---

[312]*Webster's New World Dictionary,* 2d college ed. (New York: Simon & Schuster, 1980), p. 909.
[313]Jerry M. Rosenberg. *Dictionary of Banking & Finance.* (New York: John Wiley & Sons, 1982), p. 333.
[314]*Black's Law Dictionary,* 4th ed. (St. Paul: West, 1957), p. 1186.
[315]*Ibid.,* p. 1186.

Figure 15
Seven Levels of Auditing

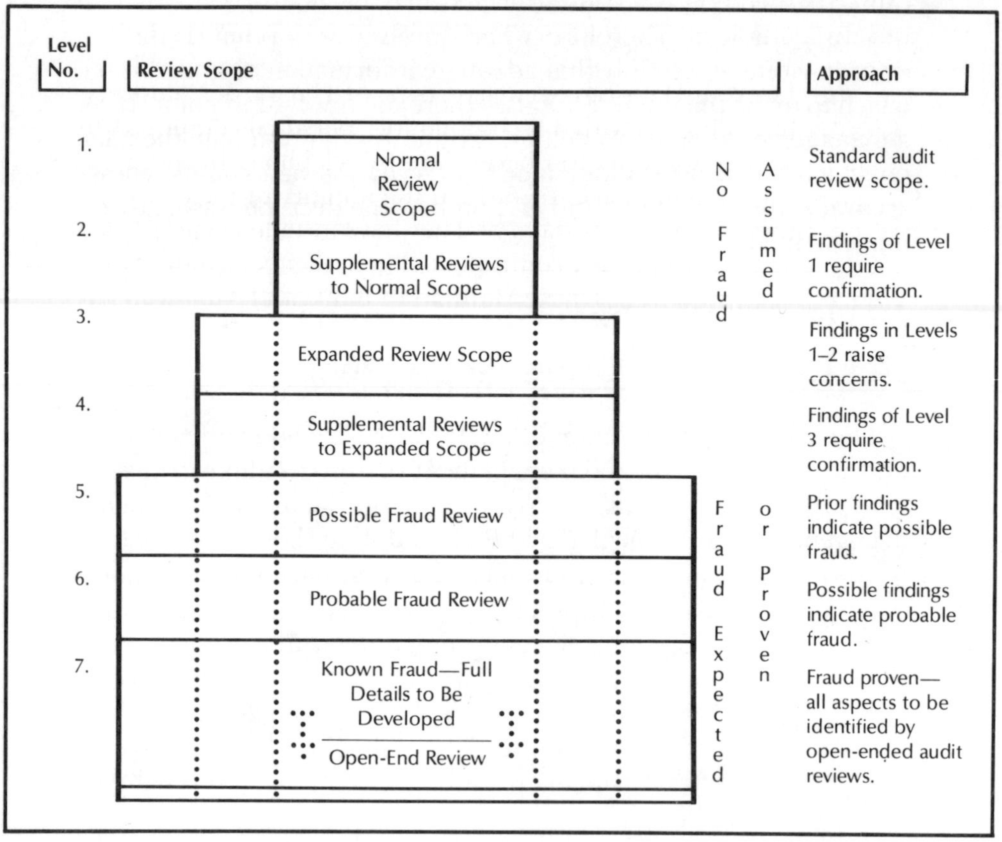

Level No.	Review Scope		Approach
1.	Normal Review Scope	N o	Standard audit review scope.
2.	Supplemental Reviews to Normal Scope	F r a u d (No Fraud Assumed)	Findings of Level 1 require confirmation.
3.	Expanded Review Scope		Findings in Levels 1–2 raise concerns.
4.	Supplemental Reviews to Expanded Scope		Findings of Level 3 require confirmation.
5.	Possible Fraud Review	F r a u d	Prior findings indicate possible fraud. (or Proven)
6.	Probable Fraud Review		Possible findings indicate probable fraud.
7.	Known Fraud—Full Details to Be Developed / Open-End Review	Fraud Expected	Fraud proven— all aspects to be identified by open-ended audit reviews.

The assumption is that the reviews under Level 1 will confirm that things are as they should be, resulting in a satisfactory (clean) report. The scope will involve "X" number of manhours to complete. If some deficiencies are identified, then Level 2 reviews would be performed to confirm that findings at Level 1 are representative or indicate that they are not as they should be, resulting in the final evaluation of the report issued. Those reviews would normally represent 1/2 "X" manhours to complete.

If the findings under Levels 1 and 2 warrant, or where there is reason to believe that mismanagement, negligence, or gross negligence has occurred, either from information developed, at Levels 1 and 2, or information from an informer, then Level 3 reviews should be done. Such scope would normally be scheduled at 2 times "X" manhours to complete. If the findings do not provide sufficient information to conclude fraud may be occurring or has occurred but leaves some unanswered questions, proceed to Level 4, and increase slightly the manhours scheduled for Level 3 to 2½ times "X." All work performed in the first four audit levels is done to confirm that things are as they should be, with deficiencies being identified in the course of the work. The deficiencies determine whether to stop at a given level or proceed to another. Keep in mind that one or more levels may be skipped when warranted. Based on the findings, the audit can proceed level by level until the auditor decides the work should be halted or furthered to Level 7. After the level by level approach, the auditor completing Level 4 would have expended 6 times "X" manhours, i.e., 6 times the manhours of Level 1.

If, after completing the audit reviews at Level 4, evidence indicates the possibility of fraud, or extremely serious conditions of mismanagement, negligence, or gross negligence, the auditor proceeds to Level 5. This level and those that follow are based on the assumption that a serious irregularity of the four types identified has occurred. Auditors would continue until (1) the assumption is proved wrong by an audit review or (2) found to be correct, and the full details would be disclosed by audit review. The manhours devoted to Level 5, where possible wrongdoing would be determined or disproved, uses 3 times "X" manhours. If the auditor proceeds to Level 6, indicating probable wrongdoing, the manpower allocated will be 4 times "X." The additional time is because Level 5 indicated further reviews are necessary to see whether a serious wrongdoing had occurred. Again, if review findings warrant, the auditor proceeds to Level 7, which *starts* with a 7 times "X" manpower commitment, the combined total of Levels 5 and 6.

The total time of Level 1 through 7 is 20 times "X." Level 7 is, of course, open-ended, so the final time committed may exceed 20 times "X" or possibly as much as two or three times that amount, depending on complexity and duration of the fraud. At Level 7 the reviews would continue until the audit is no longer considered cost effective to seek the unknown amount after all is uncovered on how the fraud was carried out. This concept is based on a "Big 8" (now fewer in number) public accounting firm partner replying to a reporter's question: "Why doesn't the auditor find more frauds earlier?" The auditor responded that "an audit expected to result in clean certified statements may be contracted for at 'X' man-hours of cost." However, "if you wanted a fraud audit performed, the cost would start at '20 X' and could ultimately be two or three times that amount." Under the seven-level concept, the auditor may start at any level and proceed level by level, or skip levels, as dictated by information developed and/or what reviews have found. Let's summarize the seven levels of audit reviews:

1. Level 1.: Normal review scope: "X" Man-hours
2. Level 2.: Supplemental reviews to
   normal scope: 1/2 "X" Man-hours
3. Level 3.: Expanded review scope: 2 "X" Man-hours
4. Level 4.: Supplemental reviews to
   expanded scope: 1½ "X" Man-hours

Total: No fraud assumed levels: 5 times "X" Man-hours

5. Level 5.: Possible fraud review: 3½ "X" Man-hours
6. Level 6.: Probable fraud review: 3½ "X" Man-hours
7. Level 7.: Known fraud review (Minimum
   shown, open-ended)   8 "X" Man-hours

Total: Fraud assumed or known
review: 15 times "X" Man-hours

Total (With Level 7 open-ended):   20 times "X" Man-hours

Now, consider various actions or lack of actions relative to:

1. Mismanagement

   (a) Misuse of rank:

   (1) To authorize nonstandard accounting entries.

   (2) To authorize personal or personally directed use of firm assets (e.g., having maintenance personnel do work at home or friend's home).

   (3) To authorize bypassing policies, procedures, and/or code of ethics.

   (b) Failure to fulfill duties and/or exercise authority and responsibilities assigned to individual in a due diligent manner.

   (c) Failure to monitor and review performance relative to authority and responsibilities assigned to subordinates.

   (d) Submission of budgets, plans, and projections based on "best guesstimates" rather than being developed through normal, prudent approaches and using appropriate methodologies and techniques.

   (e) Failure to identify risk and threats inherent in accounting, administrative, operational, or security activities, functions, products, services, entities, or facilities under individuals' direction so that appropriate cost-effective actions can be taken to control them at the levels deemed acceptable to senior management. If a senior management member, then as determined for the entire organization.

(f) Ordering the submission of financial statements that do not truly represent performance and/or current status.

(g) Misappropriation of assets for personal use, directly or by transferring funds of others into accounts that are controlled by an individual.

Note: The list is not intended to be all-inclusive.

2. Ordinary Negligence

(a) Failure to fulfill duties, and/or exercise authority and responsibilities assigned to individual with due diligence.

(b) Failure to monitor and review performance of authority and responsibilities assigned to subordinates.

(c) Failure to identify risk and threats inherent in accounting, administrative, operational, or security activities or functions, products, services, entities, or facilities under individual direction so that appropriate cost-effective actions can be taken to control them at the levels acceptable to senior management. If not a senior management member, then as determined for the entire organization.

(d) Any failure to perform in a prudent and proper manner as would be expected of a person in a responsible position. This may be as simple as perfunctorily signing an approval of transactions of any nature or assigning authority, responsibilities, and/or duties that rightfully should be retained by the individual.

3. Gross Negligence

All of the points made under segment 2 but with total or nearly total disregard for the results of their actions or lack of actions. The distinction between ordinary negligence and gross negligence focuses on lack of caring about the impact of one's actions or lack of actions on the institution.

In many instances, mismanagement and ordinary negligence can be audited on a basis of lack of controls and the need to implement them, including internal checks, to prevent repetition of negligence without discovering or reporting the conditions identified.

Some instances of mismanagement and virtually all instances of gross negligence need to be approached as though a fraud was perpetrated.

Therefore, using the format for the seven levels of auditing, audit reviews should be approached along the following lines:

1. Simple Mismanagement and Ordinary Negligence
   Start at either Level 1 or 3 and continue to expand the scope as if warranted to go through Level 4.

2. Complex or Material Mismanagement and Gross Negligence
   Start at Level 5 and continue to expand the scope as if warranted to go through Level 7.

Obviously, reviews under point 1 which, based on review findings, should be reclassified from points 1 to 2 in nature and then worked through Level 7 as found appropriate. On the other hand, reviews under point 2 which, by review findings, are not as serious as originally believed can be reduced at Level 5 or at the scope completed or where reviews have been stopped.

Possible Fraud or Actual Fraud Reviews

Principles

In ASR No. 292, issued in 1981, the Securities and Exchange Commission (SEC) states that extended audit procedures would be necessary if there were signs of fraud. It states:

> "Since routine audit procedures cannot always be relied upon to detect management fraud, the auditor must always be alert to unusual discrepancies and inconsistencies—such as improper shipping documents, illogical management explanations and major confirmation exceptions—and take appropriate steps to investigate them."

The American Institute of Certified Public Accountants (AICPA) in paragraph 5 of SAP No. 30, on "Responsibilities and Functions of the Independent Auditor," published in 1960 states:

> "The ordinary examination incident to the expression of an opinion on financial statements is not primarily or specifically designed, and cannot be relied upon, to disclose defalcations and other similar irregularities, although their discovery may result. Similarly, although the discovery of deliberate misrepresentation by management is usually more closely associated with the objective of the ordinary examination, such elimination cannot be relied upon to assure its discovery. The responsibility of the independent auditor for failure to detect fraud (which responsibility differs as to clients and others) arises only when such failure clearly results from noncompliance with generally accepted auditing standards."

SAS No. 16, on the "Independent Auditor's Responsibility for the Detection of Errors and Irregularities" (AU Section 327), issued in January, 1977, in paragraph 5, states:

> "Under generally accepted auditing standards the independent auditor has the responsibility, within the inherent limitations of the auditing process . . . to plan his examination to search for errors or irregularities that

would have a material effect on the financial statements, and to exercise due skill and care in the conduct of that examination. The auditor's search for material errors or irregularities ordinarily is accomplished by the performance of those auditing procedures that in his judgment are appropriate in the circumstances to form an opinion on the financial statements; extended auditing procedures are required if the auditor's examination indicates that material errors or irregularities may exist. . . . An independent auditor's standard report implicitly indicates his belief that the financial statements taken as a whole are not materially misstated as a result of errors or irregularities."

In SAS No. 16, "errors" and "irregularities" are defined as follows:

"The term errors refers to unintentional mistakes in financial statements and includes mathematical or clerical mistakes in the underlying records and accounting data from which the financial statements were prepared, mistakes in the application of accounting principles, and oversight or interpretation of facts that existed at the time the financial statements were prepared."

"The term irregularities refers to intentional distortions of financial statements, such as deliberate misrepresentations by management, sometimes referred to as management fraud, or misappropriations of assets, sometimes referred to as defalcations. Irregularities in financial statements may result from the misrepresentation or omission of the effects of events or transactions; manipulation, falsification, or alteration of records or documents; omission of significant information from records or documents; recording of transactions without substance; intentional misapplications of accounting principles; or misappropriation of assets for the benefit of management, employees, or third parties. Such acts may be accompanied by the use of false or misleading records or documents and may involve one or more individuals among management, employees, or third parties."

"Management fraud usually involves the deliberate misapplication of accounting principles, such as failure to provide for uncollectible accounts receivable or the deliberate overstatement of inventory. This type of irregularity is called 'management fraud' because it is perpetrated by management and because its objective is often the furtherance of a management goal, such as higher reported earnings, rather than direct personal enrichment. Such irregularities are likely to have a significant effect on financial statements. Management fraud sometimes includes defalcations or misappropriation of assets or services. Those types of management fraud are difficult to detect, because they involve management override of controls."[316]

---

[316]Sullivan, et al., *op. cit.*, p. 123.

"Employee defalcations are generally less significant than management fraud. Clever concealment of defalcations can result in overstatements of assets (paid receivables reported as still due) or understatements of liabilities (payments misappropriated and reported as paid). In many instances where defalcations have occurred, however, the financial statements are theoretically accurate, because the asset that has been misappropriated is no longer included in the balance sheet and total expenses on the income statement are correct, although amounts related to the misappropriation are misclassified. (For example, inventory that was stolen may have been properly removed from the balance sheet but charged to cost of sales rather than to a loss account.)"[317]

"How, then, does the auditor fulfill the professional responsibility with respect to significant irregularities? Simply put, with respect to defalcations the auditor is responsible for designing and performing audit procedures that professional responsibility would ordinarily dictate in a particular set of client circumstances, such as designing audit procedures with respect to cash that reflect the strengths and weaknesses of the client's internal accounting controls over cash. The question is more difficult to answer with regard to management fraud, because the result of such an irregularity is a significant misapplication of accounting principles, which the audit as a whole is designed to detect. The auditor should perform the audit with an awareness of the possibility of willful manipulation, keeping in mind the particular circumstances of the engagement."[318]

The auditor, therefore, must be (1) an excellent interviewer to draw information from the officer or staff person being interviewed, and (2) a diligent examiner in the sense of confirming by observation that what they were informed is, in fact, correct. Too often, in the pressure of meeting time schedules, the auditor may have conducted an excellent interview, as under point (1), but failed to do sufficient field review and verification work to confirm what the interviewee told them, as under point (2). In other cases, the auditor, under the same pressures, may shorten the interview to where the scope of information developed, as under point (1), is inadequate relative to the follow-up reviews, as under point (2). Thus, those reviews don't provide a sufficient level of confidence that what is happening should be happening or is being done in accordance with policies, procedures, standards, internal control/check requirements, laws, or regulations. Finally, the auditor can go through the motions of an interview, as under point (1), but it is

---

[317]*Ibid.*, pp. 123-124.
[318]*Ibid.*, p. 124.

poorly done with little or no verification, as under point (2). Because the field work is so limited in relation to actual transactions, the auditor should be extremely diligent in conducting interviews, and make sure the scope of materials covered is adequate to establish a real understanding of what should be occurring in the specific activity, function, product, or service. From that information, sufficient verification made by observation must be achieved to develop a reasonable comfort and confidence level for the environment.

Obviously, sound systems of internal controls and checks should be working to control risks and threats at or below levels acceptable to management, normally on a cost-effective basis (i.e., control values received should exceed the costs to accomplish them). In addition, fidelity bond insurance, which indemnifies a company against losses, is another protective measure by an institution.

As for fraud audits, they can be performed by both external or internal auditors, or jointly. For the external auditor, a fraud audit would be an adjunct to the normal audit scope. For the internal auditor, a fraud audit would be performed only when information received or developed in a review warranted it.

(*Note:* Refer to seven levels of auditing discussed earlier). Please note what both the AICPA and IIA say:

> "There are no professional standards with respect to fraud audits, and generally such an audit consists of an extension of ordinary audit procedures. . . . Fraud audits are not considered to be an economic method of either detecting or preventing irregularities, since the "institution" incurs a great deal of expense, and there is relatively little assurance of success. It is generally more cost effective to employ the methods of deterrence . . . described earlier . . ."[319]

Far more preferable and cost-benefit justified are the control or prevention of fraud than all the audit work needed to detect it.

If internal auditors encounter resistance to a fraud audit from management, when such an action is deemed appropriate, they should protect themselves by following the criteria set out in AU Section 327.14, which follows:

> "When the auditor's examination indicates the presence of errors or possible irregularities, and the auditor remains uncertain about whether these errors or possible irregularities may materially affect the financial statements, he should qualify his opinion or disclaim an opinion on the financial statements and, depending on the circumstances, consider withdrawing from the engagement, indicating his reasons and findings in writing to the board of directors. In such circumstances, the auditor may wish to consult with his legal counsel."

---

[319]*Ibid.,* p. 126.

The preceding statement is as important for the internal auditor as the external auditor. Why? They must be sure that everything has been done to protect them at some later date from being accused of not having been as diligent or persistent as they should have been in insisting on a fraud audit when they believed such an action was appropriate. It is jokingly referred to as "PYA" or Protect Your Assets, the most important of which is your professional reputation.

For our purposes, computer fraud is defined as an employee taking "assets of the organization through intentional misrepresentation or misapplication of information. Fraud in this case may be the modification of a system by an employee to increase payments made on his paycheck or by several employees working in collusion who make use of a system for their own purposes, such as setting up phony accounts payable records for payments to bogus companies. Finally, fraud may also be the falsification of company records by an employee for his own benefit through the insertion or deletion of personal data maintained on computer files."[320] In addition to deliberate fraud, as described, there is *inadvertent fraud,* which is "the unplanned misapplication of information due to lack of care, incompetence, or poor control—such as the incorrect position of transactions by clerical or data entry personnel. Although unintended, these processing errors can have severe implications for an organization, financial and otherwise."[321]

The "Computer Theft Iteration"[322] follows in Figure 16.

"Computers have not changed the human disposition. Fraud, theft, and embezzlement are" a continuing business risk "in the computer era. It has been argued that such crimes are even more likely now because the classic accounting controls have been diluted. Paper audit trails often have been replaced by electronic audit trails, which are not as easily verified by traditional audit methods. Speed of processing has taken precedence over effective controls . . ." To offset this fact, experts recommend that "more intensive internal auditing for firms with computerized accounting systems" be performed "as an added measure of protection."[323]

Although unauthorized break-ins by outsiders, known as "hackers," are always a threat, most computer related fraud is perpetrated by inside personnel. Therefore, the institution must have a high level of continuous EDP audits performed by qualified professionals. These audits also should be supplemented by special audit

---

[320]Hutt, Bosworth, and Hoyt, *op. cit.,* p. 34.
[321]*Ibid.,* p. 34.
[322]*Ibid.,* p. 61.
[323]*Ibid.,* p. 62.

Figure 16
Reasons for Computer Fraud

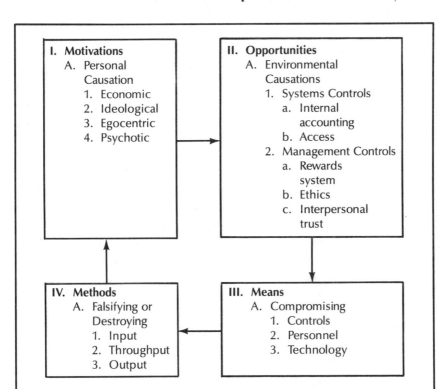

reviews by other qualified professionals, because of the high risk and the nature of the computer environment. If the internal staff is too small, a sound practice is to hire the consulting personnel of a public accounting firm to assure the quality of the day-to-day EDP audit effort. This audit of the auditors should be deemed Level 1 of the seven levels of audit. If the findings indicate possible weaknesses in the day-to-day program, a value judgment should be made on whether one or more other audit levels should be done to determine what improvements should be made to the continuing EDP audit scope. Obviously, if high concerns arise, this could entail proceeding to Level 5 or even higher to make a final determination on whether some person or group of persons has taken advantage of weaknesses to perpetrate irregularities.

In the risk-oriented internal audit environment, the auditor is continuously monitoring his efforts to determine where it is feasible on a cost-effective basis to expand the audit scope of both regular and special reviews.

Internal Audit Maximizing Coordination/ Cooperation with Public Accountants

1. Review of Internal Audit Procedures by Outside Auditor

    To the degree possible, the internal audit function should adopt the standards of the IIA, which makes it comparable as a profession to that of the independent accountant. As a result of this professionalism, independent accountants as much as possible should review and accept the work of internal auditors. Internal audit management must sell this idea continuously. Internal audit management also must strengthen, broaden, and improve the professionalism of their efforts by scheduling, through audit programs, work papers, internal control questionnaires, and reports on findings that are complete with recommendations for corrective actions. Follow-up should be conducted, where appropriate, to assure corrective actions are implemented fully and timely to protect the assets and integrity of the institution.

    My personal efforts to maximize acceptance of the internal auditor's work by the public accountants has been fundamentally to adopt the standards of the public accounting firm (e.g., program formats, work paper formats, tick-marks and cross-referencing, questionnaires, and continuing audit file). By so doing and using qualified personnel (most with public accounting experience), the result has been one of maximum acceptance of the work done by internal audit personnel under my direction. Why? Quite frankly, they are comfortable with their disciplines and formats. Also, the internal audit function being a copy of their disciplines makes them comfortable with the quality of the work, documentation of such work, and qualifications of internal audit personnel.

2. Coordinated Planning of Annual Programs

    My experience as an internal auditor in the banking and accounting industry has been that when the criteria under segment 1 are met, coordination should be maximized to avoid redundancy. Coordination takes two distinct directions:

    (a) Coordination of reviews to minimize redundancy. This entails the internal auditors performing reviews at agreed upon locations, with their work papers and programs reviewed by the external auditors who then perform the reviews at other agreed upon locations. Normally, the external auditors would inform the internal auditors about weaknesses in internal control systems, non-compliance with policies, procedures, laws, and regulations identified by their reviews. With regards to special audit reviews, such as identified elsewhere in this chapter, public accountants should be made aware of such concerns. On the other hand, public accountants should request the assistance of internal auditors where they are performing such special reviews.

(b) Cooperative audits, as indicated at the end of segment (a), involve the public accountants and internal auditors working together at a specific location. For example, my experience has indicated that internal auditors are normally far more aware of the policies and procedures of the institution. Therefore, they can perform most of the internal control questionnaire more effectively with the external auditors doing only those phases they consider critical. Otherwise, they would review and test the work of the internal auditors. Further, internal auditors are usually more skilled in sensitive areas such as (1) accounting: accruals, foreign exchange, futures trading; (2) administration: collateral maintenance, lien filing, and credit file information; and (3) operations: wire/money transfer service, cash management services, credit card, ATM, and security. On the same assignment, the public accountants can focus on risk assets, as to quality, proper authorization, and evidence of indebtedness of security documents, as appropriate. Who handles the confirmations is something to be agreed upon between the internal and external auditors.

Internal Audit Maximizing Cooperation with Regulatory Examiners

The internal audit program should be structured so it assures that all areas of reviews by the regulatory examiners are reviewed continuously and effectively and actions are taken to control or eliminate deficiencies on a cost-effective basis so they function at levels acceptable to the examiners.

Internal audit personnel should be made available to (1) assist in the review of audit documentation, on reviews performed by them, when being evaluated by the examiners to assist them in the performance of their reviews, and (2) answer questions on review findings and actions taken on deficiencies found and reported. This also would be true of loan personnel if the function is not part of the overall internal audit function but a stand-alone group, division, or department.

Internal audit personnel should develop a data-gathering telex format that should be sent to all locations when the examiners arrive to perform a review. The format should incorporate all standard data the examiners will require. As appropriate, a supplemental telex would be sent when the examiners require data over and above the standard criteria in the basic telex format.

Deficiencies, if any, found by the examiners should be followed up promptly by internal audit personnel so corrective actions can be taken quickly.

"Z-Score" Analysis

This concept is also known as "Zeta Score." It should be used in connection with credit risk of any firm where concern arises to a basic deterioration of its *(a)* cash-flow, *(b)* ability to service debt, or *(c)* profitability. The concept is built on the principles established by Edward I. Altman in his book *Corporate Financial Distress: A Complete Guide to Predicting, Avoiding, and Dealing with Bankruptcy.* It is a mathematical model based on five variables. The equation for the model is:

$$Z = 1.2X_1 + 1.4X_2 + 3.3X_3 + 0.6X_4 + 1.0X_5$$

The five variables in the equation are:

X_1 = Working capital/total assets.
X_2 = Retained earnings/total assets.
X_3 = Earnings before interest and taxes/total assets.
X_4 = Market value of equity/book value of total debt.
X_5 = Sales or revenues/total assets.

If "Z" figures at less than 2.675, a firm is considered to be a probable candidate for bankruptcy in the foreseeable future. If "Z" is 2.675 or higher, the firm is not considered a candidate for bankruptcy. This concept is not intended to be 100 percent reliable. It can, however, be an effective early-warning signal of deterioration in the financial strength of a borrower or potential borrower, particularly when the analysis is performed at two and, preferably, three separate annual dates, for comparative analysis that assists in the final evaluation.

Other Special Reviews

Some of the other special reviews that internal audit should be able to perform are:

1. Organizational integrity of an entity, facility, or unit, assuring proper segregation of duties, effective internal controls, and approval procedures.

2. Economic viability of a product or service and the level of internal controls relative to its administration, accounting, and operations.

3. Merger and acquisition studies.

4. Profit-improvement programs.

5. Coordination of efforts with risk management and security to identify and evaluate the risks and threats inherent in any activity, function, product, or service, and recommend actions that should be taken to bring them to levels acceptable to management.

Part V
A Summary

19
Summary of Approaches and Values

Risk-oriented internal auditing builds its foundation on basic principles of all other standard internal audit methods (i.e., attest, financial, operational, and management or management-oriented). These are building blocks which, if in place, permit the risk-oriented auditor to focus on risks and threats and actions dealing with them. Figure 17 illustrates this concept:

Figure 17
Risk-Based Auditing Building Blocks

Risk-Based:	Risk and Threat Identification
	Controls over risks and threats to bring to management acceptable levels
	Maintain risks and threats at levels acceptable to management
	Improve efficiency, effectiveness, and economy while controlling risks and threats
Management or Management-Oriented:	Planning: products, services, activities, functions, entities, and facilities Planning: budgeting and strategic plans
	Organizational structure: assignment of authority and responsibility
	Develop policies including code of ethics
Operational:	Administration and operations: —Transaction flows —Internal controls/checks —Procedures —Security —EDP and electronics
Financial:	Accounting and financial: —Transaction flows —Internal controls/checks —Procedures —Security —Records and reports
Attest:	Physical counts Comparison of counts to records

As you can see, risk-oriented internal auditing does not bypass or neglect any of the other basic internal audit methodologies. Instead, it uses them as a foundation on which to identify possible risks and threats relative to the aspects of accounting administration, finance, operations, and security in the institution's day-to-day business. *The focus* of risk-oriented auditing, however, is different. It is the ultimate internal audit approach because its perspective focuses on:

1. Identifying all risks and threats.

2. Taking actions to control all identified risks and threats to levels acceptable to management. Such determinations being made by management with assistance from risk management, security, and internal auditing.

3. Monitoring that the risks and threats are kept at the levels acceptable to management.

4. Maximizing efficiency, effectiveness, and economy through effective procedures that will control risks and threats.

5. Monitoring responsible management performance for any activity, function, product, service, entity, or facility to assure it is fulfilling its duties, that staffing is adequate and skills to perform tasks assigned to officials (e.g., authority and responsibility) are carried out, and policies, procedures, standards, laws, and regulations are complied with, with focus on specific risks and threats to the accounting, administrative, or operational environment.

Why is risk-oriented internal auditing more effective in achieving its stated goals than other internal audit methods? Quite simply because it is a *focused* approach, as indicated by points 1 through 5. Look at some of the weaknesses in the other internal audit methodologies:

A. Attest: This basically performs counts and compares them to the records. However, where differences are identified, no truly effective audit trail exists to assure that records reflect all entries or that all entries were processed or documented consistently. Therefore, where a difference of count to record is identified the question is asked: Is the error in the count in the inventory or in the records?

B. Financial: It concentrates on accounting and financial procedures. However, a review of the procedures has, in my experience, often disclosed that they are not written to assure there are (1) no loose ends in any part of the instructions, or (2) adequate internal checks built in at the points where the actual risks and threats either exist or should be monitored so they do not exceed the levels acceptable to management. Flow charts, often done, merely copy written procedural instructions to assure the instructions *(a)* are implemented with strict adherence to them or *(b)* provide adequate internal check requirements. Often procedures are written assuming a certain number of people are available to perform a specified number of steps. If the head count is less than anticipated in the procedure instructions, one might normally perform the work of two or, on some occasions, even more. This compromise of segregation of duties usually is not compensated for by adding additional internal checks. A sound practice is to add internal check requirements to compensate for loss of desired segregation of duties or other control aspects, resulting from organizational limitations. Therefore, such a compromise can create higher risks and threats than projected in the written procedure instructions.

C. Operational: It supplements financial auditing by broadening the base of reviews to include administration, operations, and, in certain instances, security. Unfortunately, the deficiencies indicated in segment B under points (1), (2), *(a)*, and *(b)* also are realities in this auditing environment. Such compromises here also can create higher risks and threats than those projected from the written procedure instructions.

D. Management/Management-Oriented: In this auditing approach it is normal for internal auditors to take an active role in assuring that the data base on which management decisions will be made is sufficiently broad and the information accurate. With regards to organizational structure, inherent risks, threats, and weaknesses can be identified so appropriate revisions can be made to minimize them. Also, they can assure that people assigned day-to-day authority and responsibility for any activity, function, product, service, entity, or facility, truly have the ability to fulfill their obligations. The internal auditors can assist in assuring that plans are realistic and can be achieved. They also can assist in evaluating variances in performance against plan and, as appropriate, recommend what should be done to help maximize favorable variances or reduce unfavorable variances, without increasing risks and threats inherent in day-to-day operations.

Risk-oriented internal auditing is a far more intimate approach to the task than other internal audit methods. The auditors operating in this mode must:

1. Have a reasonable understanding of whatever activity, function, product, or service on which they are conducting an audit review. From the principles and practices of the specific environment, the auditors will be able to communicate effectively with the management and staff in that audit area. They will know what standards, practices, and procedures are. They also will understand the fundamental risks and threats expected to be identified in their reviews.

2. Be fully aware of the policies and procedures of the institution, as well as laws or regulations that relate to the audit environment. The policies and procedures must be reviewed to assess their strengths and weaknesses, and to determine what should be done to comply with related laws and regulations. Also, the auditors must relate the procedures to the organization of the audit environment to see what, if any, compromises are necessary to the segregation of duties to identify whether the potential changes will increase risks and threats.

3. Broaden the familiarization phase of the risk-oriented internal audit review so that a number of officers, supervisors, and staff members are made aware of the audit so they can understand better what will or will not be done in the audit. The impact of the things being done, which might raise risks and threats, as well as things not being done, which also may raise risks and threats, should be considered when deciding on the initial audit scope.

4. Select at least one, and possibly more, transactions of each type handled and walk it through the operating environment. This intimate approach to auditing or, if you prefer, hands-on approach, is the only way to develop trustworthy information as to what is going on in the audit environment. Obviously, to hold the audit time down to that of traditional operational audits, or nearly that, the walk-through approach should be done first. Based on the findings, the compliance and substantive audit tests can be reduced from traditional levels. However, each transaction selected should add a dimension by affirming that it is being handled as a comparative transaction used for the walk-through.

5. Identify, using their hands-on approach, *(a)* organizational changes that should be made; *(b)* procedural changes, either in written instructions or in practice, with emphasis on internal checks being positioned where appropriate to monitor and control more effectively specific risks and threats. The risk-

oriented auditor also can better evaluate whether individual employees *(a)* have the required skills and have shown due diligence in performing their work, and *(b)* have received proper training and skills to carry out their assigned duties. Finally, risk-oriented auditing can evaluate whether management is truly managing or if it has delegated authority and responsibility or has failed to review, monitor, and appraise performance and compliance with policy and procedure requirements, with emphasis on assuring internal controls and checks are in place and adhered to diligently in processing work.

6. Be flexible, because they have to react to threats and risks, where identified, and determine what actions are warranted to bring risks down to a cost-effective level acceptable to management. Accordingly, when excessive risks and threats are identified the time assigned to a specific audit may be increased. That time will have to be taken from another assignment. Accordingly, effective audit planning should use the following three-tier approach:

   (a) Primary: These audits must be performed at the scheduled scope if possible. Generally, they would represent 30 to 40 percent of the human resources used in the audit plan.

   (b) Secondary: The desire is to do something in these audit areas, but they can be reduced somewhat in scope, usually up to 50 percent, to provide a minimum level of comfort and confidence. Any borrowed time here can be used for special reviews.

   (c) Tertiary: Some of these assignments can be deferred in full while others can be reduced substantially so the time can be used on special reviews.

"Special reviews," as discussed in Chapter 18, would be supplemented by taking time from certain tertiary and secondary scheduled reviews so additional work can be done on any audit assignment where risks and threats have been identified and require recommendations on how to bring them under control.

Risk-oriented auditors are usually well-received by management because they have done their homework. They have a foundation of the principles and practices of any environment they are auditing. Therefore, they are more readily accepted as a *constructive force.* They work with management to evaluate areas of concern. They attempt to have recommended solutions that are a joint effort of the audited management and the auditors. This teamwork has proved itself more effective than other audit methodologies because of its hands-on approach. The increased level of interviews with personnel who do the work is helpful in finding ways things might be made more efficient and better controlled. By walking through transactions, the auditor becomes familiar with strengths, weaknesses, and inefficiencies. Other audit approaches do not provide this tact. In the final analysis, risk-oriented auditing strives truly to be "a management tool" and "of assistance to all levels of management," as the creed of IIA points out.

Appendices

Appendix A

Standards for the Professional Practice of Internal Auditing

The following is a Summary of General and Specific Standards for the Professional Practice of Internal Auditing, from pages 3 and 4 of the publication of The Institute of Internal Auditors, Inc., as named in the title of this appendix. The publication can be obtained by ordering it directly from The Institute of Internal Auditors, Inc., Altamonte Springs, Florida.

100 INDEPENDENCE—INTERNAL AUDITORS SHOULD BE INDEPENDENT OF THE ACTIVITIES THEY AUDIT.
    110 ORGANIZATIONAL STATUS—The organizational status of the internal auditing department should be sufficient to permit the accomplishment of its audit responsibilities.
    120 OBJECTIVITY—Internal auditors should be objective in performing audits.

200 PROFESSIONAL PROFICIENCY—INTERNAL AUDITS SHOULD BE PERFORMED WITH PROFICIENCY AND DUE PROFESSIONAL CARE.
    THE INTERNAL AUDITING DEPARTMENT
    210 STAFFING—The internal auditing department should provide assurance that the technical proficiency and educational background of internal auditors are appropriate for the audits to be performed.
    220 KNOWLEDGE, SKILLS, AND DISCIPLINES—The internal auditing department should possess or should obtain the knowledge, skills, and disciplines needed to carry out its audit responsibilities.
    230 SUPERVISION—The internal auditing department should provide assurance that internal audits are properly supervised.
    THE INTERNAL AUDITOR
    240 COMPLIANCE WITH STANDARDS OF CONDUCT—Internal auditors should comply with professional standards of conduct.
    250 KNOWLEDGE, SKILLS, AND DISCIPLINES—Internal auditors should possess the knowledge, skills, and disciplines essential to the performance of internal audits.
    260 HUMAN RELATIONS AND COMMUNICATIONS—Internal auditors should be skilled in dealing with people and in communicating effectively.

270 CONTINUING EDUCATION—Internal auditors should maintain their technical competence through continuing education.

280 DUE PROFESSIONAL CARE—Internal auditors should exercise due professional care in performing internal audits.

300 SCOPE OF WORK—THE SCOPE OF THE INTERNAL AUDIT SHOULD ENCOMPASS THE EXAMINATION AND EVALUATION OF THE ADEQUACY AND EFFECTIVENESS OF THE ORGANIZATION'S SYSTEM OF INTERNAL CONTROL AND THE QUALITY OF PERFORMANCE IN CARRYING OUT ASSIGNED RESPONSIBILITIES.

310 RELIABILITY AND INTEGRITY OF INFORMATION—Internal auditors should review the reliability and integrity of financial and operating information and the means used to identify, measure, classify, and report such information.

320 COMPLIANCE WITH POLICIES, PLANS, PROCEDURES, LAWS, AND REGULATIONS—Internal auditors should review the systems established to ensure compliance with those policies, plans, procedures, laws, and regulations which could have a significant impact on operations and reports and should determine whether the organization is in compliance.

330 SAFEGUARDING OF ASSETS—Internal auditors should review the means of safeguarding assets and, as appropriate, verify the existence of such assets.

340 ECONOMICAL AND EFFICIENT USE OF RESOURCES—Internal auditors should appraise the economy and efficiency with which resources are employed.

350 ACCOMPLISHMENT OF ESTABLISHED OBJECTIVES AND GOALS FOR OPERATIONS OR PROGRAMS—Internal auditors should review operations or programs to ascertain whether results are consistent with established objectives and goals and whether the operations or programs are being carried out as planned.

400 PERFORMANCE OF AUDIT WORK—AUDIT WORK SHOULD INCLUDE PLANNING THE AUDIT, EXAMINING AND EVALUATING INFORMATION, COMMUNICATING RESULTS, AND FOLLOWING UP.

410 PLANNING THE AUDIT—Internal auditors should plan each audit.

420 EXAMINING AND EVALUATING INFORMATION—Internal auditors should collect, analyze, interpret, and document information to support audit results.

430 COMMUNICATING RESULTS—Internal auditors should report the results of their audit work.

440 FOLLOWING UP—Internal auditors should follow up to ascertain that appropriate action is taken on reported audit findings.

500 MANAGEMENT OF THE INTERNAL AUDITING DEPARTMENT—THE DIRECTOR OF INTERNAL AUDITING SHOULD PROPERLY MANAGE THE INTERNAL AUDITING DEPARTMENT.

510 PURPOSE, AUTHORITY, AND RESPONSIBILITY— The director of internal auditing should have a statement of purpose, authority, and responsibility for the internal auditing department.

520 PLANNING—The director of internal auditing should establish plans to carry out the responsibilities of the internal auditing department.

530 POLICIES AND PROCEDURES—The director of internal auditing should provide written policies and procedures to guide the audit staff.

540 PERSONNEL MANAGEMENT AND DEVELOPMENT—The director of internal auditing should establish a program for selecting and developing the human resources of the internal auditing department.

550 EXTERNAL AUDITORS—The director of internal auditing should coordinate internal and external audit efforts.

560 QUALITY ASSURANCE—The director of internal auditing should establish and maintain a quality assurance program to evaluate the operations of the internal auditing department.

Appendix B

SAS No. 55: The Auditor's New Responsibility for Internal Control

"The auditor's responsibility for considering internal control in a financial statement audit has expanded. As of January 1, 1990, *Statement on Auditing Standards no. 55*, 'Consideration of the Internal Audit Structure in a Financial Statement Audit,' replaces section 320, 'The Auditor's Study and Evaluation of Internal Control,' of SAS no. 1 (AU section 320 of AICPA Professional Standards)."

"SAS no. 55 expands the auditor's responsibility in two ways. First, it broadens 'internal control' to 'internal control structure.' Second, it increases the knowledge the auditor must have about internal control.

"INTERNAL CONTROL STRUCTURE. The internal control structure consists of the control environment, the accounting system and control procedures"..."This broader concept recognizes that policies and procedures an entity establishes within each of these areas are forms of control that can have a significant direct effect on several major audit planning matters.

"The three components of internal control structure are an important source of information about the types and risks of potential material misstatements—including management misrepresentations—that could occur in financial statements. Additionally, these policies and procedures are a primary source of information about the specific processes, methods, records and reports used in preparing the entity's financial statements. Both types of information are essential considerations when designing audit procedures"..."AU 320 also discussed the three internal control structure elements. However, it provided very limited guidance about the control environment and accounting system and how they affect planning. In addition, included only control procedures within the concept of control."

"INCREASED KNOWLEDGE OF INTERNAL CONTROL. SAS no. 55 requires the auditor to obtain a sufficient understanding of the control environment, the accounting system and control procedures to plan the audit. This means understanding how internal control policies and procedures are designed and determining whether they're in operation."

"AU section 320 was more limited: It required auditors to obtain general knowledge of the control environment and flow of transactions through the accounting system. This knowledge helped the auditor to determine whether control procedures might exist that could be relied on. In the absence of reliance, this knowledge helped the auditor design substantive tests."

"AU section 320 didn't require an understanding of the control environment or accounting system to help identify possible misstatements. It also didn't require any understanding of control procedures unless the auditor planned to rely on them."

"Without doubt, auditors implementing SAS no. 55 will ask, 'What's an understanding of the internal control structure sufficient to plan an audit?' The answer will vary from entity and requires the auditor's judgment. SAS no. 55 provides three major considerations to help auditors formulate their judgments:

WHAT KNOWLEDGE OF EACH ELEMENT SHOULD INCLUDE. SAS no. 55 provides specific guidance. For example, it says the auditor should obtain sufficient knowledge of the control environment to understand management's and the board of directors' attitude, awareness and actions concerning the control environment. The standard also requires the auditor to obtain sufficient knowledge of the accounting system to understand:

— The classes of transactions in the entity's operations that are significant to the financial statements.

— How those transactions are initiated.

— The accounting records, supporting documents, machine-readable information and specific amounts in the financial statements used in processing and reporting transactions.

— The accounting process involved from the initiation of a transaction to its inclusion in the financial statements, including how the computer is used to process data.

— The financial reporting process used to prepare the entity's financial statements, including significant accounting estimates and disclosures."

"As far as specific control procedures are concerned, SAS no. 55 recognizes that as auditors obtain an understanding of each element, they are also likely to gain insight about control procedures. For example, in learning about the cash accounting system, auditors usually become aware of whether bank accounts are reconciled."

"In some audits, the knowledge of control procedures acquired in understanding the control environment and accounting system will be sufficient; in others, the auditors will need to devote additional effort to understand control procedures. . . . "

"The Auditor's Judgment. In determining whether there's sufficient understanding to plan, auditors consider their assessments of inherent risk, judgments about materiality and the complexity and sophistication of the entity's operations and systems. As inherent risk assessments increase, an amount the auditor considers material becomes smaller or as an entity's operations and systems become more complex, it may be necessary to devote more attention to obtaining knowledge of each internal control structure element to gain sufficient understanding to plan the audit. . . . "

"The Use of Other Sources. An understanding of the internal control structure usually isn't the only source of knowledge the auditor uses to identify the types and risks of possible misstatements and to design substantive tests. Although this understanding is significant, knowledge can also be gained from other sources—such as prior audits. The understanding of the internal control structure needed to plan will vary with the planning knowledge obtained from other sources."

"The auditor may use a variety of ways to obtain knowledge about design of policies and procedures and whether they're in operation. These include asking appropriate management, supervisory and staff personnel, inspecting documents and records and observing the company's activities and operations."

"The nature and extent of the procedures the auditor chooses to perform will vary depending on the specific internal control structure policy or procedure involved, his or her assessments of inherent risk, judgments about materiality and the complexity and sophistication of the entity's systems. For example, the auditor may conclude that the inherent risk assessment or the materiality judgment for the prepaid insurance account doesn't require specific procedures to understand the control structure."

"In selecting procedures to obtain the understanding, it's very important to know what 'placed in operation' means and how it differs from 'operating effectiveness.' This distinction is critical to proper implementation of SAS no. 55."

"Placed in Operation means the entity is actually using the policy or procedure—that is, it doesn't exist only in theory or on paper. Knowing what policy is in use is critical to audit planning because only policies and procedures in use affect the types and risks of misstatements and the design of substantive tests."

"Operating Effectiveness refers to how a policy or procedure is used, the consistency with which it's used and who's applying it. For example, an auditor may find through interviews with personnel, observing the processing of" . . . "transactions and inspecting" . . . "files that prenumbered" . . . "invoices are used. This may not

293

tell the auditor, however, about operating effectiveness: How often are such statements not prepared? How often do errors occur in their preparation? Are they sometimes prepared by unauthorized personnel? For public accountants? In obtaining a sufficient understanding of the internal control structure to plan an audit, the auditor isn't required to evaluate operating effectiveness." Such understanding is, however, required of internal auditors'.

"SAS no. 55 requires auditors to document their understanding of the control environment, accounting system and control procedures. This differs from AU section 320, which required documentation of control procedures only if the auditor planned to rely on them. AU section 320 didn't require any documentation of the control environment or accounting system."

"The new standard, however, allows flexibility in the form and extent of documentation. Generally, the more complex an entity's internal control structure and the more extensive the procedures performed to obtain understanding, the more extensive the auditor's documentation should be."

"ASSESSING CONTROL RISK. After obtaining the understanding, the auditor assesses control risk. Formally defined, control risk is the risk that a material misstatement that could occur in a financial statement assertion will not be prevented or detected on a timely basis by the entity's internal control structure policies or procedures. Stated simply, control risk is the likelihood that a material misstatement will get through the internal control structure into the financial statements. The auditor assesses this risk by evaluating the effectiveness of the policies and procedues in the control environment, accounting systems and control procedures set up to prevent or detect misstatements."

"This requirement to assess control risk is not new. It was first established in 1983 by SAS no. 47, *Audit Risk and Materiality in Conducting an Audit*. But SAS no. 55 adds a requirement to assess control risk in relation to the financial statement assertions set forth in SAS no. 31, *Evidential Matter* (that is, existence or occurrence, completeness, rights and obligations, valuation or allocation and presentation and disclosure). Also, the auditor must consider the control environment and accounting system, as well as control procedures, in making that assessment. Thus SAS no. 55 completes the link between the internal control structure, assessing control risk and obtaining evidence about financial statements assertions."

"DETERMINING THE ASSESSED LEVEL OF CONTROL RISK. The conclusion from assessing control risk is called the 'assessed level of control risk.' The level may vary from maximum to minimum; it can be stated in quantitative terms—such as percentages—or qualitative terms—for example, maximum, substantial, moderate or low."

"The answers to two questions determine the assessed level of control risk:

1. Does an entity have internal control structure policies or procedures that pertain to a financial statement assertion?

2. How effective is the design and operation of those policies or procedures in preventing or detecting misstatement in the assertion?"

"Internal auditors should review to determine all risks and then determine the appropriate audit scope or need for enhancements to or new policies and procedures to establish internal controls and hold the risks to the levels determined as acceptable by management.

"Under SAS no. 55, the auditor isn't required to assess control risk at below the maximum level for any assertion" . . . "Even when potentially effective policies and procedures exist, an auditor may decide not to test their effectiveness because doing so would be inefficient. In such circumstances, the auditor assesses control risk for those assertions at the maximum level. Auditors also assess control risk at the maximum level when they obtain evidence that policies and procedures relevant to an assertion aren't designed or operating effectively."

"When auditors assess control risk at below the maximum level, SAS no. 55 requires them to identify internal control structure policies or procedures relevant to the assertion and perform tests of both design and operation effectiveness. These 'tests of controls' include procedures such as inquiry, observation, inspection of documents and reperforming a policy or procedure by the auditor. The auditor uses the resulting evidence to assess whether control risk for the assertion is below the maximum level."

"The auditor considers two potential sources of evidence about the effectiveness of the design and operation of internal control structure policies and procedures: (1) the understanding of the internal control structure and (2) any planned tests of controls performed concurrently with obtaining the understanding."

"UNDERSTANDING THE INTERNAL CONTROL STRUCTURE. In many audits, obtaining the understanding requires substantial audit effort that may provide considerable knowledge about the effectiveness of the control environment, accounting system and certain control procedures" . . . "Although SAS no. 55 doesn't specifically require auditors to evaluate effectiveness of the design and operation of policies and procedures when obtaining the understanding, it does require them to obtain evidence about the effectiveness of both design and operation to assess control risk at below the maximum level. This may raise a question about how the understanding can provide evidence to support an assessment of control risk at below the maximum level."

"The answer is that some procedures performed to obtain the understanding may provide evidence about the effectiveness of design or operation for some policies and procedures even though they weren't specifically planned to do so. This evidence may be sufficient to support an assessed level of control risk below the maximum level."

"PLANNED TESTS OF CONTROLS. Often, when beginning an audit, the auditor expects to be able to obtain the evidence necessary to support an assessment of control risk at below the maximum level for certain assertions. Consequently, for audit efficiency, the auditor may plan to perform specific tests of controls to gather this evidence as he obtains an understanding of the internal control structure. The auditor uses the evidence from these tests, along with any evidence about the effectiveness of policies and procedures obtained from the understanding, to determine the assessed level of control risk for financial statement assertions."

"After assessing control risk using evidence from those two sources, the auditor may believe a further reduction in control risk for some assertions could be supported by obtaining additional evidence. If that would improve audit efficiency, the auditor performs these additional tests.

"DOCUMENTING THE CONTROL RISK ASSESSMENT. SAS no. 55 requires the auditor also to document the basis for conclusions about the assessed level of control risk. When the assessment is below the maximum, this documentation generally includes tests of controls applied to internal control structure policies or procedures, their results and the auditor's evaluation of the policies' or procedures' effectiveness. However, when the auditor concludes that control risk is at the maximum level, SAS no. 55 requires only the conclusion itself to be documented—not the reasons why that conclusion was reached." The internal auditor, however, should go further and indicate actions required to bring such control risk(s) down to the levels determined by management as acceptable.

"USING THE ASSESSED LEVEL OF CONTROL RISK. The assessed level of control risk for an assertion relates directly to the substantive tests the auditor plans and performs. The logic is simple: The more effective the internal control structure, the lower the risk of misstatement. The lower the risk, the less evidence the auditor needs from substantive tests to form an opinion on the financial statements. Consequently, as control risk decreases, the auditor may modify substantive tests by:

—Changing the nature of substantive tests from a more effective to a less effective procedure—such as using tests directly toward parties within rather than outside the entity.

—Changing the timing of substantive tests—performing them at an interim date rather than at year-end.

—Changing the extent of substantive tests—to a smaller size, for example."

"ENHANCING AUDIT EFFECTIVENESS. SAS no. 55 is one of the nine 'exception gap' standards recently approved by the ASB. Its objective is to enhance audit effectiveness by improving audit planning and sharpening the auditor's assessment of control risk. To achieve this objective, the standard increases the auditor's responsibility to obtain knowledge about an entity's internal control. Moreover, it establishes and explains the relationship between the internal control structure and assessing control risk and financial statement assertions."

> *Note:* The preceding text, in quotation marks, was taken from the article, "SAS No. 55: The Auditor's New Responsibility for Internal Control," by Robert H. Temkin, CPA, a partner of Ernst & Young (then Arthur Young & Co.), and Alan J. Winters, an employee of the AICPA. The article was published in the *Journal of Accountancy*, May 1988; pp. 86-98. The AICPA, which published the foregoing periodical, notes that "views, as expressed in" the "article, do not necessarily reflect the views of the AICPA. Official positions are determined through certain specific committee procedures, due process and deliberation."

Bibliography

A Guide for Studying and Evaluating Internal Accounting Controls—Banking. (Chicago: Arthur Andersen & Co.), 1980, pp. 7, 10.

A Guide for Studying and Evaluating Internal Accounting Controls—Savings and Loan Associations. (Chicago: Arthur Andersen & Co.), 1982, p. 9.

Anticipatory Auditing Seminar—Reference Manual. Developed by the First National Bank of Chicago and promoted in seminars by Bank Administration Institute, p. 4.

Arens, Alvin A., and James K. Loebbecke. *Auditing—An Integrated Approach.* (Englewood Cliffs, N.J.: Prentice-Hall), 1976, pp. 6, 170, 172, 174, 258, 259.

Aspinwall, Richard C., and Robert A. Eisenbeis, eds. *Handbook for Banking Strategy.* (New York: Wiley-Interscience), 1985, p. 357.

Banking Terminology. (Washington D.C.: American Bankers Assn.), 1981, pp. 74, 118.

Bittel, Lester, and Jackson E. Ramsey. *Handbook for Professional Managers.* (New York: McGraw-Hill), 1985, pp. 487, 806.

Black's Law Dictionary, 4th ed. (St. Paul: West), 1957, pp. 493, 504, 614, 722, 724-726, 779, 790, 791, 1023, 1109, 1149, 1186, 1287.

Bologna, Jack. *Corporate Fraud—The Basics of Prevention and Detection.* (Stoneham, Mass.: Butterworth), 1984, p. 18.

Bolonga and Lindquist. *Fraud Auditing and Forensic Accounting—New Tools and Techniques.* (New York: Wiley), 1987, p. 27.

Brown, Gene R. "Changing Audit Objectives and Techniques." *Accounting Review,* October 1962, pp. 697, 700, 708.

Cashin, James A., editor-in-chief. *Handbook for Auditors.* (New York: McGraw-Hill), 1971, pp. 1-12. Based on article by C.A. Moyer in the *Journal of Accountancy,* published by the American Institute of Certified Public Accountants, December 1952.

——————— , *Handbook for Auditors.* p. 1-4. Based on "The Philosophy of Auditing," written by R. K. Mautz and Hussein A. Sharaf. Taken from a publication of the American Accounting Association, 1961, p. 14.

——————— , *Handbook for Auditors.* pp. 1-7, 1-8, 1-9, 1-11, 1-12.

Colton and Kraemer, eds. *Computers and Banking—Electronic Funds Transfer Systems and Public Policy.* (New York: Plenum Press), 1980, 150-152.

Eason and Webb. *Nine Steps to Effective EDP Loss Control.* (Bedford, Mass.: Digital Press), 1982, pp. 67-68.

Edmunds, Robert A. *The Prentice-Hall Standard Glossary of Computer Terminology.* (Englewood Cliffs, N.J.: Prentice-Hall), 1984, pp. 74, 97, 98, 100, 118, 294, 340, 429, 432, 434, 446, 455.

Flesher and Siewart. *Independent Auditor's Guide to Operational Auditing.* (New York: Ronald Press), 1982, pp. vii, 3-6, 8.

Garcia, F. L. *Encyclopedia of Banking and Finance,* 7th ed. (Boston: Bankers Publishing), 1973, pp. 64, 65, 157, 197, 243, 275, 498, 585, 756, 813, 855.

Heeschen, Paul E., and Lawrence B. Sawyer. *Internal Auditor's Handbook.* (Altamonte Springs, Fla.: The Institute of Internal Auditors), 1984, p. 143.

Hutt, Arthur E., Seymour Bosworth, and Douglas B. Hoyt, *Computer Security Handbook*, 2d ed. (New York: Macmillan), 1988, pp. 3, 11, 12, 34, 84, 87, 88, 90, 384, 385.

Jones, Reginald H. "Audit of the Future." Unpublished speech to the New York City Chapter of The Institute of Internal Auditors, February 1969.

Kohler, Eric L. *A Dictionary for Accountants*, 4th ed. (Englewood Cliffs, N.J.: Prentice-Hall, 1970). 1970, pp. 27, 29, 39, 69, 100, 101, 201, 240-242, 289, 377, 423.

Kuong, Javier F. *Computer Auditing, Security & Internal Control Manual*. (Englewood Cliffs, N.J.: Prentice-Hall), 1987, pp. 3, 6, 7, 9, 12, 16, 17, 219, 227-229, 244, 247.

Maynard, H.B., ed. *Handbook of Business Administration*. (New York: McGraw-Hill), 1970, pp. 9-78.

Montgomery, Robert H. *Auditing Theory and Practice*, 8th ed. (New York: Ronald Press), 1912, p. 13.

Moulton, Rolf T. *Strategies and Techniques for Preventing Data Loss or Theft.* (Englewood Cliffs, N.J.: Prentice-Hall), 1986, pp. 15-17, 19, 86, 87, 121.

"The Philosophy of Auditing." Subject of an American Accounting Association meeting in Chicago, 1961, p. 5.

Prochnow, Herbert V. *Bank Credit*. (New York: Harper & Row), 1981, pp. 2, 75, 76.

Reports, Conclusions, and Recommendations. From American Institute of Certified Public Accountants Commission on Auditors' Responsibilities, 1978, p. 7.

Risk Management Glossary. (New York: Risk and Insurance Management Society), 1985, pp. 66-68.

Rosenberg, Jerry M. *Dictionary of Banking and Finance*. (New York: John Wiley & Son), 1982, p. 333.

Sawyer, Lawrence B. *Elements of Management-Oriented Auditing*. (Altamonte Springs, Fla.: The Institute of Internal Auditors), 1983, pp. 1, 2, 4-7.

Sayle, Allan, Jr. *Management Audits—The Assessment of Quality Management Systems.* (New York: McGraw-Hill), 1981, p. 4.

Seidler and Carmichael. *Accountants' Handbook,* 6th ed., v. 1. (New York: Ronald Press), 1981, p. 10-3.

Seglin, Jeffrey L. *Bank Administration Manual*, 3rd ed, revised. (Rolling Meadows, Ill.: Bank Administration Institute), 1988, pp. 22, 23, 29, 30, 184, 378-380.

Standards for the Professional Practice of Internal Auditing. (Altamonte Springs, Fla.: The Institute of Internal Auditors), 1981, pp. 100-1, 200-1, 300-1, 400-1, and 500-01.

Stettler, Howard F., *Systems Based Independent Audits*. (Englewood Cliffs, N.J.: Prentice-Hall), 1977, pp. 6, 86.

Steven, Anton. "Operational Audits of Construction Contracts." *The Internal Auditor.* v. XXX, May-June 1973, p. 10.

Sullivan, Jerry D., Richard A. Gnospelius, Philip L. Defliese, and Henry R. Jaenicke. *Montgomery's Auditing*, 10th ed. (New York: Ronald Press), 1985, pp. 9-11, 25, 123, 127, 187, 214, 283, 328, 329, 382, 392, 417, 418, 422, 423, 529-531, 533, 534, 535, 1005, 1008.

Watne and Turney. *Auditing EDP Systems.* (Englewood Cliffs, N.J.: Prentice-Hall), 1984, pp. 14, 98, 99, 101, 103, 105.

Webster's New World Dictionary, 2d college ed., (New York: Simon & Schuster), 1980.

Webster's Ninth New Collegiate Dictionary. (Springfield, Mass.: Merriam-Webster), 1986.

Index

About the Author

William T. Thornhill has a long, impressive career in a variety of management assignments. He holds a bachelor's degree in business administration and a master's degree in accounting, having attended Strayer Junior College, Maryland University, and American University. He holds four professional certifications in auditing, computer systems development and management, credit management, and is a fraud examiner. He started Thornhill Consulting Services in 1985 to enable him to focus on training development and teaching and consulting in organization, internal controls, strategic planning, external controls, risk management, and fraud (e.g., prevention, detection, and control).

While at Arthur Andersen & Co., at their Professional Education Center, in St. Charles, Illinois, he developed and presented training methods to internal and client personnel in the United States and abroad.

As a vice president at First National Bank of Chicago, he headed the credit card and international operations divisions; was managing director of its two Jamaican subsidiaries; introduced operational auditing when setting up the international and holding company group of the audit department; headed the teams writing the first two departmental manuals (e.g., international and real estate), and performed merger and acquisition studies or handling loan workout situations.

Earlier in his career, Thornhill was controller and later treasurer of a "Fortune 100" finance company; vice president—operations of two finance subsidiaries and, later, assistant controller of a "Fortune 100" company. Before that, he was a regional general auditor (foreign supervisory auditor) for an international joint venture of Exxon and Mobil; and started his career with Ernst & Young, working in auditing and consulting.

As an author, he has had more than 100 articles and one monograph published as well as parts of four books for AMACOM, and complete books for Prentice-Hall, Inc., Bank Administration Institute, and Bankers Publishing, before writing this book.

Over the years, Thornhill has belonged to various professional organizations, including Bank Administration Institute (BAI), Risk and Insurance Management Society (RIMS), as an associate, Financial Managers Society of S&Ls (FMS), The Institute of Internal Auditors, Inc. (IIA), the Association of Systems Management (ASM), the International Credit Association (ICA), the National Association of Accountants (NAA), and the National Association of Certified Fraud Examiners (CFE).